THE COMMANDER

THE COMMANDER

FAWZI AL-QAWUQJI AND THE FIGHT FOR ARAB INDEPENDENCE, 1914–1948

•

LAILA PARSONS

HILL AND WANG

A division of Farrar, Straus and Giroux   New York

Hill and Wang
A division of Farrar, Straus and Giroux
18 West 18th Street, New York 10011

Library of Congress Cataloging-in-Publication Data
Names: Parsons, Laila, author.
Title: The commander : Fawzi al-Qawuqji and the fight for Arab independence,
    1914–1948 / Laila Parsons.
Description: New York : Hill and Wang, 2016. | Includes index.
Identifiers: LCCN 2015043497 | ISBN 9780809067121 (hardback) |
    ISBN 9780374715380 (e-book)
Subjects: LCSH: Qāwuqjī, Fawzī, 1890–1977. | Generals—Syria—Biography. |
    Israel-Arab War, 1948–1949. | BISAC: BIOGRAPHY & AUTOBIOGRAPHY /
    Military. | HISTORY / Middle East / General.
Classification: LCC DS98.3.Q23 P37 2016 | DDC 956.04092—dc23
LC record available at http://lccn.loc.gov/2015043497

Designed by Jo Anne Metsch

www.fsgbooks.com
www.twitter.com/fsgbooks • www.facebook.com/fsgbooks

1 3 5 7 9 10 8 6 4 2

FOR ROB

CONTENTS

LIST OF ILLUSTRATIONS

PREFACE

The windswept town of Rutba lies in the far western desert of Iraq, just a few miles from the Syrian border to the north, the Saudi Arabian border to the south, and the Jordanian border to the west. The Damascus to Baghdad road runs east through Rutba toward the Euphrates River and the city of Ramadi. At Ramadi it crosses the Euphrates and then heads southeast through Falluja, through the suburb of Abu Ghrayb, and finally into the metropolis of Baghdad. On May 9, 1941, around the old fort in Rutba, fighting erupted between Arab nationalist rebels and the British army. Just over one month earlier, a group of officers in the Iraqi Army had mounted a successful coup against the British-controlled Iraqi government and laid siege to the British air force base at Habaniyya, west of Baghdad. The British landed troops at Basra in southern Iraq and sent a force of two thousand men and five hundred vehicles into Iraq from Transjordan in the west through the town of Rutba. The British air force and infantry troops took only a few weeks to quell the rebellion. The

rebel leaders fled the country, and the former pro-British regime was
reinstalled.

Fawzi al-Qawuqji, the commander of the Arab force charged with
the task of defending the Rutba fort from the British advance, retreated
east with two hundred men toward the town of Hit on the Euphrates, just
north of Ramadi. From there Qawuqji continued to undertake guerrilla
operations against British forces, even though the rebellion had been
almost entirely crushed. One of his goals was to sabotage the oil pipeline
that ran from the oil fields of Kirkuk through the town of Haditha and
west out into the desert, ending up in another Middle Eastern city then
under British control, the port of Haifa, which lay on the green hills of
the eastern Mediterranean. Qawuqji appears briefly in the flurry of British telegrams about the revolt and its possible consequences for British
interests in the region. His attempt to disrupt the flow of oil, so crucial
for the war then being fought in France, Italy, and North Africa, grabbed
the attention of British officials, who described Qawuqji as a "scallywag
of particular cunning" and recommended that he be "liquidated." By
contrast, the men who fought alongside Qawuqji praised him as an
Arab nationalist hero who fought on despite overwhelming British military force.

By 1941 Qawuqji was an old hand at confronting colonial armies. He
fought as a young officer in the Ottoman army against the British advance
into Palestine in the fall of 1917, he played a central role in the mass rebellion against French colonial rule in Syria in 1925, and he was one of the
leading rebels in the revolt in Palestine against British occupation in
1936. After 1941 he went on to lead the Arab Liberation Army in the
Arab-Israeli War of 1948. This book tells Qawuqji's story in an effort to
open up his world and describe the Arab Middle East in the first half of
the twentieth century from the inside out.

Qawuqji's world was dominated by the disintegration of the Ottoman
Empire in the wake of British and French military conquest; the drawing of new borders—by men in Paris and London—of the new states of
Syria, Palestine, Jordan, Lebanon, and Iraq; the imposition of British
and French colonial rule over those newly created states under the League

of Nations mandate and protectorate system; the emergence of armed resistance by Arab men (and a few women) against that rule; and the creation of the state of Israel in 1948. British and French soldiers and politicians in this period made decisions that entirely determined the futures of people in the Middle East; these include Mark Sykes, Georges Picot, Lord Balfour, Henri Gouraud, John Bagot Glubb, Alec Kirkbride, and Percy Cox. Few in the West remember these individuals now, but their names resonate in Beirut, Damascus, Baghdad, Ramallah, and Amman. So too do the names of the Arab fighters who resisted the British and French occupying armies: Yusuf al-'Azma, Sa'id al-'As, Sultan al-Atrash, 'Abd al-Qadir al-Husayni, 'Izz al-Din al-Qassam, Adib Shishakli, Ramadan Shallash, Ibrahim Hananu, and Fawzi al-Qawuqji.

Fawzi al-Qawuqji's life was the story of one individual, not the history of a nation. He found himself in particular places, made particular choices, and even fought particular battles, largely as a result of personal circumstances. But his story is also part of a larger narrative of Arab resistance against British and French colonial rule in the first half of the twentieth century. The events of Qawuqji's life are recognizable to most Arabs, for whom Western colonialism and its responses, Arab nationalism and Islamism, form the political backdrop of their daily existence. *Al-Jazeera* talk shows, newspaper editorials, popular books, and dramatized TV series continue to depict the legacy of colonialism. Many people have their own stories of grandfathers and great-grandfathers killed in the fight against colonial forces. The history of colonialism in the region is held on to with such tenacity because most Arabs feel that little has changed. When the United States invaded Iraq in 2003, the Westerners fighting around Rutba were no longer the British soldiers of 1941 but the American soldiers of the First Marine Expeditionary Force from Camp Pendleton, in California. The arrival in Iraq's western desert of these British and American uniformed men from Newcastle and San Diego appears as a continuum of foreign invasion and occupation.

Qawuqji's story is not a simple one of heroic resistance against colonial armies. It is complex and full of contradictions. We find him fighting with colonial forces rather than against them. We find him committed to the old Ottoman Turkish order in the region, rather than to the Arab Revolt against the Ottomans. He detested European control over Arab lands, yet he was a Germanophile, spending the latter years of World War II in Berlin hoping that a German victory in the Middle East would bring the end of British and French colonial rule and the beginning of true Arab independence. He succeeded to the highest military ranks in his struggle against foreign occupation yet failed to push colonial troops out of Arab land. Because of this failure, many people in the Middle East regard Qawuqji and others like him as harbingers of an era of fruitless military adventures stretching from 1948 until today. For others, particularly those of an older generation, Qawuqji retains the status of a Garibaldi, struggling on against all odds in the fight for Arab independence.

Some of the contradictions in Qawuqji's life story reflect larger historical trends: the wrenching transformation of the Arab peoples from Ottoman subjects to colonial citizens in the 1920s and 1930s; the co-opting of many Arabs into the ranks of their colonizers; the persistence of Germany as a counterbalance to British and French military power; and the emergence of Palestine as a central symbol of Arab nationalism. These broad historical themes—Ottomans into Arabs, European colonialism versus Arab nationalism, Germany in the Middle East, Palestine—form the backdrop of Qawuqji's life. Although this book narrates the main events of his professional life, it is not a conventional biography. Instead, the goal has been to evoke, through a detailed description of the experiences of one individual, the historical landscape of the early-twentieth-century Arab Middle East. My hope is that I have done this in a way that will be easily recognizable to the majority of people living there today.

AUTHOR'S NOTE

I have used a wide range of original sources to construct the narrative in this book. A detailed account of these sources can be found at the end of the book, under the section entitled "Notes on Sources."

THE COMMANDER

1

OTTOMAN OFFICER

An Arab cadet in Istanbul—Posting in Mosul—From the
Iraqi front to the Palestinian front—Reconnaissance and the
Iron Cross—German officers and Jamal Pasha—The Arab
Revolt—Retreat and famine

"I opened my eyes to the world and found myself in the Ottoman military
school system." This sentence opens Fawzi al-Qawuqji's memoirs. Childhood games with his brothers, Qadri, Zafir, Yumni, and Bahjat, and his
sisters, Fawziyya and Badriyya, in the alley outside his home; the smells
of his mother's cooking; visits to the family's orchard of orange and lemon
trees; glimpses of the small religious college where his great-grandfather
the scholar Abu al-Muhassin al-Qawuqji used to teach; eating special
sweets with his father on a trip to Libya: none of these memories is
mentioned in his self-narrative. He saw himself as the product of Ottoman
military education.

This was understandable. Qawuqji's father, 'Abd al-Majid al-Qawuqji,
had served in the Ottoman Army, as did some of Qawuqji's brothers,
including his younger brother Yumni, with whom Qawuqji was particularly close. 'Abd al-Majid and his wife, Fatima al-Rifa'i, raised their
children in a simple house on a small alley in the Attarin district of the
Arab port city of Tripoli, in today's Lebanon. They did not have the means

to send their sons to the elite Ottoman civil school system. That system was reserved for the children of landowners or important merchant families. The military school system was free, and families with little income saw it as a practical way to ensure that their sons were educated and provided with a profession. The Qawuqjis were typical of military families in the late-nineteenth-century Ottoman Empire: neither wealthy nor poor, they were part of a respectable lower-middle-class Arab Sunni community in Tripoli.

AN ARAB CADET IN ISTANBUL

Qawuqji underwent officer training at the War College in Istanbul in the early 1900s. The Ottoman government had introduced the new military school system decades earlier, in the mid-nineteenth century. By the early 1900s thousands of boys from all over the Ottoman Empire had attended their local military school for free, and a select few, like Qawuqji, went on to train as officers in the War College itself. The military schools were expanded by the Ottoman sultan Abdul Hamid II, who saw them as a crucial element in his plan to modernize the institutions of the Ottoman state. In the 1890s, during a state visit to Washington, D.C., Sultan Abdul Hamid presented the American government with a gift, a series of albums containing photographs of the Ottoman Empire. The albums highlighted the Ottoman government's modernization drive, with photographs of new hospitals, factories, mines, harbors, railway stations, and government buildings. The albums also contained hundreds of photographs of the military schools. Some were exterior shots of the school buildings, which were nearly all neoclassical in style. Others showed cadets at drill practice on the training grounds of the schools, officer instructors in their classrooms, and dining tables laid for dinner (figure 1).

The military schools depicted in the albums ranged across the Ottoman Empire, from Istanbul itself, to Van in eastern Anatolia, to Damascus and Baghdad in the Arab provinces of the empire, all the way to Sanʿa in Yemen. The War College in Istanbul took pride of place. Another photo-

FIGURE 1

graph (figure 2) shows officers and cadets gathered in front of the War College in the early 1890s. Taken by a photographer from Istanbul's Abdullah Frères Studio, it captures the self-confidence that these men felt about their future in the Ottoman Army.

For Qawuqji and the other cadets, daily life in the War College was highly regimented. He spent his nights on a raised bed in a long gallery with dozens of other boys, listening to the horns of steamships moving slowly up the Bosphorus just half a mile from the windows of his dormitory. In the mornings he washed and dressed himself in his formal cadet's uniform, stiff wool trousers and a frock coat with a high collar. At mealtimes he ate with the other cadets in a vast dining room, on raised tables laid with separate plates and knives and forks. Meals were simple—stewed beans, mutton, rice—except during Ramadan, when special dishes were prepared and Ramadan sweets were handed out. His days were punctuated by the rhythm of daily prayers in the mosque that sat inside the walls of

FIGURE 2

the college. But he spent most of his waking hours sitting at a wooden desk, facing a blackboard, and learning the standard military curriculum, taught either by a staff officer or by a religious scholar ('alim). His classes were conducted mainly in Ottoman Turkish and included oratory, theology and ethics, military theory, and history, as well as German and French.

Paintings of military heroes lined the walls of his classroom: a picture of Mehmet the Conqueror, the Ottoman sultan who captured Constantinople from the Byzantine Empire in 1453, hung next to portraits of Napoleon and Bismarck. Each classroom also had an official military map showing the Ottoman Empire stretching from the Balkans in the northwest to Mesopotamia in the east, to Egypt, Sudan, and the Arabian Peninsula in the south. The great metropolis of Istanbul, home of the War College itself, lay at the center of these maps. Often the maps did not reflect the true extent of Ottoman territorial control. Much of the Balkans was lost by the end of the nineteenth century, and Egypt was now ruled by the British, who pushed every day against the borders of the empire. Many cadets knew that the cartographic representation in their classroom differed from the reality on the ground, where the Ottoman Empire was increasingly besieged by French and British assaults. Some maps also included the empire's new communications infrastructure then under construction, particularly the telegraph and the railway that by the early 1900s could take you from Istanbul to Ankara and Konya in central Anatolia and all the way to Damascus. Four hundred miles of new line pushed south from Damascus toward the holy cities of the Hijaz, and a branch line connected Damascus and Haifa.

Cavalry practice took Qawuqji outside the classroom into the hills just outside the city. Young cadets normally trained with decades-old Mauser rifles from Germany, although they were not allowed to use live ammunition. The few Ottoman cadets sent off to Germany came back with stories of different training practices. Everything in Germany was elaborately and precisely organized, and German cadets trained in battle scenarios using the latest model of the Mauser loaded with live ammunition. German cadets also ate good food in ornate dining rooms, wore uniforms made of fine cloth, and danced with pretty girls in elegant ballrooms.

The Ottoman cadets' sense that emulating such European practices put them in the vanguard deepened as they moved through their days sleeping on raised beds, eating at raised tables, and studying German and French at raised desks set in rows. These experiences set the cadets apart from most other Ottoman subjects. Other aspects of Qawuqji's daily life remained familiar from his childhood in Tripoli: the food he ate, the prayers he attended, and the classes he took in theology and ethics, grounded in the rich traditions of Islamic learning.

The stone neoclassical building of the War College stood on a hill overlooking the Bosphorus. The barracks of Tashkishla, which served as the city's garrison, lay to the south of the college. Abdul Hamid's walled palace lay to the north, and the cadets could see the older palaces and gardens of Dolmabahce and Chiragan on the shore of the Bosphorus below. The bars and restaurants of the European district of Beyoglu were within walking distance, as was the harbor area of Galata (figure 3), whose side streets were famous for their beer halls and brothels worked by Christian prostitutes.

Cadets often sneaked out for a night on the town, avoiding detection by one of the college monitors lest they lose points on the sections of

FIGURE 3

their report cards labeled "Moral Conduct." The cadets moved past public buildings built in the same neoclassical style and with the same dressed stone as the college itself: the railway station at Haydarpasha, the customs office at the port where the steamships docked, and Abdul Hamid's new municipal buildings. This gave them a sense of the empire's new direction.

The cadets at the War College were almost all Sunni Muslims, from every province of the Ottoman Empire. In his memoirs Qawuqji speaks of his Arab, Turkish, Albanian, and Circassian peers, all of them looking up to the Ottoman sultan as their leader. They shared a firm sense of being part of a new class of Ottoman soldiers who would spend their professional lives in the Ottoman Army. But social hierarchy did exist. In some cases the teachers treated the Turkish-speaking cadets from Istanbul and Anatolia with greater respect than the Arabic-speaking cadets from the Arab provinces of the empire. Although Qawuqji does not mention it in his memoirs, he complained in later years that certain cadets were served better food than he was. When he asked why, he was told that it was because they were Turks and he was an Arab.

During 1908 and 1909 Qawuqji's vague sense of social difference started to connect with the turbulent politics in Istanbul. In 1908 the constitutionalists, the so-called Young Turks, took power from Abdul Hamid II, who was committed to reforming the infrastructure but not the principle of the direct rule of the sultan. The Young Turks were a group of progressive medical students and military cadets. Their movement stemmed from previous reform-minded groups, which had been driven underground after Abdul Hamid abolished the new Ottoman constitution in 1878. They wanted to replace the system of absolute monarchy with a constitutional monarchy. Many of them also rejected the Ottoman character of the empire, focusing instead on the use of specifically Turkish symbols to build a new Turkish-centered nationalism.

Qawuqji was startled that some of his teachers heralded the overthrowing of Abdul Hamid as the beginning of a new era:

I was getting on with the business of going from class to class when suddenly one day an officer came rushing in, all agitated, and shouting, "The army of freedom has entered Istanbul and freedom and justice and equality and fraternity are declared in the State!" I laughed to myself and wondered: What is the army of freedom? And what happens when it enters Istanbul? And what does freedom mean? Was it lost and have we suddenly found it? The officer kept talking at us in this way, and we listened to him as if we were listening to a lecture on Arabic literature given in Chinese by a Chinese professor.

Political events crashed through the walls of the college into Qawuqji's world. By his own account, he now began to see differences between Arabs and Turks. After 1908 Qawuqji started hearing of the formation of secret Arab organizations. He noticed that the Turkish students seemed to feel connected to one another through what he calls a new bond. This new bond differed from the older, looser connection that the Turkish students had previously felt to other Ottoman subjects. To illustrate his point, Qawuqji tells the story of a fight between a group of Turkish soldiers and a group of Arab soldiers:

> I heard one of them saying with great enthusiasm and seriousness, "I am Turkish," and the other replying immediately with pride, "I am Arab," and the Arab students rushed to support their colleague. And it was as if this moment of truth, which was released into the skies above the War College, had put an end to the bond that had tied us to the Ottoman state. From that moment we began to feel that we had an independent Arab nation and that behind it were a community and a history and a time-honored glory.

Political identities are not formed overnight. This young Arab cadet had many years of bloody fighting ahead of him defending the Ottoman Empire against British and French invaders. Even after the end of World War I and the collapse of the Ottoman state, Qawuqji nurtured the connections and broad networks that he had inherited as an Ottoman cadet and officer. But the fight that broke out in the college between Arab and Turkish cadets in the wake of the Young Turks' revolution of 1908 was still a pivotal event in Qawuqji's life. The most worrying question he now asked himself was whether professional success in the Ottoman Army would depend on merit or on being an Arab or a Turk. This doubt about his promotions unsettled his mind as he struggled with more immediate issues, such as his place in the yearly ranking of cadets, the state of his moral report card, and worries about where his first posting would be once he graduated from the War College in 1912.

POSTING IN MOSUL

It was the custom of the Ottoman Army at that time to assign some of the War College's graduating officers to a particular corps by the drawing of lots. Qawuqji drew a corps stationed in Mosul in 1912, as did his close friend from the War College, Ahmad Mukhtar al-Tarabulsi. The normal route from Istanbul to Mosul was southeast through Aleppo and Dayr al-Zur. The two friends decided to go a different way. They went by boat from Istanbul to Samsun, on the northern coast of Anatolia, and then traveled by wagon due south to Diyar Bakr. From Diyar Bakr they floated down the Tigris all the way to Mosul, paddling a raft made of goatskins that were stretched and filled with air (*kalak*). The journey took fifty-three days, forty-one from Istanbul to Diyar Bakr and twelve on the river between Diyar Bakr and Mosul.

Qawuqji describes this trip in some detail, and the way he narrates it, his journey from Istanbul to Mosul symbolizes his transition from Ottomanism to Arabism. He tells how he and Tarabulsi decided to take this alternative route across Anatolia because they wanted to acquaint themselves with the traditions of the Anatolian Turks and to compare them with the traditions of the Arabs through whose lands they would pass as they moved south down the Tigris toward Mosul. Qawuqji encountered different groups of people along the way and realized with increasing clarity that there were substantial differences between the Turkish- and Arabic-speaking peoples. As they floated south down the Tigris, and the rocky hills of central Anatolia gave way to the grasslands of the rolling countryside north of Mosul, the people living on the banks of the river rushing out to greet them spoke Arabic, not Turkish:

> The sights of Anatolia and its houses passed by us in a uniform way, until we got back onto the raft again and it took us southward with the flow of the Tigris. We found ourselves in a new world: the Arab tribes (*qaba'il*) living on the banks of the river provided us with what we needed and gave to us the fruits of their lands. They would sing to us and recite poetry, poetry of war and poetry of the nation, songs and poems that stirred our spirits. For this was our language, heard in so many different dialects, and this was a shared feeling. These Arab customs showed them in every way to be part of our nation.

The romantic image of Arab tribesmen shouting out greetings from the banks of the Tigris, welcoming the two young officers with bountiful offerings and songs of war and nation, seems to spring less from a personal account of an experience of travel than from Qawuqji's later desire to render a public story of Arab nationalism. A major component of Qawuqji's brand of nationalism is the notion that the tribes represent the essence of the Arab nation. This does not mean that we must be skeptical of Qawuqji's claim that he really experienced a feeling of kinship when he heard the people on the banks of the river speaking Arabic rather than Turkish and when he saw that their customs were more akin to his own than to those of the Turkish villagers he had encountered earlier. And yet one suspects that this young man, who had spent his early childhood in an urban environment in the port city of Tripoli and his young adulthood in the War College in Istanbul, where he was taught in Turkish and surrounded by fellow cadets who came from every corner of the Ottoman Empire, probably had more prosaic encounters with the tribes on the banks of the Tigris than his lyrical description implies. Where is Qawuqji's anxiety that the rains might swell the waters of the Tigris to such a degree that it would be dangerous to continue? Where is his preoccupation with ensuring that they had enough food to last the rest of the journey? Where are his growing feelings of intimacy with his friend, who shared the grueling journey with him for over forty days? These stories are absent. The nationalistic narrative of 1912 that Qawuqji tells as a 1970s memoirist is much more important to him than what would have seemed to him like trivial details. Qawuqji journeyed through the lands of the Ottoman Empire when it was a borderless patchwork of different linguistic and religious communities. But the journey also took place at a time when the Ottoman polity was beginning to reconfigure itself along national lines. For example, 1912 was smack in the middle of the Balkan wars of independence from the Ottoman state. From the vantage point of the 1970s, 1912 stood out as a moment when the Arab nation was emerging toward its natural fulfillment. Since the late nineteenth century a handful of Arab subjects of the Ottoman Empire, mainly intellectuals and military officers, had articulated the new idea of Arabism, which emphasized the differences between Turkish and Arab cultural and political identities and promoted the Arabic language over Ottoman

Turkish, the language of the state. Popular support for the idea of Arab-ism, though still restricted to a minority of Arabs, grew after 1908 as a response to the Young Turks and their focus on a Turkish-centered Ottoman identity. Some Ottoman Arabs formed small secret societies like al-Fatat (The Youth) and al-'Ahd (The Covenant), whose members discussed the possibility of Arab autonomy within the structure of the Ottoman Empire. To the Qawuqji of the 1970s, mindful of half a century of Arab nationalism's bitter disappointments, the tribes rushing out to greet him and the Arabness they represented were a glimpse back to a future now lost.

Qawuqji's destination, the city of Mosul, straddled the banks of the Tigris about 250 miles northwest of Baghdad. Then the capital of the Ottoman vilayet of Mosul, the city had a mixed population of Arabs, Kurds, Assyrians, Armenians, and Turkomans. Under the Ottoman Empire it served as an important center of trade because of its strategic location on the caravan route linking India and Persia with the Mediter-ranean. The main market in Mosul lay inside the eight gated thick stone city walls. It was known for its metalwork, spices, leatherwork, and lux-ury goods. Mosul was famous for its mosques—particularly the mosque of Nabi Younis—as well as for the ruins of the ancient city of Nineveh. The city had famously fertile soil; one of its epithets was The Green (al-Khadra').

Qawuqji also states in his memoirs that following the abolition of the Ottoman caliphate in 1924, Mosul became the "the city that the late Rashid Rida had suggested as the center of the new Islamic caliphate because it was encircled by the borders of the neighboring Islamic lands, such as Turkey, Iran, and Syria." The institution of the caliphate originated in the seventh century and emerged as an Islamic system of governance that designated the caliph the leader of all Muslims. During the Ottoman period, which lasted from the early sixteenth century to the establishment of the Turkish Republic in 1923, the Ottoman sultan also designated himself as caliph and nominal head of all Muslims. Many Muslim Arab nationalists mourned the end of the caliphate in 1924, and efforts to restore it were part of the struggle for Arab independence from British and French colonialism in the post-Ottoman period. Like Qawuqji, Rashid Rida, the early-twentieth-century journalist, Muslim reformer, and Arab nationalist, was from Tripoli. Like Rida, Qawuqji saw no contradiction between the revival of the caliphate and Arab nationalism. Both were aspects of the same anticolonial effort. As was the case with many others of his era, Qawuqji does not fit squarely into either category: secular nationalist on the one hand, or Islamic revivalist on the other. For him, the restoration of the true Arab caliphate and the promotion of the tribes as the essence of the Arab nation were part of the same project. Arab nationalism meant different things to different people. For many, particularly Arab Christians and other minorities, Arab nationalism was a modern secular ideology, which promoted the Arabic language and Arab cultural heritage. Most Christians and even some Muslims were not particularly drawn to an Arab nationalist rhetoric that employed Islamic themes. For many others, particularly for Sunni Muslims like Qawuqji, Islam was integral to their understanding of Arab nationalism; they felt comfortable with, and inspired by, Islamic symbols.

The tribes as the essence of Arabness is a central theme of Qawuqji's depiction of his evolution from Ottoman man to Arab man. He traces his dawning awareness of Arab identity to his days in the War College and the fact that the Turkish officers around him started to identify themselves not as subjects of the Ottoman Empire but as belonging to Turan, as the heirs of the Turkic peoples of Central Asia. As Qawuqji tells it, the Arabs had to respond by articulating how they too were not Ottomans but Arabs: "The particularism of the Turks increased over time, and their assertion of their links to the Turan intensified just as our desire to locate the spring of our Arabness intensified. And we had to search for an ancestry to connect to and be proud of so that whenever the Turks said, 'We are Turanids,' we would say, 'And we are Qahtanid.'"

According to Qawuqji's genealogy of Arabness, the Qahtan, a pre-Islamic southern Arabian tribe, are cast as the original Arabs. They are juxtaposed with the 'Adnan, a northern tribe that is said to have been Arabized at a later period. The term "Qahtan" enjoyed a brief period of popularity in the early days of Arab nationalism. The soldier-nationalist

'Aziz 'Ali al-Masri, who also studied at the War College in Istanbul, founded a group called al-Qahtaniyya in 1909 with a view to promoting the creation of an autonomous Arab enclave within a kingdom over which the Turkish sultan would be sovereign. In 1914 al-Qahtaniyya became al-'Ahd (The Covenant), the secret club of Arab officers in the Ottoman Army mentioned above, and Qawuqji joined it during his time in Mosul. But Qawuqji's preoccupation with the differences between Arabs and Turks was not the only thing on his mind as he struggled to establish himself as a junior officer in the Mosul garrison.

The citadel and the parade ground were in the northern part of the city. This is where the governor had his offices and where Qawuqji went for drills and other official garrison business. Like other officers, he was billeted outside the citadel area and lived in a house in one of the neighborhoods near the banks of the Tigris. At the top of the photograph of Mosul (figure 4), taken a few years after Qawuqji's time there, the Tigris winds southward.

Qawuqji's neighborhood (*mahalla*) provided him with the daily needs of life. It had a public bathhouse and a weekly market, and it was structured around a mosque complex that, in addition to serving as a place for public prayer and the celebration of religious holidays, provided a small hospital and school. Qawuqji had the choice of drawing water directly from the Tigris or paying a few piasters for a weekly delivery of water by mule. The officers' pay was often in arrears, and sometimes they depended on the goodwill of their neighbors for food and other amenities.

Among its many responsibilities, the Mosul garrison was tasked with collecting taxes. Troops fanned out into the countryside around Mosul to force reluctant tribesmen to pay up. The garrison's role in tax collecting was a local effect of the centralization and modernization drive undertaken by the Ottoman state in the late nineteenth and early twentieth centuries. It was also a way for officers to cope with the problem of late salary payments. Once they collected taxes from the tribes, they could skim a little off the top, often to send home to their wives and children. This was common practice in garrison towns across the empire that were close to large tribal federations. The tribes were notorious for not paying

FIGURE 4

their taxes, and local governors often had to call in the army to enforce tax collection in tribal areas.

The troops were also called on to settle disputes between tribes and to prevent tribal raiding, which had gone on for centuries as part of a complex system of social and economic checks and balances in tribal society. The various arms of the Ottoman state made increasing efforts to control this raiding. The need was particularly acute when raiding affected local merchants, who—in the eyes of the local governor, responsible to Istanbul—represented the mainstay of the region's taxpayers. In the four years before Qawuqji arrived in Mosul, the Shammar and Dulaym tribes stole thousands of goats that were owned by merchants from Aleppo and Mosul and were pastured by the settled village communities along the banks of the Tigris. The Ottoman governor received complaints not only from aggrieved merchants but also from tribal shaykhs demanding the freedom to pursue traditional practices that were crucial to their economic independence. Both merchants and tribes practiced animal husbandry, a key component of the Mosul economy, and this led to sometimes destructive competition between the two constituencies.

Soon after Qawuqji's arrival the commander of his battalion, Asad Bey, called him into his office in the citadel. Asad Bey explained that two units of the garrison had been sent to the summer grazing pastures of the Shammar tribe, in order to force it to pay the taxes that it owed. Not only did the Shammar refuse to comply, but they were causing havoc in the grazing area of the Jubur tribe. Asad Bey dispatched Qawuqji with twenty-five cavalry soldiers to extract the taxes from the Shammar and at the same time protect the grazing lands of the Jubur. This was Qawuqji's first big responsibility after graduating from the War College. The shopkeepers of Mosul were thus treated to the spectacle of a troop of Ottoman cavalry-men, riding out of the walled city across the old stone bridge and disappearing north toward the grazing lands of the Jubur.

Qawuqji and his troops forced Shammar tribesmen to pay their taxes and to return the goods that they had stolen from the Jubur, and his narrative follows a pattern that repeats itself throughout his memoirs: he pulled off an unexpected feat by taking imaginative risks. In this case he tricked the shaykh of the Shammar into believing that he was surrounded by an entire battalion of Ottoman soldiers who would capture and kill the whole tribe unless he returned the stolen goods. Qawuqji's gamble paid off, but it landed him in trouble with his commanding officer. As rumors of Qawuqji's success against the Shammar spread, other tribes in the area asked him to settle their raiding disputes, and as a result, he stayed away from the garrison for long stretches.

Apart from his army duties and his reconciliation efforts among the tribes, Qawuqji actively participated in a secret society of Arab army officers who met regularly to discuss the threat posed to Arabs by the increasing Turkification of the Ottoman bureaucracy, including the officer corps of the army, in the wake of the 1908 revolt. One night in Mosul a stranger came to Qawuqji's billet on the banks of the Tigris. The stranger whispered that if Qawuqji really believed in his nation, he would get up and follow him without asking why. He then blindfolded Qawuqji and led him through the night to another house. When they arrived, the man removed the blindfold, and there before Qawuqji was a group of men sitting around a table upon which lay a copy of the Quran, a sword, and a pistol. They asked him to swear in front of the group that he would commit himself to working toward the freedom of the Arabs, and he duly did. The blindfold was put back on, and Qawuqji was led back home.

In spite of his dramatic initiation, Qawuqji felt skeptical about the effectiveness of these groups. His doubts became particularly acute after the dissolution of a plan to send him to the Arabian Peninsula to garner support there for the Arab nationalist cause. Hearing news from Istanbul of the Young Turks' increasing hold on power, Qawuqji worried that the group he had joined was just talk and no action:

> It dawned on me that the organization of our group was not like the organization of the Turkish Committee of Union and Progress, which was planning and putting things into effect. Meanwhile we were perfecting our plans, and talking, and not doing anything. I asked myself: Are we less capable than the Turks? Or are the Turks braver than we are? Or are we just dreamers and the Turks doers? And all this in spite of the fact that Arabs are intellectually superior to Turks? And the answer came to me that this is what will be revealed in the long days ahead.

Competition with Turkish fellow officers was not restricted to politics. One thread that runs through Qawuqji's account of his Mosul days is his attraction to a beautiful young Arab woman who lived in one of the houses in his neighborhood. Both he and some Turkish officers billeted nearby vied for her attention as she walked through the alleys to go to market. Qawuqji was convinced that he had a better chance than the Turkish officers because like her, he was an Arab and was therefore better acquainted with the style of courtship that she was used to. After returning from Mosul from his time with the tribes, he sensed that his reputation in his neighborhood had soared, particularly because of his being able to get the Shammar to pay their taxes. This caused him to imagine that he might have, in his words, "found favor with her." So he wrote her a letter. Unfortunately his attempt to woo her was horribly bungled. At the same time he wrote to her he also wrote to his father in Tripoli. But he put the wrong letter in the envelope and ended up receiving an angry reprimand from his father by return post: What was he doing spending all his time running after women? He had not raised a son with such morals! Qawuqji was shocked and hurt by his father's response, but soon afterward he received a letter from his mother, telling him that young men were going off to fight on various fronts. Even his father, she told him, in spite of his age, had left to fight on the Erzurum front. It was 1914, and the Ottoman Empire had joined Germany in the war against Britain and France. Qawuqji's mother hoped for glory for him in the days ahead.

For Qawuqji, World War I did not begin with Archduke Franz Ferdinand's assassination in Sarajevo, or with the negotiations and alliances between the Ottoman state and imperial Germany or with the passage through the Dardanelles of the SMS *Goeben* and the SMS *Breslau*. It began in the late fall of 1914 with the British invasion of Iraq and their occupation of Basra and al-Qurna. Five hundred miles southeast of Mosul, Basra lay on the banks of the Shatt al-'Arab. Fed by the Tigris and the Euphrates, which came together just a few miles north of Basra at the small river town of al-Qurna, the Shatt al-'Arab is a broad waterway that flows into the Persian Gulf and today marks the boundary between Iraq and Iran.

In early November 1914, following a heavy bombardment by the Royal Navy, British troops landed at an old fort on the Fao Peninsula, just south of Basra. From there they pushed the Turkish defenses back until they captured Basra on November 21. The main goal of the British campaign was to protect British oil interests in the Persian Gulf. To that end they pushed farther up the Shatt al-'Arab in order to secure the oil works near al-Qurna. After several battles with the Turkish Thirty-eighth Infantry Division, the British seized control of al-Qurna itself by the second week of December.

FROM THE IRAQI FRONT TO THE PALESTINIAN FRONT

In early January 1915 the Ottoman Army sent Qawuqji from Mosul to al-Qurna in command of a small cavalry unit. Qawuqji's unit was itself part of Sulayman Askeri Pasha's Thirty-eighth Infantry Division, tasked with defending the mouth of the Euphrates from British advance. Qawuqji was wounded defending a line that ran along an irrigation canal in the Ruta region northeast of the town. Sulayman Askeri Pasha (who later committed suicide because of his failure to defend al-Qurna) was also wounded. Both he and Qawuqji were part of a convoy of casualties making their way approximately three hundred miles north to the hospitals of Baghdad. For Qawuqji the battle for al-Qurna marked the beginning of four years of fighting against the British conquest of Ottoman Arab lands. He watched soldiers of the British and Australian armies invade and conquer al-Qurna in southern Iraq, Bir Sabʻa in the desert in southern Palestine, Jerusalem, Ramallah, Baysan, and finally Damascus. This struggle against the British march through the Ottoman Middle East was the story of World War I for Qawuqji and thousands of other Ottoman Arab soldiers. Of course the better-known story about Arabs in World War I is that of the pro-British Arab Revolt of 1916, helped by the British officer T. E. Lawrence. But in military terms the Arab Revolt was a sideshow. Far more Arab soldiers in fact fought on the Ottoman side, resisting British advances.

After recovering in Baghdad from the wounds he received in the battle of al-Qurna, Qawuqji was ordered to rejoin his unit, which by this time had moved to the Gaza–Bir Sabʻa line that was holding back the British advance from Egypt into southern Palestine. Defending Bir Sabʻa was not Qawuqji's first choice. He managed to get himself discharged from the hospital on the basis of his rejoining his unit but instead headed toward Mount Lebanon and arrived eventually at Jamal Pasha's headquarters in Jounieh, a coastal town just north of Beirut. Jamal Pasha was the Turkish

Ottoman commander in overall charge of operations in the Levant. Once there Qawuqji asked to be attached to a cavalry unit that would defend Jounieh in the event of a British or French assault on the port. Jounieh was only a day's ride from his hometown of Tripoli, and it was also attractive to Qawuqji because of his involvement with a group of politically active Ottoman Arab officers based near Beirut. One of Jamal Pasha's preoccupations during this early period of the war was to preempt the clustering of politicized Arab officers in individual military units. He wanted them spread out across the various fronts, where they would be less likely to crystallize into anything that might thwart Ottoman objectives. Qawuqji, who was known to be politicized by this time, was thus denied his request to join the cavalry unit to defend Jounieh. He was dispatched instead to rejoin his unit in the small desert town of Bir Sabʻa in southern Palestine.

Qawuqji took some time to get to Bir Sabʻa. In the Middle East of 1915, trains sometimes took days to show up and, once they appeared, only crept along temporary tracks that had been laid in a hurry for army mobilization. Soldiers often spent days in the cities of transit—Istanbul, Jerusalem, Aleppo, Damascus—waiting for trains to take them on the next legs of their journeys. In 1915 there were also very few spur lines, so much of the travel inland was done on horseback across rough country or by horse and wagon on dirt tracks. These delays provided an opportunity for Qawuqji to stay for a while with friends in a village near Nablus and to meet up in Jerusalem with a woman who had joined him from Beirut. In Jerusalem he also socialized with a group of German officers staying at the same hotel. This was the first of Qawuqji's encounters with German officers during the war. He was struck by how much less supercilious they were toward him than the Turkish officers he had dealt with. His overriding memory of those few days in Jerusalem was of being treated by the German officers as if he were one of them.

Qawuqji finally arrived in Bir Sabʻa in early March 1916. Bir Sabʻa was the end of the Ottoman line of defense that began in the city of Gaza, thirty miles to the west on the coast of the Mediterranean. Bir Sabʻa

FIGURE 5

was a small town of just a few hundred people; its buildings, including a
police station, had been planned according to a small grid drawn up for
the Ottoman state by architects in the late nineteenth century (figure 5).

The town was designed to serve primarily as a garrison to control
the Bedouin tribes of the Naqab (Negev) Desert of southern Palestine.
In late 1915 a small railway station had been built there to serve the spur
line, which was an essential supply line to Ottoman troops stationed
at the last outpost of the Gaza–Bir Sabʿa defenses. Here is how Qawuqji,
who had spent most of his life in the bustling cities of Tripoli, Istanbul,
and Mosul, describes the town: "Bir Sabʿa was a pit surrounded on all
sides except the north by sand dunes and arid uninhabited desert, except
for the few places that had freshwater wells and were where the tribes
came to water their livestock. It was constantly exposed to sand storms,
which sometimes filled the sky and covered the tents so that they came
to resemble a momentary sand hill made by the wind."

Presenting his papers to his commanding officer, along with a pro-
fuse apology for his tardiness, Qawuqji began his posting to Bir Sabʿa. It

remained his base until the British army pushed him and his comrades north to Jerusalem in the fall of 1917.

RECONNAISSANCE AND THE IRON CROSS

Apart from maintaining the trenches and guarding supply lines, there was not much to do at the Bir Sab'a end of the line except to wait for the much-talked-about British attack. Reconnaissance operations were the surest route to glory; these were how you earned the respect of your fellow officers and your troops. From the moment he arrived in Bir Sab'a, Qawuqji pestered his commanding officer to be allowed to take a small cavalry unit out on a reconnaissance mission. When his commanding officer finally relented, Qawuqji's ignorance of this new terrain and of reconnaissance tactics in general soon became evident. He headed straight into a British ambush and returned with some of his cavalrymen killed and others wounded. But with time his reconnaissance skills improved, and he became famous in the Bir Sab'a military camp for his tactics. After one particularly successful foray he was awarded the Ottoman Medal of War. Qawuqji's aptitude for risky adventures, which had served him so well in forcing the Shammar to pay their taxes during his prewar posting in Mosul, features prominently in his narrative of his wartime experiences.

Qawuqji's exploits were also recognized with another medal, the German Iron Cross. The photograph of him in his Ottoman Army uniform (figure 6) shows his medals. The top of his Iron Cross is visible on the left of the row of medals.

In late October 1917 the British-Australian assault on the Gaza–Bir Sab'a line hit the Ottoman Army hard and pushed Qawuqji and his unit north toward Jerusalem and Ramallah. Nestled in the Judean Hills due north of Jerusalem, the small village of Nabi Samuel was regarded by the Ottoman general staff as the key to Jerusalem's defense: whoever had control of Nabi Samuel commanded an important road into Jerusalem and a strategic high point overlooking the city. Nabi Samuel

FIGURE 6

changed hands many times over the course of the battle for Jerusalem and eventually ended up under British control. This in turn led to General Edmund Allenby's capture of the city. During one of the Ottoman counterassaults on Nabi Samuel, Qawuqji was appointed the liaison between the German and Turkish units involved in the attack.

That particular autumn the Judean Hills were treacherous terrain. Torrents of rain had made the rock-strewn ground slippery, and there were few paths between the small villages. Horses could not be ridden but had to be led in single file, so that to reach Nabi Samuel, most of the men in Qawuqji's unit, some with no shoes or just cloth tied to their feet, had to walk over miles of rough wet ground. The German unit that was attached to Qawuqji's led the attack. It began in the early evening, and by nightfall they had managed to take control of sections of Nabi Samuel from the British, so that part of the village was in their hands and part was in enemy hands. The positions of the combatants were so close that it was impossible to put up barbed wire to demarcate their positions. The commander of the German unit decided that the wisest course was to withdraw that night under the cover of darkness. But Qawuqji had fought hard to take the parts of the town that they held, and he persuaded the German commander to let him take some men and advance on the British positions. At one in the morning on the night of December 6, 1917,

Qawuqji roused his men, and they all drank tea with some rum mixed in. They then crept over the village's ruined walls, which had been shelled the previous day by Turkish artillery.

> We threw all the hand grenades that we had so that the sound of them tore through the silence. Then we struck like lightning at the British lines, and the voices of the German soldiers were raised in a loud "Hurrah." The bayonets did their work, and it was not long before the British troops left alive were defeated and withdrew from this area of the front on the enemy's right flank. Then we started in with rifles and light artillery, and quickly the entire enemy line of the village fell.

Qawuqji subsequently received the Iron Cross for his role in this attack, even though the British retook the village the following day. General Allenby entered Jerusalem on December 11, 1917 (figure 7). In Qawuqji's words, it was "the most important political event of that year."

The British capture of Jerusalem sealed the British army's conquest of Palestine. Only five weeks earlier the British government had issued the Balfour Declaration, in which Palestine was promised as a "national home for the Jews." European Jews committed to Zionism had lobbied for many years to secure British support for their project of settling Jews

FIGURE 7

in Palestine. In 1917, at the moment of the British conquest, Jews made up 11 percent of the population of Palestine. Some of them were from religious communities that had lived there for generations. Others were recently arrived Europeans, committed to the political goal of settling in the area of the Middle East that they regarded as the ancient kingdom of Israel, the original home of the Jews. The remaining 89 percent of the population were Palestinian Arabs. Many Palestinians were farmers and lived in the thousands of villages scattered across Palestine. But there was also a significant urban population living in Palestinian cities and towns like Jerusalem, Jaffa, Haifa, Acre, Nablus, Nazareth, and Safad. The Balfour Declaration would have remained just words on a piece of paper without the British military occupation of Palestine, which was to last thirty-one years. Qawuqji watched the British conquest unfold with his own eyes. He had probably not even heard of the Balfour Declaration, remote as it was from the realities of his life in the war. But in March 1948, after a long career spent fighting against British and French colonialism all over the Middle East, he was to return to the Judean Hills above Jerusalem in order to lead the fight in the 1948 Arab-Israeli War.

GERMAN OFFICERS AND JAMAL PASHA

Several weeks after the fall of Jerusalem, with his unit based in Ramallah, just north of Jerusalem, Qawuqji met the German general Otto Liman von Sanders. Germany was allied with the Ottoman Empire, and following Allenby's victory, von Sanders had taken control of the Ottoman Army in Palestine, replacing his predecessor, Erich von Falkenhayn. Von Sanders directed the overall Ottoman campaign in Palestine and the Sinai. This placed him above Jamal Pasha in the chain of command. Frustrated by the state of German-Ottoman reconnaissance, which was mostly limited to sporadic sorties by the Albatross airplanes of the small German air force there, von Sanders ordered Qawuqji to infiltrate British lines and bring back a report on their maneuvers, weapons stockpiles, and lines of supply. This Qawuqji did, slipping behind the lines at night, hiding throughout the day on top of a small wooded hill, and noting down British movements. Reconnaisance missions such as these were part of a pattern of special tasks that Qawuqji undertook for German officers during the war. Von Sanders was the most famous of these officers, but the closest relationship that Qawuqji formed was with von Leyser, with whom he worked closely in the early days of the Bir Sab'a campaign. Von Leyser was a German cavalry officer who had been appointed to organize the lines of the military encampment between Bir Sab'a, the trenches, and the old fort of al-Nakhil. Qawuqji's commanding officer, Asad Bey, assigned him to serve as a special assistant to von Leyser. Qawuqji remembered some German from his days in the War College in Istanbul, but through his dealings with von Leyser and with other German soldiers connected to von Leyser, his German quickly became quite good. Qawuqji's special relationship to von Leyser also freed him from his normal duties, and this in turn enabled him to try to reestablish contact with old friends among the group of Arab army officers whom Jamal Pasha had dispersed all over the empire. Qawuqji even succeeded in using his influence with von Leyser to arrange for some of these friends to be transferred to the Bir Sab'a front.

When Jamal Pasha made a much-publicized visit to the Palestine front in 1916, he stopped at Bir Sab'a to inspect the troops. Von Leyser accompanied him on the inspection, and Qawuqji served as a translator between von Leyser and Jamal Pasha. When Jamal Pasha realized that there were quite a few Arab officers in the inspection line, he became increasingly agitated. A series of awkward conversations between Jamal Pasha and Qawuqji followed. They ended with Jamal Pasha's storming off the parade ground and insisting on talking privately to von Leyser and Qawuqji. In one of the German medical tents nearby, Qawuqji and Jamal Pasha had a long and angry conversation in Turkish, during which Jamal Pasha accused him of being a pro-Arab agitator. When Qawuqji explained to von Leyser that the conversation between him and Jamal Pasha had nothing to do with the troops or the state of the military preparations at Bir Sab'a but was focused instead on "Syrian politics," von Leyser was so furious that he stormed out of the tent. For von Leyser, Jamal Pasha's suspicions about the loyalty of Arab officers were a dangerous distraction from the joint Ottoman-German goal of winning the war.

After Jamal Pasha left to inspect troops elsewhere on the Palestine front, Qawuqji worried about the repercussions for him and the other Arab officers at Bir Sabʿa. He knew that a concentration of Arab officers under German rather than Turkish command would preoccupy Jamal Pasha's mind, given his anxieties about Arab loyalty to the Ottoman state. What made this all the more tense was Jamal Pasha's execution of Arab anti-Ottoman activists in Damascus earlier that summer. Photographs of these executions were published in the Arabic press, and this in turn led to strained relations between Arab and Turkish officers in the Ottoman Army. One blurred photograph (figure 8) shows the corpses of the Arab nationalists hanging on a scaffold while Ottoman officers stand by.

Soon after Jamal Pasha's inspection, and to hardly anyone's surprise, he issued an order to disperse the Arab officers at Bir Sabʿa to other fronts. The incident on the parade ground among Qawuqji, von Leyser, and Jamal Pasha marked the beginning of a series of events that culminated in Qawuqji's arrest for crimes against the Ottoman state and von Leyser's maneuvers to free him from military detention and return him to the front. Qawuqji's persecution as an Arab officer in the Ottoman Army brought him closer to von Leyser and other German soldiers and rein-

FIGURE 8

forced the feeling he had experienced in the hotel in Jerusalem on the way to Bir Sabʿa: that he could trust the German officers and that they treated him as one of their own. His connection to von Leyser made him an object of suspicion among the Turkish officers, particularly as relations between the Germans and the Ottomans deteriorated after the war had turned in favor of the entente. By the summer of 1916 the Ottoman government had become concerned that some Ottoman subjects were switching sides. The year before, the government had designated the entire Ottoman Armenian population in eastern Anatolia a potential fifth column and begun the deportation of those Armenians, leading to the deaths of hundreds of thousands. Arab subjects of the Ottoman Empire were generally regarded as loyal to the Ottoman side and not targeted to the same degree as Armenians had been. But Arab defections to the entente, although small in number, were symbolically important. In June 1916 the pro-British Arab Revolt broke out in the Hijaz. Jamal Pasha's draconian tactics in the Levant, including his execution of the Arab nationalists in Damascus in the summer of 1916, further alienated the Ottoman Empire's Arab subjects. In this climate, given the growing uncertainty among Ottoman Turkish officers about the loyalty of non-Turks, Arab officers such as Qawuqji came to be the focus of intense suspicion. The truth remains that Qawuqji stayed loyal to the Ottoman Army until the end of the war, despite his resentment toward some Turkish Ottoman officers who had treated him badly.

One experience that bonded Qawuqji to von Leyser was their common misfortune to have been in a train crash between Bir Sabʿa and Jerusalem. Von Leyser had been summoned to Istanbul to receive new orders to assume command of another unit. To Qawuqji's delight, von Leyser requested that he accompany him; here was a chance to get out of Bir Sabʿa and back to civilization, at least for a while. But Qawuqji had also just received new orders, to present himself at a military court in Jerusalem, with no details concerning the charge. They boarded the train together at Bir Sabʿa. The engine was pulling one passenger car, containing von Leyser, Qawuqji, and forty other soldiers, and several cars filled with artillery shells. The train moved quickly, and as it started to climb toward Jerusalem, it approached a series of bends where the track was being repaired. The workmen had not cleaned up properly, and some tools had been left on the line. Although red flags were put up, these were too far from those points on the track where the men had been working, and the driver missed the warning. Von Leyser, standing at the window staring at the desert hills, suddenly called out to Qawuqji and jumped from the train. Before Qawuqji had a chance to think, he was thrown into the air and heard a massive crack as two of the carriages carrying shells rolled over. Qawuqji lay covered in dust, waiting for the shells to explode. When he felt it was safe, he crawled over to von Leyser. The rest of the German soldiers were trapped in the overturned car. After a few hours a wagon came by and took them back to Bir Sabʿa. The German soldiers were only lightly wounded, but the driver and engineer had been killed.

In the following weeks Qawuqji, accused of disregarding the laws of the Ottoman state, appeared in court. Both Qawuqji and von Leyser knew that this charge arose from Jamal Pasha's visit to Bir Sabʿa, where the Ottoman general felt threatened by the presence of so many Arab officers in one unit and became suspicious of Qawuqji's special relationship with a German officer. Von Leyser used his influence with the Ottoman authorities to protect Qawuqji from these charges. Among Qawuqji's private papers is a letter that von Leyser wrote for him in mid-1917, testifying to his loyal service in the Ottoman Army:

Syria 18/5/17

This is to confirm that First Lieutenant Fawzi Bey served with me in his capacity as companion and aide from 1/3/16 until 12/5/17. I can testify to the fact that he offered outstanding service to his country during this period and distinguished himself with unusual energy and experience . . . [H]e is of good character and intelligent and perceptive, and he has perfected the German language in a few months in a way that has amazed everyone. I am recommending this young 23-year-old cavalry officer to future commanders with pride and honor, certain that he will be of indispensable service to the Ottoman state . . .

Signed: Von Leyser
Commander of Battle Formation, Sinai Front
Cavalry Officer, the State of Germany

Qawuqji's friendship with von Leyser and other German officers only deepened when von Leyser refused to abandon him, despite the insistence of Turkish officers that Qawuqji be condemned as an Arab traitor against the Ottoman state.

THE ARAB REVOLT

Like hundreds of other Arab officers in the Ottoman Army during World War I, Qawuqji did not join the pro-British Arab Revolt that originated in 1916 in the Hijaz and that has been made famous by the involvement of the British officer T. E. Lawrence. In fact very few Arab officers from the eastern Arab provinces of the empire (today Syria, Lebanon, Jordan, Israel/Palestine, and Iraq) joined the revolt. Many who joined, such as Ja'far Pasha al-'Askari and Salah al-Din al-Sabbagh, did so only after having been taken prisoner by the British. The ranks of the Arab Revolt were filled with tribesmen from the Arabian Peninsula, led by Amir (Prince) Faysal, the son of Husayn bin 'Ali, the sharif of Mecca. Husayn bin 'Ali had agreed to throw in his lot with the British in exchange for their promise that he and his sons would become leaders of an independent Arab state following the defeat of the Ottomans. But these tribesmen felt little connection to the tens of thousands of Ottoman Arab soldiers who hailed from villages and towns in the eastern Arab provinces. It is true that as the British pushed the Ottoman Army out of Palestine and advanced on Damascus, some Arab soldiers deserted the Ottoman Army and joined the Arab Revolt. Qawuqji did not join but clearly felt the need to explain his reasons. In a long passage in his memoirs, he explains that he viewed the Arab Revolt as an expression of British and French interests and that the specific objective of the British was to gain support for Allenby's push to Damascus, not to secure Arab independence from Ottoman rule. He saw "Lawrence's Arabs" as just another colonial unit of the British army, much like the Indians, Australians, or Canadians. Qawuqji's feelings are understandable. In 1916 and 1917 it would have seemed like an enormous step for an Ottoman career officer, who had been trained from childhood to think of his future in terms of advancement in the Ottoman Army, to walk away and join a bunch of desert tribesmen who for one reason or another had thrown in their lot with the British.

In October 1917 both morale and supplies were low in the Bir Sabʿa trenches, and British and Australian attacks grew more frequent. As Qawuqji woke up one morning, Bir Sabʿa filled with the dust of enemy cavalry, just beyond the reach of the Ottoman guns. Asad Bey asked Qawuqji to take a small number of men out to find out what was going on. Qawuqji took just two men to a small hill. As they started to ascend, two soldiers from the Australian Light Horse Brigade popped up from behind the brow of the hill and pointed their rifles at them. Qawuqji immediately raised his hands as if in surrender and shouted, "We are Arabs." He did this so that the Australian soldiers would think that he was an Arab soldier fleeing the Ottoman Army to join them. As they were being led into the Australian camp, they moved slowly behind the two Australians and then jumped on their horses and galloped as fast as they could down the hill and back behind the Turkish lines, where they were able to provide Asad Bey with some details of the Australian position. Qawuqji's loyalty to the Ottoman Army when desertions of Arab soldiers were becoming more frequent is a sign of how firm Qawuqji's link to the Ottoman state seemed at the time.

RETREAT AND FAMINE

At the end of October 1917, following the final British attack on Bir Sabʿa, Qawuqji's unit began its long retreat across Palestine and Syria, first to

Jerusalem (where he'd won the Iron Cross fighting at Nabi Samuel), then to Ramallah, to Baysan in the Galilee, to Darʿa, Kiswa, Damascus, al-Rabwa, Majdal ʿAnjar, and Riyaq, and finally to Homs. There he was given permission to leave the disintegrating Ottoman Army and journey home across the Lebanese mountains to Tripoli. Qawuqji witnessed the devastation that four years of war had brought to the population:

> Death had taken over every patch of land, so that these luminous Arab lands had become a grave for the living, with no sound and no movement. The people were no longer interested in news of the war or who was winning but rather were focused on the immediate needs of their next hour. No one was able to find out about the necessities of life, which were usually brought to them by the harvest. And it wasn't much better at the front. Famine covered everything.

The starvation afflicting both the Ottoman Army and the local population was made even more painful by the comparison with the British army, which was well-supplied. British soldiers were fed and clothed and wore leather shoes, unlike the bare feet and rags of the ordinary Ottoman soldiers. At dusk Qawuqji could see the British soldiers playing football far away in their camp, while soldiers in his camp were frantically digging trenches in an attempt to defend the towns they kept falling back from.

In late September 1918 Qawuqji's unit was ordered to retreat from Baysan, where they were still resisting Allenby's advance, to Darʿa in Syria, as part of a last-ditch effort to defend Damascus. Qawuqji's commander received orders not to attack the enemy and to proceed to Darʿa as quickly as possible. While they were camped on the east side of the Jordan River, just south of Baysan, Qawuqji heard about a small group of Turkish Seventh Army officers who had been cut off by the British advance and were in danger of being taken prisoner. Commanding the Seventh Army was Mustafa Kemal, hero of Gallipoli and later known as Ataturk, the founder of the modern Republic of Turkey. Qawuqji rushed to his commanding officer and requested permission to rescue the group of Turkish officers. Because the unit had clear orders to proceed to Darʿa as quickly as possible and not to engage the enemy, his request was turned down. He then went straight to the commander of the infantry, Rida Bey, who agreed to shell the British while Qawuqji sent two small companies across the Jordan to bring back the besieged officers. When one of the companies returned with the officers, it emerged that Mustafa Kemal was among them. Hearing of Qawuqji's role, Mustafa Kemal went to thank him. Qawuqji recorded his words in his memoirs: "You have not only saved the leaders of the Ottoman Army, but you have saved the honor of the army. In fact your actions should be a model for all officers."

Qawuqji's unit reached Damascus in late September 1918, just a few days before the arrival of the British and their allies from the Arab Revolt. Mustafa Kemal and some German officers commandeered as their headquarters the Victoria Hotel, which lay just to the west of the Hijaz railway station. Qawuqji was billeted in a smaller hotel nearby. Walking around the city for the first time in many years, he was shocked by its state: "I was wandering around the city that years of war had cut me off from, and I felt something unnatural in its spirit. People were full of anxiety, and the streets were clogged with soldiers who knew nothing about the fate of their units or what lay ahead. Anarchy ruled everywhere."

Shortly after arriving, Qawuqji went to the public bath (hammam) to wash and shave. While there, he heard shooting and people shouting. Rushing back to his hotel, Qawuqji saw soldiers frantically tearing off their military uniforms and racing toward the railway station. The British army and its Arab allies were in the outskirts of Damascus. The British military map (figure 9) shows the assault on Damascus on September 30, 1918.

Qawuqji ran down to the railway station, but it was so packed with soldiers trying to leave Damascus that it looked, in his words, "like a slice of watermelon in the desert covered with flies." Realizing that it was hopeless to leave by rail, he made his way back toward the barracks of Marja. In Marja Square he watched the flag of the Arab Revolt raised as speakers called on the people of Damascus to welcome Amir Faysal and the Arab Army as the new leaders of Syria. Hoping to join one of the

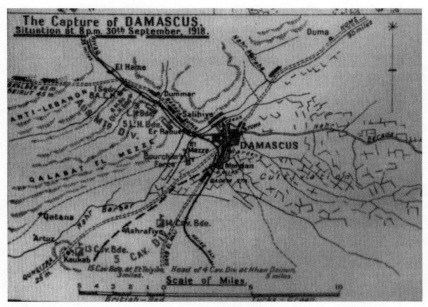

The Capture of DAMASCUS.
Situation at 8 p.m. 30th September, 1918.

FIGURE 9

Ottoman columns retreating toward Aleppo, Qawuqji then walked north. He ended up in Majdal 'Anjar, a town in the eastern Biqa' Valley a few miles northwest of Damascus. Majdal 'Anjar was full of Ottoman soldiers all trying to get home. German officers blocked them, insisting that they defend Majdal 'Anjar against the British advance. Some had camped in the pass at the entrance to the town. Qawuqji tried to warn one of the German officers that the British were very close and that the troops should be allowed to disperse, but it was too late. British planes flew low over the troops and fired on them with machine guns. Qawuqji had never seen an aerial attack of this intensity before, and he was horrified by the devastation it wrought. He never forgot the image of soldiers running to hide in the trees of a nearby orchard and being mowed down from the air, the orchard filling with dead and wounded men.

Qawuqji ran northward away from the orchard and with the surviving troops staggered into the small town of Riyaq. It was in chaos. The townspeople, desperate after years of famine, were stealing from the army's own scant supplies. Qawuqji sat amid the mayhem on a crate of champagne that had been abandoned by some German officers. In his memoirs he says that he felt as if he were sitting on one of the last pillars of the crumbling Ottoman Empire. He started to wonder what the future held for the Arabs. Would the British make good on their promise to give the Arabs independence in return for the support they had shown in the Arab Revolt? Qawuqji dug into the crate of champagne and drank down a whole bottle, banishing thoughts of the future from his mind. A few days later he was in Homs, where Mustafa Kemal was headquartered in the railway station, organizing the retreat of the Ottoman Army.

> I went to him. Restlessness and pain showed in his face and in his movements and he said: "So it is over. Our fate is in the hands of our enemies. Each man must do what he can to save what he can. I hope one day that the Arabs achieve a free state in which they can play a new role, and if you hear one day of things going on in Anatolia and you are not doing anything important in your country, come to us."

Qawuqji's story of his final encounter with Mustafa Kemal comes after his many vivid accounts of the collapse of the Ottoman military and civil infrastructure. This encounter is presented as the meeting of two battle-worn soldiers, burdened with the responsibility of salvaging the Turkish and Arab nations. In fact the establishment of the new republic of Turkey was still five years away, and the independence of most of the ex-Ottoman Arab provinces had to wait until the mid-1940s. The end of the Ottoman Empire did not happen neatly in a single moment. Qawuqji's story of his conversation with Mustafa Kemal in Homs is another example of the way Qawuqji's 1970s memoirs project backward, seeking to locate the origin of the division between the fate of Turkish Anatolia and that of the Arab provinces of the Ottoman Empire.

A few days later Mustafa Kemal went north to Aleppo, where he remained while the Treaty of Mudros was signed on October 30, 1918. The signatories agreed that hostilities would end at noon the following day.

Turkey was required to open the Dardanelles and the Bosphorus to Allied warships and its forts to military occupation. It was also required to de-mobilize its army, release all prisoners of war, and evacuate its rule in the Arab provinces, the majority of which were already under Allied control. Qawuqji left Homs and headed west, homeward to Tripoli. He arrived just in time to see British troops move in and take over his birthplace.

2

■

SYRIA IN REVOLT

An Arab army—Gouraud's ultimatum—A French cavalry officer—The road to rebellion—Sultan al-Atrash—Planning—A false start—*Hama est révolté*—To Damascus—Leadership in the Ghouta—A Syrian in the kingdom of Ibn Saʿud—Reforming the king's army—Arrested

In 1941, twenty-three years after the British army occupied Damascus, Qawuqji sat down at his desk in his apartment on Cuxhavener Street in the Hansaviertel in Berlin. There he drafted a long report for the German Foreign Ministry entitled "The Customs and Traditions of the Tribes of Syria and Iraq." Qawuqji had been asked to provide background information necessary for the logistical planning of a German invasion of Syria. Before its destruction during the Allied bombing of Berlin between 1943 and 1945, the Hansa quarter was a quiet bourgeois neighborhood, whose streets were lined with late-nineteenth-century, ornately designed apartment buildings. From the window of one of these apartments on Cuxhavener Street, Qawuqji looked down on well-tended trees and boys on bicycles going by. He was a long way from the mountains and deserts of Syria and Iraq. In his report he drew on his participation in the Syrian Revolt of 1925–1927 to furnish the Germans with details about the locations and political affiliations of the Syrian tribes whose support he relied on during the revolt. He described the people and geography of, in his words, "the beautiful mountainous regions of Syria," such as Jabal Druze, Jabal al-Zawiya, and Jabal Qalamun, focusing on the tribes that were most likely to support a German invasion—a German invasion that by his reckoning would end British and French imperialism in the region and guarantee the full independence of Syria and Iraq.

The document repeats language that Qawuqji used in another report that he had drafted fourteen years before, in 1927. Entitled "Reasons for the Revolution," this earlier report went to his contacts in Turkey as part of his attempt to garner Turkish support for the Syrian Revolt, which was beginning to falter by 1927. Under the subheading "The Geography of Syria" he describes the Syrian mountain ranges as a natural stronghold: "Based on its natural formations, Syria is considered to be an impenetrable site capable of defending itself. In it is a range of mountains that run parallel to its seashore right up to its northern borders. This range dominates the big cities of Beirut, Tripoli, Latakia, and many other cities."

What comes through in these two documents is his deep affection for the land of Syria. Historians have debated at length about what "Syria" meant to most people in the 1920s, 1930s, and 1940s. Was Qawuqji what some historians call a Greater Syrianist? In other words did he believe that the natural borders of Syria included what are today Lebanon, Jordan, and Israel/Palestine? We know from his memoirs that he opposed the colonial division of ex-Ottoman Arab lands into different mandate protostates. But nowhere does Qawuqji describe precisely where "Syria" began and ended, in, for example, 1922, or 1935, or 1941. What we can be certain of is his strong feeling of attachment to Syria, however it was defined. During the Syrian Revolt of 1925–1927, he fought hard for Syria's independence from the French, whom he regarded as foreign land grabbers. The failure of the revolt, and his exile from Syria in 1927, were devastating to him. In the years right after the collapse of the revolt, during his period of exile in the Hijaz, a province of today's Saudi Arabia, Qawuqji named his daughter Suriya. He always insisted on a pronunciation that emphasized the first syllable: SU-ri-ya, the Arabic for Syria, as opposed to the much more common girl's name Surayya.

Qawuqji features prominently in one of the first comprehensive histories of the Syrian Revolt. Written by the Syrian historian Muhyi al-Din Safarjalani, the book was published in Damascus in the early 1960s during the heyday of Syrian nationalism. The author's father had been a close friend of 'Abd al-Rahman Shahbandar, one of the leading figures of the revolt. Safarjalani spent years doing research, including collecting the testimonies of many of the major participants. The book has a special introduction by Shahbandar, recorded in 1938 more than twenty years before its publication. After Shahbandar's introductory words there is a short section entitled "The Words of the Arab Freedom Fighters," which includes the testimonies of other leaders of the revolt, such as Sultan al-Atrash, Fawzi al-Qawuqji, and Nasib al-Bakri. Full-page studio photographs of these men accompany many of the testimonies.

The Syrian Revolt of 1925–1927 marked Qawuqji's transition from pursuing a settled professional career as a cavalry officer in a state army to leading a peripatetic life of rebellion and exile. This chapter tells the story of that transition.

AN ARAB ARMY

After the Treaty of Mudros was signed on October 30, 1918, the rump state left behind from the Ottoman Empire opened the Dardanelles and the Bosphorus to Allied warships and its forts to Allied troops. The Versailles Peace Conference, just a few months away, began the process that transformed the Allied military occupation of Arab lands into the mandate system. Under the mandate system, Britain and France divided the Arab lands of the Ottoman Empire between themselves, creating the new states of Syria, Lebanon, Transjordan, Palestine, and Iraq. Britain ruled Transjordan, Palestine, and Iraq. France ruled Syria and Lebanon. In Anatolia, Mustafa Kemal used what was left of the Ottoman Army to lead a successful war of resistance—the Turkish War of Independence—against the Allied occupation, and he established the Republic of Turkey in 1923. The last Ottoman caliph was exiled from Turkey a year later. The map (figure 10) shows the new borders of the postwar era.

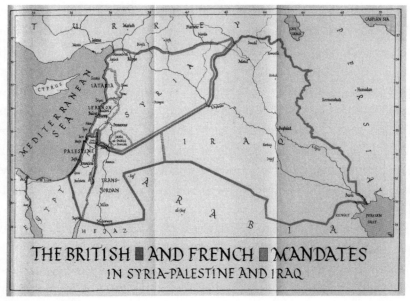

THE BRITISH ■ AND FRENCH ■ MANDATES
IN SYRIA-PALESTINE AND IRAQ

FIGURE 10

Many Arab men and women also resisted the Allied occupation of Arab lands and launched revolts against British and French occupation. Amir Faysal, who had led the pro-British Arab Revolt during World War I, tried to defend Syria against French control. He even ruled as king of Syria for a few months in 1920. Like Faysal, most Arabs strongly opposed the plans that were being drawn up for them at Versailles, but they did not have the military resources to defeat the British and French armies. Britain and France finally implemented the mandate system in the Arab lands of the ex-Ottoman Empire in 1923.

Qawuqji stayed with his unit in the Ottoman Army until the very end of the war. In the closing months of 1918 he had nothing to do but go home to his parents' house in Tripoli. He had seen the destruction that the war brought to Damascus, where rubble filled the streets and people starved as a result of years of famine. Tripoli, by contrast, had escaped the worst devastation. But food supplies were low, and the sudden disappearance of the Ottoman Army and Ottoman government infrastructure created anxiety and uncertainty about the future. Just a few days after his homecoming, some old childhood friends invited Qawuqji to a party. They wanted to chat and play some music. Qawuqji was withdrawn at the party, brooding over the long years of war and the collapse of his future as a cavalry officer in the Ottoman Army. In the middle of the party, just as the music was starting up, the unusual sound of car horns came in from outside the windows. Qawuqji rushed to the balcony of his friend's house, which overlooked Midan al-Taal, the main square of Tripoli. He watched as a column of British cars, followed by a British cavalry unit, wound its way into the square. He stayed on the balcony, joined now by his friends, as horses, cars, and men in British army uniforms gathered below him.

This was a deeply upsetting sight for Qawuqji, who had devoted the previous four years of his life to fighting against the British army's advance through Palestine, only to see them now laughing and shouting to one another in English as they milled around the center of his childhood home. This is what he says in his memoirs about the way he felt at that moment:

> As they gathered there, I felt as if the torrent of blood that had flowed between us during those four years of war had not stopped. The scene had a huge impact on me: the young men of the town playing music and having fun while the enemy moved its army and supplies and equipment into my town. What did the future hold? And what would protect my country from the greed of these conquerors?

One of Qawuqji's biggest worries in the years right after the war was that Arab soldiers could not fight as effectively as Turkish soldiers. This lack of confidence had been gnawing at him at the War College in Istanbul, and it intensified during his experiences with some Turkish officers he had served under during the war. Eventually stories about the anticolonial rebel 'Abd al-Karim al-Khattabi's battles against the French in Morocco during the early 1920s transformed Qawuqji's view of the fighting capabilities of Arab soldiers, but in late 1918, as the Turks fought their own war against the continued Allied occupation of Anatolia,

Qawuqji expressed pessimism about the Arabs' capacity to do the same: "I came out of the war with a low opinion of the Arab soldier and his abilities in warfare, and this was matched by my high esteem for the courage of the Turkish soldier, particularly when it came to defense."

Qawuqji knew that if he wanted to continue his career as a soldier, a career that he had been trained for since he was a small boy, he faced two choices: like many Arab ex-Ottoman officers, he could go north to Anatolia and join the reconfigured Ottoman Army, led by Mustafa Kemal, in its fight against the British and French for the independence of Anatolia, or he could stay close to his family and friends and throw in his lot with Amir Faysal and the Arab Army in Damascus.

Some historians refer to the time between Faysal's entry into Damascus in October 1918 and his expulsion by the French Army nearly two years later, in July 1920, as the period of Faysal's rule. Other historians argue that this is a misnomer. It is true that Faysal based himself in Damascus with a staff of Arab officers who had served with him during the Arab Revolt. He was also the nominal head of an Arab government. But there were many groups, both in Damascus and in other parts of the country, that felt little or no allegiance to this stranger from the Hijaz, who, backed by pro-Arab British officials like T. E. Lawrence, had set himself up as king of Syria. His territorial control was limited, and there were occasions during his brief rule when he required protection against those who regarded him as illegitimate. Many in Syria, and particularly members of the big landowning classes, saw him as an uncivilized tribesman, who had betrayed the Ottoman caliphate. Loyalty toward the caliph and the Ottoman Empire was still very strong in this early postwar period. Some British officials worked hard at Versailles in 1919 to fulfill the promises that had been made to Faysal concerning the independence of Syria. But the French also wanted Syria, and the British government refused to place the local interests of Faysal and his Syrian and Lebanese supporters above its geopolitical alliance with the French. In April 1920 the Allied Supreme Council met at San Remo and agreed to allocate the mandates of Syria and Lebanon to France.

It is difficult to know exactly how Qawuqji felt about Faysal's bid to rule Syria in 1918. Qawuqji's memoirs were compiled during the early 1970s, a time when Syrian nationalist historians described the Faysal period as the birth of Syrian nationalism. Qawuqji certainly felt a strong bond with the Arab officers who had joined the Arab Revolt during the war. These ties originated in their common experience of education and service. Many Arab ex–Ottoman Army officers who had not joined Faysal during the war were nevertheless willing to join his Arab Army in the wake of the collapse of the Ottoman state. Faysal and his officers welcomed these recruits into their ranks.

Faysal made a tour of the important cities of Syria in the late fall of 1918. He began in Aleppo and then proceeded to Homs, Tripoli, and Beirut. The photograph (figure 11) shows a woman from Aleppo watching Faysal's procession from her balcony as it passed through the city in late 1918.

In his memoirs Qawuqji describes Faysal's visit to Tripoli in some detail. The visit marked the beginning of Qawuqji's allegiance to the new Arab Army in Syria. Faysal was received by a small group of British officers, and he stayed in the house of the mufti of Tripoli, al-Sayyid ʿAbd al-Hamid Karami. Faysal's open connection to the British unsettled those like Qawuqji who had returned home from the front after fighting

FIGURE 11

to the end on the Ottoman side. At the same time, heads of Tripoli's leading families went to Karami's house to greet Faysal and to show that he was welcome. Qawuqji was not among this delegation, but Faysal sent a special request by messenger asking Qawuqji to come see him. Qawuqji agreed. He went to Karami's house with three friends, all of whom had also stayed loyal to the Ottoman Army throughout the war. Here is how Qawuqji describes his encounter with Faysal:

> We entered to where Amir Faysal was sitting, and we greeted him with a military salute. He returned the greeting and began to talk, saying, "I do not criticize, nor do I condemn any soldier who stayed with the Turkish Army. Your struggle is to your credit because you fought side by side with the Turks with faith and honor, and it was your right to do this. The fate of this country, of which you are a part, has been put in our hands and I call upon you to serve it." These words of Faysal's lifted our spirits, and we could do nothing but accept his invitation to serve under his command with joy and satisfaction.

As a result of this meeting, Qawuqji left Tripoli to return to Damascus. What had seemed to him like an empty future was now filled by what he hoped would be an important role in the new Arab Army in Syria. He allowed himself to feel the promise of this new future. After all, the British had promised Faysal's father, Sharif Husayn, an independent Arab state if he supported them during the war. With the departure of the Ottomans and with the support of some British officials, Syrians established a parliament and worked toward drafting a constitution. More important for Qawuqji, fellow ex-Ottoman officers who shared his background and experiences busied themselves constructing a new army. The Ottoman Army no longer existed, and being a soldier was what Qawuqji knew how to do, so he joined the office of Yasin al-Hashimi, minister of war in the new Syrian protogovernment. Hashimi had fought in the Ottoman Army and was one of the few Arab officers who had commanded a corps in the Ottoman Army. He remained loyal to the Ottoman Army until the very end of the war and had been wounded fighting against fellow Arabs serving in Faysal's forces.

It was not easy to bring together hundreds of officers and ordinary troops who had been fighting against one another only a few weeks before. The men felt anxious about the actual details of their new career. For example, the Ministry of War had to settle the question of which officers held which rank. This mattered not just for reasons of prestige but because rank was directly linked to salary. Should the ranking system of the Ottoman Army count for more than the ranking system of the army of the Arab Revolt? Many of the officers who had stayed loyal to the Ottoman Army believed that their fellow officers who joined the Arab Revolt had been overpromoted in an unofficial army. They argued that the only ranking system that counted was that of the Ottoman Army, which was grounded in imperial history and in the law of the sultan and caliph. By contrast, those officers who had joined the Arab Revolt and had fought hard to take Damascus alongside the British felt that they should maintain their ranks, particularly given that this new army, and the future toward which they all were directed, were a direct result of their efforts. As it turned out, officers who had fought in the Arab Revolt were usually given higher ranks than those who had remained with the Ottoman Army. Qawuqji was able to navigate his way skillfully through these difficulties and achieve the respectable position in the army of *ra'is*, or captain, which provided a salary he could live on. In late 1919 the General Command, headed now by Yusuf al-ʿAzma, Hashimi's successor, appointed Qawuqji commander of the First Company of the Cavalry Brigade. Qawuqji also took part in producing the first modern army manuals to be printed in Arabic. He was to use these manuals a few years later, when he worked to train armies in the Arabian Peninsula and Iraq.

The Center for Historical Documents in Damascus possesses a very blurred photograph (figure 12) of Qawuqji's identity card from the Arab Army dated 1920. The card lists basic information, including his brigade (cavalry), his rank (captain), his nationality (Arab), his religion (Islam), his

FIGURE 12

military education (War College in Istanbul), his place of birth (Tripoli), and so on. In the photograph he is clean shaven and looks very young. He is wearing his new army uniform: a high-collared shirt and tie, a dress coat with brass buttons, and the hat of the Arab Army.

Historians of this period are interested in the categories listed on ID cards like these. For example, the card divides religion from nationality. This was something new that was not practiced by Ottoman institutions. It is also interesting that the designated nationality is "Arab," not "Syrian." This appears to support the view of some historians that it is incorrect to talk about "Syrian" nationalism until later in the 1920s. Scholars tend to assume that documents like these can tell us something about how people felt about their identity at a given moment. But if we focus in a little closer, we can picture Qawuqji in the high-ceilinged room of the Damascus headquarters of the Arab Army, waiting to have his form filled out and his photograph attached. This young man in his early twenties was proud and relieved to be obtaining proof of membership in a new and important institution, all at a time of post-Ottoman chaos. The Ottoman Army's former Arab officers—at least those who wished to continue in a formal military career—saw the Arab Army as their best option, compared with joining the new Turkish Army fighting in Anatolia or one of the European armies occupying most Arab lands. Existential questions about his identity—whether he felt himself to be more "Arab" or "Syrian" or "Muslim"—were probably not preoccupying Qawuqji at that moment.

One of the Arab Army's primary tasks in 1919 was to maintain order, particularly in rural areas. Brigandage and tribal raids were serious problems after the war. Adding to the sense of apprehension was the fact that Faysal's attempts to secure international support for an independent Arab state at the peace negotiations in Versailles grew more and more hopeless as the French government negotiated hard for control of Syria. French negotiators at Versailles appealed to facts on the ground. The French Army, which had been based in Lebanon since October 1918, threatened the occupation of inland Syria. French forces concentrated in the town of Zahle in the Biqa' Valley, just a few miles from the main road between Damascus and Homs. To solidify its positions, the French Army sent French liaison officers to other towns in al-Biqa', such as Ba'albak and Rashayya. Toward the end of 1919, Yusuf al-'Azma, the new commander of the Arab Army, sent Qawuqji and his small cavalry company to al-Mu'allaqa, a town in the Biqa' that had come under the control of French troops led by a particularly aggressive French intelligence officer, whom Qawuqji refers to as Captain Hak. Qawuqji spent several weeks in al-Mu'allaqa trying to establish Arab Army control over the town and to prevent armed brigands from the countryside joining the French Army for money. Even within the Arab Army, some officers began taking a French conquest of inland Syria as a fait accompli, believing that it was hopeless to try to resist. One group of Arab Army officers saw the French as a less bad alternative to the British. This was the case with many Iraqi officers, who were all too aware of the British army's brutal suppression of a popular Iraqi uprising in 1919 and 1920.

GOURAUD'S ULTIMATUM

In December 1919 the British forces withdrew from Syria, leaving the way open for the French to take their place. On April 25, 1920, the Supreme Inter-Allied Council granted France the mandate over Syria and Lebanon. On July 14, 1920, Henri Gouraud, who had been named high commissioner of Syria, issued an ultimatum to Faysal forcing him to choose between submission and abdication. Gouraud (figure 13) had earned a reputation as a tough and imperious French colonial officer.

The leaders of the Arab Army disagreed about how to respond to the ultimatum. Some argued that it was smarter to negotiate with the French rather than try to fight one of the most powerful imperial armies in the world. Others, including 'Azma, the commander of the army, urged their comrades to follow the Turkish model and fight for independence while there was still a chance—that is, before the French Army had installed itself in Damascus.

Qawuqji remained distant from the debates of these weeks, focusing instead on maintaining security in the area that lay in the path of the French advance. For him, France was embodied in the person of Captain Hak, the French intelligence officer roaming around in al-Mu'allaqa. Qawuqji managed to throw him out of the main government building in al-Mu'allaqa and posted guards around town with the order to stop any Frenchman trying to pass. When Captain Hak rode into town one day and attempted to reach the government headquarters, Qawuqji's men seized him and refused to let him through until Qawuqji gave permission. Even then Captain Hak was only allowed to meet with Qawuqji surrounded by his men, who were armed. When Captain Hak complained that he would report Qawuqji to the Arab Army headquarters in Damascus, Qawuqji told him to go ahead. He was just carrying out the will of the Arab Army.

In Damascus the days following Gouraud's ultimatum were filled with anxiety and disorder. The shadow of France's imperial designs on Syria fell across the city. Huge popular demonstrations were directed against

FIGURE 13

Faysal, who was accused of collaborating with foreign invaders. Faysal struggled to prepare for the military defense of Syria, at the same time leaving open the possibility of peaceful negotiation. The mass conscription that Faysal had imposed a few weeks earlier also caused riots. Many Syrians associated conscription with the trauma of *seferberlik*, the forced enlistment that the Ottoman state had imposed on the Arab provinces during World War I. People were particularly angry about the *badal*, a fee that the rich could pay to exempt them from conscription.

The leaders of the Arab Army, most notably Hashimi and 'Azma, disagreed about whether they were ready to fight the French. 'Azma believed that the Arab Army had the capacity to fight and win. Hashimi was busy recruiting more men from across the country, including from the Bedouin tribes, arguing that in its current state the Arab Army could hold out for just a few days against a French advance. Knowing of Qawuqji's successes in al-Muʿallaqa and that Qawuqji commanded the loyalty of the men who were serving with him there, Hashimi summoned Qawuqji, who had by this time returned to Damascus, to a meeting with King Faysal. Qawuqji went to Faysal's headquarters in Damascus, close to Marja Square. Qawuqji entered the house and found Faysal sitting in his office, looking haggard. Faysal shook Qawuqji's hand and told him that the situation was extremely serious. He asked Qawuqji to take his men and go immediately to join Nuri Shaʿlan, the shaykh of al-Ruwala, one of the three large nomadic tribes that camped near Damascus in the summer. The tribes in Syria enjoyed a reputation for being protective of their independence, and tribal leaders such as Shaʿlan were more concerned for the welfare of their tribesmen than with who ruled in Damascus. But Shaʿlan had entered Damascus with Faysal in December 1918, thus temporarily expressing his support for Faysal's rule. Faysal believed that Shaʿlan's men could be invaluable allies if they agreed to join the Arab Army in the fight against the French.

Faysal ordered Qawuqji to take his company and some of Shaʿlan's men and get behind French lines. Qawuqji spent the following days roaming the countryside outside Damascus with his small company, trying to join up with Shaʿlan. During the third week of July 1920, Shaʿlan told Qawuqji through a messenger that he had doubts about the Arab Army's ability to defend his people and his livestock against the French advance. He refused to offer his support. Qawuqji, having failed in his mission, rushed back to help defend Damascus. But the main battle between the Arab Army and the French was already over. ʿAzma, in command of a few hundred regular soldiers from the Arab Army, along with some untrained citizen volunteers from Damascus, had ridden out to the town of Maysalun, which lay just twelve miles outside Damascus in the pass that leads into the Lebanese mountains, to face the French. Along with two hundred of his men, ʿAzma, then only thirty-six, was killed in the battle that took place on July 24, 1920. Today in Syria, ʿAzma is viewed as a national hero for his role in trying to resist the French advance, and his statue stands in a major square in central Damascus.

The battle of Maysalun was a rout. The lightly armed Syrians were outnumbered by the French, who had tanks and aircraft. ʿAzma's retreating troops were bombed from the air, and Damascus fell into chaos. Qawuqji arrived in Damascus on the evening of the battle of Maysalun. After a few hours spent trying to protect Faysal's headquarters and other areas of Damascus from thugs roaming the streets, looking for things to loot, he returned to the barracks in order to get some sleep, having spent the previous days with no rest. When he woke up on the morning of July 25, French troops were already marching into Damascus: "I woke to the sound of the voices of the enemy who had filled Marja Square. The capital of the Umayyads, the capital of King Faysal, had fallen under enemy occupation. The spectacle of the French entering Damascus was even worse than the spectacle of the British and the Arabs entering Damascus [eighteen months before]."

Faysal and a small entourage were forced to leave the city. They traveled first to Darʿa, one hundred miles southwest of Damascus, and tried to regroup. But the French threatened to bomb Faysal's headquarters. On August 1, 1920, Faysal and his entourage left for the port city of Haifa, on the coast of Palestine, which was under British control. They then traveled on to Cairo, where they stayed for several months at the expense

FIGURE 14

of the British Foreign Office. As a consolation prize, and because they believed that Faysal could help suppress anti-British feeling in Iraq, the British crowned Faysal king of Iraq a year later in August 1921. He remained king of Iraq until he died in September 1933. The photograph (figure 14) shows him at his coronation in Baghdad.

Qawuqji stayed in Damascus. After a year he joined the new French-run army in Syria, the Syrian Legion. He did not see Faysal again until he himself was forced into exile to Baghdad in 1932.

A FRENCH CAVALRY OFFICER

One of Gouraud's first acts upon becoming high commissioner of Syria and Lebanon was reorganizing the Syrian Legion, a small locally recruited force that had served with the French Army. The Syrian Legion had its origins in the Légion d'Orient, which had been formed in the Levant during World War I as a proxy army for the French. As a result of clashes between Armenians and Syrians, the Légion d'Orient was divided in 1919 into two separate armies, the Armenian Legion and the Syrian Legion. The Armenian Legion was sent to fight against Mustafa Kemal's forces in Anatolia, while the smaller Syrian Legion, which numbered about six hundred men, remained in Lebanon. Christian troops formed the majority of the Syrian Legion, but Gouraud wanted both to expand the numbers of the Syrian Legion and to diversify its ethnic and religious makeup. In 1921 the legion was reorganized and came to include 'Alawis, Circassians, Druze from the Hawran, and some Sunnis. Members of religious and ethnic minorities sometimes joined the legion because they believed that the French could guarantee their community's security better than a Sunni nationalist government could. Most joined because it was a way out of the poverty that still crippled most of the population in the postwar era.

Qawuqji's private papers contain a copy of his recruitment booklet (*Copie du Livret Matricule*) in the French Syrian Legion. It records that he was born on October 6, 1894, in Tripoli, the son of 'Abd al-Majid Qawuqji and Madame Fatima, and that he was married on September 2,

1918. His physical characteristics are listed as follows: blond hair that does not fall on the forehead, an oval face, blue-gray eyes, a straight nose, height of one meter seventy-five centimeters (five feet nine inches), scars on his right wrist, and traces of a wound on his left ankle. This information is dated February 6, 1922. At the bottom of the page is a chronology of his progress through the Syrian Legion:

Appointed for two years, July 19 1921.
Second Captain (auxiliary basis), July 1 1921.
Transferred to the Cavalry Regiment of the Syrian Legion,
    February 1 1922.
Removed from control on said day.
Reappointed for two years from 1 July 1923.
Reappointed for two years effective 1 July 1925.
Deserter 5 October 1925.

The photograph of Qawuqji's ID card in the Arab Army, now in the Center for Historical Documents in Damascus, and this recruitment booklet from the Syrian Legion, now in the French military archives, have clear dates associated with them. These are the kinds of documents that permit historians to point at a moment in the past that they can be sure is true. We can say with certainty that Fawzi al-Qawuqji was at some point in 1920 an officer in Faysal's Arab Army. We can also say with certainty that by July 1921 he was an officer in the French Syrian Legion. The evidence for this is these two archival documents just described. But it is much trickier to explain why he joined the French Syrian Legion, given that he was fighting against it just a few months before. In his memoirs Qawuqji claims that from the very beginning he was motivated by the desire to infiltrate the ranks of French officers so that he could gain their trust and eventually rebel against them. This might be true. But it is more likely that he simply needed a job in the wake of Faysal's departure from Syria and the disbanding of the Arab Army. The Syrian Legion offered him rank, salary, and a military life. And the fact that he had married in 1918—a fact recorded in his French recruitment booklet but not in his own memoirs—made this offer difficult to turn down. Qawuqji's first wife was a cousin, and his parents had arranged the marriage. Her name was Ruhaifa, and she bore Qawuqji two children in the 1920s. The first child was a son named Majdi, and the second a daughter named Haifa. Typical of many arranged marriages of the time, the marriage between Qawuqji and Ruhaifa was one of social convenience, not of companionship, and it seems Ruhaifa remained living in Tripoli.

People who knew Qawuqji have said that when he joined the Syrian Legion, he believed that he was joining a national army. In 1921 he could not imagine that Syria would continue to be under French control as late as 1946. The decision haunted him later in his life. In 1948 those who tried to discredit him as a potential field commander of the Arab Liberation Army did so by labeling him a collaborator, citing the fact that he was one of the only ex–Arab Army officers to have served in a reasonably high rank in the French Syrian Legion.

The French benefited politically from recruiting as many officers from the Arab Army as possible. In the summer of 1921 Qawuqji was at home in Damascus when a policeman knocked on his door and asked him to accompany him to the headquarters of the French Army, now located in the same house where Faysal had been based. Qawuqji entered what had been Faysal's hall, passing by Moroccan soldiers who stood guard at the door. When he entered, he saw that the man who had called the meeting was Captain Hak, with whom he had clashed in al-Muʿallaqa. Captain Hak let him feel the full force of the reversal in their roles by saying: "Do you now see how an Arab army is not able to beat a great army like ours?" He then argued that officers like Qawuqji must trust the French government. Captain Hak claimed that the French Army simply wanted cooperation with the people of Syria, so that the French government could guide Syria to independence. Then he took Qawuqji into what had been Faysal's office to meet Captain Hak's superior, Commander Arlabus. Arlabus was sitting in Faysal's chair. Everything in the room was exactly as it had been a year before, when Qawuqji had sat in the same room, meeting with King Faysal. Arlabus also tried to convince Qawuqji of the purity of French intentions and explained that they needed stalwart

Syrian men to help them run the country. A few days after this meeting Qawuqji received an order appointing him to a cavalry company in Hama, an important town on the banks of the Orontes River, in west-central Syria.

At the beginning of his deployment in Hama he was offered the rank of second captain. He refused because he had been a full captain in the Arab Army. A brief period of negotiation followed, during which he argued that his medals and his rank from the Arab Army should be transferred to the Syrian Legion. At some point after this he was made captain of his own cavalry *escadron*, or squadron. The Syrian Legion took the unusual step of naming the squadron after him, Escadron Feuzi. In March 1922 he received a letter from Georges Catroux, the military governor of Syria, congratulating him on holding the rank of captain of his own squadron: "It is appropriate that the squadron be in your name, which is unusual, so that you would know the degree of trust and appreciation you are enjoying, whether for peaceful services or for military ones."

The French archives for this period document a string of professional successes achieved by Qawuqji in the Syrian Legion. A telegram dated July 26, 1921, and signed by Catroux, confers on him the Croix Chevalier Légion d'Honneur, the Legion of Honor (Knight class) for his service in wartime. In December 1921 he received a letter from Lieutenant Colonel de Saint Hillier, commander of the Second Sepoys, commander at arms in Hama, and president of the Racetrack Committee, congratulating him on the performance of his horsemen in cavalry races:

I wish to congratulate you on the manner in which the Syrian horsemen of your squadron presented themselves on the racetrack. The hard course of 16,000 meters [ten miles] that they completed, made more difficult by the wet and slippery ground, highlighted the quality of the horses and the energy and stamina of these military units. I particularly appreciate the support you provided to the committee in organizing this meeting, and I thank you on my own behalf and on behalf of the members of the committee.

But his memoirs reveal a parallel narrative, in which Qawuqji grows more and more uneasy about his relationship with his French commanding officer in Hama. Qawuqji refers to him as Captain Mike. Captain Mike imprisoned a number of men from leading Hama families because they had refused to carry out his orders. He prevented some of the tribes from grazing their flocks in their usual pastures out of fear that they might support the uprising of Ibrahim Hananu to the north of Hama. According to Qawuqji, Captain Mike also raised taxes and stirred up sectarian conflict. Moreover, Captain Mike was famous for his dog, which he used in order to threaten people. French colonial officers often used dogs to help control their colonized subjects. A notorious French military governor, based in southern Lebanon, would call villagers into his office and intimidate them with his dog. The contradiction between this kind of brutish behavior and the French rhetoric of their Mission Civilisatrice fueled Syrian resentment. There were so many complaints about Captain Mike's uncivilized behavior from Hama families, including families with great influence in the town, such as the Kaylani family, that he was transferred out of Hama and replaced by the much smoother Commander Morbieu. Qawuqji worked closely with Morbieu and acted as his special adviser.

We cannot know exactly when Qawuqji started to think about rebelling and giving up what was obviously a successful career as a cavalry officer in the Syrian Legion. Saʿid al-Tarmanini, one of Qawuqji's closest confidants in Hama and the man with whom he planned the rebellion, said years later that Qawuqji "wanted freedom from the life he was living by replacing it with a life of honor and dignity." In the early 1920s many young Syrian men still fought against French control of their land. The most famous of these were figures like Ibrahim Hananu, Salih ʿAli, and Ramadan Shallash, all of whom led anti-French revolts and scored successes against the French Army. Just north of the borders of French Syria, Mustafa Kemal battled the French and the Greeks in Anatolia. Some historians cast the rebellions of Hananu, ʿAli, and Shallash as the first stirrings of Syrian nationalism. Other scholars believe that these ex-Ottoman officers continued to fight for the integrity of the Ottoman polity against foreign invaders, looking north to Mustafa Kemal as a model. They claim that these rebellions in the early 1920s should be understood in the context of Ottoman continuity rather than Syrian nationalism. It is clear that Qawuqji was moved by and connected to Mustafa Kemal's struggle against the French in Anatolia. He was proud of what ex-Ottoman Turkish officers were achieving militarily just a few hundred miles to the north of Hama. Here is how he describes his feelings at the time:

> The revolt of Mustafa Kemal in Anatolia had reached its most dangerous hours. We were now convinced that the Turks would win in the end after we had initially thought that Mustafa Kemal's movement was yet another armed movement that the victorious Allied forces from the Great War would successfully suppress. With this victory the Turks secured for themselves freedom and independence, and their victories made a huge impression on me and on many others. We began to look at the situation of the Arabs, and we began to feel that we had lost our warlike qualities that were rooted in a long history.

It was not just the rebellions close to home that made an impact on Qawuqji. French and Arabic newspapers in Syria were full of what was called in Arabic the War of the Countryside, the struggle of the Moroccan rebel ʿAbd al-Karim al-Khattabi. In the early 1920s Khattabi led his Berber irregular troops to several victories over both the Spanish and the French in Morocco. (A combined European force finally defeated him in 1926.) This also had an impact on Qawuqji. He mentions " ʿAbd al-Karim, hero of the countryside" many times in his memoirs. In the memoirs and in Arab nationalist publications from the era, ʿAbd al-Karim al-Khattabi is cast as an Arab hero who brought dignity back to the Arabs by fighting against foreign invaders.

Mustafa Kemal's victory in Anatolia and the rebellions of Salih ʿAli, Ibrahim Hananu, and Ramadan Shallash provide the broad context for Qawuqji's decision to rebel against the French Army. We also know something of the immediate context—namely, the ugly behavior of some of the French officers in Hama. In addition, Tarmanini's explanation that

Qawuqji "wanted freedom from the life he was living by replacing it with a life of dignity" brings the broad context and the immediate context together. But there must have been much more in the details of Qawuqji's life as an officer in the French Army in Hama, details now lost to the past, that led to a deep personal alienation from the French world that he had chosen in the summer of 1921.

THE ROAD TO REBELLION

Hama is about 130 miles north of Damascus on the banks of the Orontes River. In the early 1920s Hama was Syria's third-largest town, with about fifty thousand inhabitants, and it served as a market center for the farming communities of the surrounding area. It was perhaps best known for the large wooden waterwheels and aqueducts that channeled the waters of the Orontes to the fields and gardens of the town. Boys loved to play on these waterwheels by grabbing on to spokes and then dropping into the river as the spokes rose. Hama was also famous in Syria for the beautiful gardens and for the grand eighteenth-century houses owned by landowning families such as the 'Azms, Kaylanis, and Barazis. The photograph of Hama (figure 15) was taken from a hill overlooking the city. It shows the minaret of the Great Mosque on the banks of the Orontes River. Opposite the Great Mosque, on the other side of the river, is one of the medieval Arab waterwheels.

Almost entirely Sunni Muslim, Hama also had a small Christian community that lived in its own neighborhoods. Hama was known to be a more religiously conservative place than Damascus, for example. The religious scholars ('ulama') formed the backbone of a largely pious community struggling to carry on with daily life in the face of war and foreign occupation. Striding through the town in their uniforms, eating and drinking in the shaded cafés that lined the river, Syrian Legion troops drew the gaze of Hama's inhabitants. Qawuqji was well-known among the Hamawis as the Sunni Arab from Tripoli, who held the highest rank of any Arab man in the French Army in Hama.

FIGURE 15

Over the course of 1923 and 1924, Qawuqji's behavior began to change. Dressed in his army uniform, he started attending mosque on Fridays. He went on hajj, or pilgrimage to Mecca, sometime in 1924, and he spent some of his free time visiting leading religious scholars in Hama. As a Sunni Muslim Qawuqji was a somewhat unusual figure because most Arab officers serving in the French Army were from Syrian minorities, such as the Christians or the 'Alawis. The French generally regarded the Sunnis as more hostile than other Syrians, and French colonial officials deliberately promoted the minorities as a way of securing power in local communities. Splitting off the minorities from the Sunni majority in Syria also served French interests because it hindered the development of a unified Syrian nationalism that might one day rise up against French rule. But even aside from the fact that Qawuqji was a Sunni, it was odd in this period for army officers of any religion to be ostentatiously pious.

When Morbieu, the French commanding officer of the Hama garrison, asked Qawuqji why he was visiting leading religious scholars and attending mosque, Qawuqji replied that in order to do his job properly, he needed to ingratiate himself with Hama's conservative religious establishment. He told Morbieu that the religious scholars were spreading rumors that Qawuqji was an unbeliever, seduced by foreign French ways.

Qawuqji also made contact with some young Hamawi men, who were known to have anti-French leanings. In the beginning only a few men came to these meetings. Qawuqji lists their names in his memoirs: ʿAbd al-Salam al-Farji, Muhammad ʿAli al-Daghistani, ʿAbd al-Qadir Maysir, Tahir al-Daghistani, and Saʿid al-Tarmanini. Tarmanini's account of his involvement in the Hama rebellion has never been published, but it exists in manuscript form in the Center for Historical Documents in Damascus.

Tarmanini explains that in 1924 Qawuqji returned from his pilgrimage to Mecca with a renewed commitment to Islam and a vow to fight to overthrow French colonialism in Syria. He describes how Qawuqji started going to mosque in order to meet with religious scholars and encourage them to preach holy war (jihad). Tarmanini only knew of Qawuqji at that point as the "Arab man from Tripoli" in the uniform of a French officer. One morning Tarmanini was sitting on a wall near the citadel, looking out over the city of Hama, when a tall man approached him. It was one of the Daghistani brothers, whom he knew from the neighborhood. The man said that he had been sent by Captain Fawzi al-Qawuqji with an invitation for Tarmanini to meet with Qawuqji in his home after evening prayers (salat al-ʿasha') the next day. Tarmanini asked why he was being given this invitation. Daghistani replied that he had no idea and had just been sent to deliver the message. Then Daghistani left, having given Tarmanini the address of the house and directions for how to get there. Tarmanini was worried because he knew Qawuqji as a French officer. Even though he had seen Qawuqji in the mosque, he was skeptical of his displays of piety, which he assumed were motivated by the desire to uncover information for his French superiors. But driven by curiosity, he decided to go. The next day, after evening prayers, he arrived at the house. After looking up and down the alley to make sure that no one could see him going into the house of an officer in the French Army, he knocked on the door. Qawuqji opened the door himself and showed him into the inner room, in the middle of which stood a table with a Quran on it. Tarmanini recognized ʿAbd al-Salam al-Farji, whom Qawuqji introduced as his brother-in-law. When Tarmanini realized that Farji was married to Qawuqji's sister, he felt calmer. He knew Farji a little and respected him. The family connection between Farji and Qawuqji made him feel that he might be able to trust Qawuqji.

Qawuqji began speaking breathlessly about the misery of the French colonization of Syria and about his admiration for the great nationalist hero in Morocco ʿAbd al-Karim al-Khattabi. Qawuqji explained to Tarmanini how the French Army had put all its resources into trying to suppress Khattabi's uprising. He went on to say that if there were a similar uprising in Syria, the French would not have the capacity to fight on two fronts. They would be forced to negotiate with whoever led the rebellion and quit Syria. Here is how Tarmanini relates what happened next:

> I couldn't believe that I was hearing this from Captain Fawzi, who was so beloved by the French that he was considered to be more French than the French. After a silence that lasted for more than five minutes, Qawuqji continued by saying that I, Fawzi al-Qawuqji, am ready to undertake my national duty and take all the necessary steps to announce the revolt in this city in cooperation with you and with whomever you choose from your trustworthy friends. You are the first person with whom I choose to discuss this serious matter. For this reason I want to hear your true position so that I am clear on the issue. I ask this of you because I am not hiding anything from you. The situation is extremely dangerous, and it will require courage and sacrifice. For this reason your answer should be clear and frank.

Tarmanini replied that he was ready to join Qawuqji, but he raised serious concerns about Qawuqji's pro-French reputation. Qawuqji agreed that this was an obstacle, but he reassured Tarmanini that he would do everything he could to change local opinion about him. Then Qawuqji, Tarmanini, and Farji made a solemn oath on the Quran to work together to plan and execute the rebellion.

Tarmanini lists the names of some of the men, including teachers, religious leaders, journalists, and doctors—whom he and Qawuqji recruited in the months before the rebellion: Some of these names are well-known in Syria today. For example, Tarmanini mentions Munir al-Rayyis, who wrote a three-volume memoir about life as a journalist and rebel. He knew Qawuqji well and worked alongside him in many of the anticolonial rebellions that Qawuqji was involved in following the events in Hama in 1925. Rayyis first met Qawuqji briefly in Damascus, following the withdrawal of the Ottoman Army in the very early days of Faysal's rule. He had been impressed by Qawuqji's stories of the war, in particular his story of having saved Mustafa Kemal's life. Rayyis was a few years younger than Qawuqji, but that meant his experience of World War I had differed from Qawuqji's. Rayyis was at school during the war and had not fought, and so he admired Qawuqji's experience in battle. When rumors spread that a rebellion in Hama was being planned, Rayyis, who came from Hama, immediately made contact with Tarmanini, a close friend of Rayyis's older brother Nazim. When Tarmanini told him that Qawuqji was secretly involved in the planning and was also recruiting actively among local troops in the French Army, Rayyis was thrilled. Events in the Hawran Plateau and the Druze Mountain, approximately two hundred miles south of Hama, sparked these young men into action.

SULTAN AL-ATRASH

The Hawran Plateau spreads out below Mount Hermon, which today lies on Syria's southwestern border with Lebanon and Israel. Southwest of Hawran lies the high volcanic massif of the Druze Mountain (Jabal

Druze), home of Syria's Druze, a minority Muslim Shiʿa sect. Trouble had broken out between the French Army and the Atrash family, one of the leading Druze families in the area, in the early 1920s. As a result, the French were keeping a close eye on Hawran and periodically sent surveillance planes to check on the inhabitants. On July 19, 1925, some Druze farmers from Hawran shot down one of these surveillance planes. The next day Sultan al-Atrash rode into the town of Salkhad with a group of fighters and claimed occupation of the town. Sultan al-Atrash, like many others from Hawran, had been drafted into the Ottoman Army in 1910 and sent to the Balkans. He had then gone on to fight in the Ottoman Army during World War I, as had most of the men who joined the revolt against the French in Syria. These ex-Ottoman military networks played an important role in the spread of the revolt. Sultan al-Atrash in particular became an icon of resistance against the French in the years that followed the revolt. The photograph of him (figure 16) was taken in

FIGURE 16

Transjordan in late 1926 after he was forced to flee Syria as the revolt was failing.

The events in Hawran on July 19 and 20, 1925, were followed by a widespread rebellion there against the French during the summer and early fall of 1925. The first few weeks of the rebellion saw many Druze victories against the French Army. By August 1925 Sultan al-Atrash had made contact with the leading Syrian nationalists 'Abd al-Rahman Shahbandar and Nasib al-Bakri, who were based in Damascus. Atrash believed they would be interested in exploring ways in which the rebellion could be organized to spread beyond Hawran. Shahbandar was president of the People's Party, and Bakri was a member. Both were from elite Damascene families that had supported Faysal's rule, and Bakri had in fact served as Faysal's envoy to Hawran. The People's Party had emerged only that summer as an official party. It stood for the independence of Syria within its natural borders, which were defined as stretching from 'Aqaba (the southern point of what is today Jordan) to the Taurus Mountains (today the northern border with Turkey). In other words, the People's Party did not recognize the colonial division of what it regarded as historic Syria into the mandate states of Syria, Transjordan, Lebanon, and Palestine. This was a particularly Syrian brand of Arab nationalism, one that transcended ethnic and religious divisions. In the wake of Atrash's appeals, Shahbandar committed the People's Party to the revolt: "We are ready for death, all of us, in the cause of raising the beacon of the nation and the homeland. We will participate in the uprising and join Jabal Druze."

By the end of August 1925, after the French failed to force a peace settlement on the Druze in Hawran, the revolt had spread to Damascus. Groups of armed men formed in Damascus neighborhoods and surrounding villages, especially in the villages of the Ghouta, the lush orchards that bordered the city. Some Bedouin tribes also started to signal their willingness to join the revolt. With all this in view, Qawuqji and Tarmanini accelerated their plans for rebellion in Hama.

PLANNING

Qawuqji had already worked hard to ensure support among the religious scholars of Hama. He regularly attended mosque and interjected during the Friday sermon (*khutba*) to ask for clarifications on certain theological matters. He did this so that he would be noticed by the mosque attendees. At the same time, he sought the support of a few key soldiers in his cavalry company: Michel Nahas, Ahmad al-Firkali, and ʿAli al-Maghribi. Qawuqji names these men in particular in his memoirs. He says that they all showed bravery and heroism over the course of the revolt itself and remained loyal to him until the end. Qawuqji's statement about loyalty is striking. When trying to explain why rebels picked up arms and fought in this period, contemporary historians consider various possible factors: Were they driven by feelings of hatred toward the foreign occupiers? By Syrian nationalism? By money? By fear that if they refused to join, they would be punished by rebels? It is hard to ascertain an individual's particular set of motivations. Different men fought for different reasons. And even a single person may have had several reasons that motivated him to leave his home and go onto the streets to fight. But we do know that certain individuals had the charisma or legitimacy to command the loyalty of enough other men that they were able to lead large groups. This kind of loyalty is systematized and institutionalized in state armies. But among men fighting outside the parameters of a state army it becomes even more fundamental. Qawuqji possessed the ability to attract the loyalty of others. He had it in Hama in 1925, in Palestine in 1936, in the Iraqi desert in 1941, and in the hills of the Galilee in 1948. The sources only hint at the human fabric of this loyalty, but it is not hard to reconstruct what it was made of: shared experience, friendship, family ties, common beliefs, trust, and so on. These factors sometimes, but not always, overlapped with the broader categories of identity that preoccupy contemporary historians, categories such as class, religion, and geographical origin.

Qawuqji brought Nahas, Firkali, and Maghribi, each of whom served in Qawuqji's unit in the Syrian Legion, into the countryside to help him garner the support of the tribes living near Hama. Qawuqji was convinced of the importance of bringing the tribes into the fight against colonialism. We know of his experience working with Iraqi tribes from his days as a young cadet stationed in Mosul. Faysal had acknowledged this experience when he chose Qawuqji as the person most capable of recruiting tribesmen to fight against the French in the summer of 1920. Qawuqji's narrative of the events in Hama in early October 1925 shows that he viewed the tribes as the heart of the effective resistance. In his memoirs he describes the tribes outside Hama as "the flame of the fire of the revolt." He is deliberately vague about the precise manner in which he recruited the tribes, preferring instead a more romantic portrayal. In his preface to the memoirs of his friend and fellow soldier Sa'id al-'As, he used exactly the same phrase, "the flame of the fire of the revolt." But in this preface, written much earlier, he provided more details about how he had procured tribal support. The earlier account describes the promises Qawuqji made to them: that they would no longer be taxed and that the shaykhs and their fighting men would receive salaries once the revolt was over. Tarmanini's account is even more specific about salaries: fifty gold liras per month for the shaykhs of each tribe, fifteen gold liras per month for each tribesman who had a horse, and ten gold liras per month for tribesmen who would fight on foot. But Qawuqji also threatened the shaykhs, saying that if they did not join in the revolt, they would become the target of the revolutionary army in place of the French. Qawuqji was to use threats like this throughout the revolt.

Qawuqji also understood the importance of obtaining the allegiance of the elite families in the town. He visited Najib al-Barazi, who told him that he supported the revolt in principle but that Qawuqji should wait until after the harvest in September before executing his plans. According to Qawuqji, Barazi promised to do what he could to drum up support and money for the revolt. For his part, Tarmanini went to see Mukhlis al-Kaylani, the head of another powerful family in Hama. Kaylani also promised to give financial support to the revolt as long as his role was kept absolutely secret from the French. Kaylani expressed doubts to Tarmanini about the feasibility of overthrowing the French Army in Hama without support from outside. Qawuqji also sent Tarmanini to Damascus to see Shahbandar and another important member of the People's Party, Nabih al-'Azma. Qawuqji gave Tarmanini responsibility for ensuring that the People's Party was behind the plans for revolt in Hama. Tarmanini secured the party's support on this trip. He also took time to go shopping and bought four pairs of sturdy wire clippers, which were later used to cut the telegraph lines in Hama, just before the revolt was launched, so that the French would be delayed in calling for reinforcements. In addition, Qawuqji sent men to Homs, Ba'albak, Tripoli, and even Palmyra and Dayr al-Zur, to garner support for the revolt and encourage others to launch parallel revolts.

Tarmanini also made an important journey to Bhamdoun to visit the famous anti-French rebel and ex-Ottoman officer Ibrahim Hananu, in order to ask his advice and get his blessing for the planned revolt in Hama. Bhamdoun was a small Christian town on the road between Damascus and Beirut. Hananu was in the hospital in Bhamdoun and received Tarmanini in his hospital room. Hananu listened carefully as Tarmanini described their plans. He then replied by saying that revolt against the French Army was a very risky and hazardous undertaking (*mughamara*). He spelled out for Tarmanini the price of failure. Finally Tarmanini asked Hananu what he knew about Qawuqji and if he thought that Qawuqji could lead the revolt. Hananu said that he knew Qawuqji to have been an effective officer in the Ottoman Army. He gave his blessing to Qawuqji's leadership and to the Hama revolt, and he wished them luck. Tarmanini returned to Hama and presented this news to Qawuqji. Qawuqji, delighted by Hananu's enthusiasm about his leadership, embraced him. Hananu's anticolonial credentials were rock solid, and his endorsement played a big role in dispelling any remaining doubts about the genuineness of Qawuqji's commitment to the revolt.

Even more important than obtaining Hananu's blessing was making contact with Sultan al-Atrash. Qawuqji sent Munir al-Rayyis and Mazhir al-Siba'i to Hawran to find him. Rayyis was a journalist and a well-educated man who had passed through the Ottoman civil school system sponsored by the Ottoman state. More prestigious than its military counterpart, the civil system, in particular the well-known Damascus school Maktab al-Anbar, trained the intellectual elite of Syria. Siba'i, like Sultan al-Atrash and Qawuqji himself, had attended the War College in Istanbul and had fought alongside Mustafa Kemal's forces in Anatolia in the early 1920s. He had also joined Ibrahim Hananu's revolt in northern Syria before he ended up in Hama in 1925.

When Rayyis and Siba'i arrived in Hawran toward the end of the summer of 1925, they found some of their friends from Damascus there already, including Shahbandar himself. Rayyis related the oral message from Qawuqji to Shahbandar, and then Shahbandar arranged for a meeting between Siba'i and Sultan al-Atrash. Shahbandar chose Siba'i over Rayyis for the meeting because the former had much more experience in battle and would thus be better qualified to discuss and settle upon the logistical aspects of any agreement. Atrash and Siba'i met in the village of Rasas, just south of al-Suwayda, the main town of Hawran. Siba'i presented the oral message from Qawuqji. In his memoirs Rayyis lists Qawuqji's requests:

1. Qawuqji asked the leaders of the revolt in the [Druze] Mountain not to make any agreements with the French after the outbreak of revolt in Hama without also consulting the leaders of the Hama rebellion.
2. He asked that the leaders of the revolt in the [Druze] Mountain appoint a time for their mobilizations and the execution of their plans.
3. He asked if they knew of a place where they could withdraw in the event of the failure of their revolt in the heart of the city or the massing of French troops against them. Should they withdraw with their forces to the Zawiya Mountains and other areas in the north that are good for revolt and ignite the revolt there? Or should they instead withdraw to the south and join the revolt in the [Druze] Mountain?
4. He requested that the leadership in the [Druze] Mountain draw

up a plan to launch an attack on the French in the area of Damascus a day or two before the outbreak of revolt in Hama because such a thing would have a big effect in all areas of Syria, would raise the morale of the people, and would increase enthusiasm for revolt against the French.

Sultan al-Atrash agreed to all the conditions and sent word back to Qawuqji that the appointed time of the revolt should be in the month of October. He also said that should Qawuqji and his men need to take refuge in the Druze Mountain in the event of the failure of the revolt, they would be welcomed as brothers. This message, which was written, not oral, was sent, by way of various messengers, back to Hama, to Tarmanini's house, where Tarmanini kept it hidden under the floor. Rayyis and Siba'i stayed in Hawran. During the final weeks of that summer they fought with Atrash's forces against the French. It is clear that these men, who were willing to risk their lives to rid Syria of the French, were united by anti-French sentiment. What is more difficult to establish is which sort of regime they wished to replace French rule with. Some, like Shahbandar and Rayyis, were constitutionalists. They aimed to establish an independent, secular, undivided Syria with a strong constitution. During Faysal's rule in Syria (1918–1920), Faysal led a Syrian parliament that debated many topics, including the drawing up of a Syrian constitution. Many politically minded intellectuals looked back on that period as a moment when Syria was on track to becoming an independent state complete with an elected parliament and a negotiated constitution. This moment of promise had been shut down by the French when they occupied Damascus in July 1920. Other men, like Sultan al-Atrash and Qawuqji himself, were less interested in what might follow French withdrawal. Their focus was on ridding Syria of the French. Any attempt to put together a detailed program for a postindependent Syria provided the occasion for disagreement and distracted from the immediate task.

A FALSE START

When Qawuqji received the letter from Atrash in late September, he called a meeting of those planning the revolt, including Tarmanini. At the meeting they agreed that the night of the Prophet Muhammad's birthday (*Mawlid al-Nabi*), when the streets would be noisy and full of people, was the best date for the launching of the revolt. In all the commotion, rebel movements would be less conspicuous. According to Tarmanini's account, this meeting was followed by a series of smaller meetings devoted to planning the seizure of French military positions in Hama. The revolt would begin at midnight on Mawlid al-Nabi. By that time thirty men under the command of Mustafa 'Ashur would have been stationed in the orchards of 'Adsa, just outside Hama; fifteen men would have been stationed in the house of 'Abd al-Rahman al-Mut; and thirty men from Homs, under the command of 'Abd al-Hadi al-Ma'sarani and Fu'ad Raslan, would have been stationed on the outskirts of Hama. 'Abd al-Qadir al-Malishu was responsible for taking three or four men to cut the telegraph lines at least two hours before midnight. Tarmanini was responsible for checking that everyone was in place, ready for the attack by midnight. In addition, Qawuqji was supposed to be meeting with Barazi in order to make sure that Barazi would be implicated in the revolt from the outset and would therefore be committed to seeing it through.

When the night of Mawlid al-Nabi arrived on September 30, 1925, Malishu and his men used the clippers that Tarmanini had bought in Damascus to cut the telegraph wires at around 10:00 p.m. Then two things went wrong. Tarmanini heard that everyone was in position except the thirty rebels under the command of Mustafa 'Ashur, who had not shown up in the orchards of 'Adsa. Tarmanini rode out to the orchards himself to check and found no one there. In addition, Qawuqji had gone to the Barazi family home in Hama expecting to meet Barazi and others, but there was no one there either. When Qawuqji heard from Tarmanini that 'Ashur's men had also not shown up in the orchards of 'Adsa, he called off the plan even though the telegraph wires had already been cut. Fearing that the cutting of the telegraph wires would alert the French to their plan, Tarmanini urged him to carry on. But Qawuqji decided it was too risky to move ahead without 'Ashur's men and without the support of Barazi and his men.

Qawuqji knew that he had to reset the date of revolt quickly before momentum was lost. The new date was decided: four days later, October 4, 1925. Tarmanini and Qawuqji agreed that they would meet in the early morning of the fourth for the final planning of the revolt, which would begin that evening. At the meeting they settled upon the steps to be taken during the hours leading up to the revolt. The rebels were to gather in both Makram al-Kaylani's house in the Hadir quarter of the town, where Qawuqji would be based, and in Tarmanini's house in the Suq quarter. The first operation would be to take over the two police stations and the stores of weapons and ammunition in both the quarters. Once this had been accomplished, they were to march on and attack the Serail, the main French government building in the center of Hama. The Serail included government offices, army barracks, and an arsenal. They also agreed that Qawuqji would send a small unit of men to protect the Christian areas of Hama from indiscriminate attacks. This was because local Christian communities were suspected of being pro-French and Sunnis sometimes targeted Christian houses and businesses during times of trouble.

Specific times were set for each stage of the revolt. The two men were careful to record the plan in their respective notebooks and make sure that their written plans exactly corresponded. Fearful that some of the conspirators, especially the leaders of the tribes, would lose their nerve and back out at the last minute, Qawuqji took an action to ensure that everyone remained committed. He sent two men from his cavalry unit, Nahas and Firkali, to where some French units were based just outside Hama. He ordered them to capture a French soldier so that Qawuqji could parade this officer in front of the shaykhs and some of the Syrians serving in his own cavalry unit. This would show them that the revolt had started for real and that there was no going back. Qawuqji mentions this kidnapping only briefly in his memoirs as one small, albeit crucial, piece of his plan. Tarmanini also includes a short account of the kidnapping in his memoirs. By far the most detailed narrative is the French soldier's own official report, which is now housed in the French military archives in Vincennes, a Paris suburb. At the end of the report the officer signs his name as M.D.L. Gerbail. M.D.L. stood for *maréchal-des-logis* (marshal of lodgings), a rank in the French Army approximating the rank of sergeant.

Nahas approached Gerbail in his barracks. He informed Gerbail that he had orders from Capt. Fawzi al-Qawuqji for Gerbail to accompany Nahas by car to where Qawuqji was based, about five miles northeast of Hama. Nahas told Gerbail that he would be back in his barracks within an hour. They went together in the car, with Firkali driving. About three miles into the journey Nahas stopped the car in order to urinate. Firkali also got out of the car. Together the two men slapped Gerbail in the face and told him to put his hands up. They then took all the money that he had in his wallet. Gerbail had over two thousand francs in his wallet that day because he was the paymaster for his unit and had received the troops' pay package only that morning, a fact that Nahas and Qawuqji must have known. Nahas then announced that the main cities of Syria—Damascus, Homs, and Aleppo—were in revolt and that Hama was on the point of revolt. He told Gerbail that Captain Qawuqji had sent Nahas to save Gerbail's life. When Gerbail protested that if this were really the case, they would have left him with his unit, not kidnapped him, Nahas put him back in the car and drove him for several hours south, to a small village. Qawuqji was waiting for them. He spoke to Gerbail in a calm manner, trying to reassure him that he would not be harmed. Qawuqji, Nahas, and Gerbail then left by car to meet with some tribal shaykhs who had agreed to join the revolt. They had a meal with the shaykhs. According to Tarmanini, Gerbail was too frightened to eat, but Qawuqji persuaded him to have a little meat with rice and yogurt. The news that Qawuqji and his men had kidnapped a French officer spread quickly. The kidnapping signaled that Qawuqji was serious and that the revolt had begun.

The next morning, October 4, 1925, Qawuqji and Tarmanini put their plan into action. They gathered with their men at 1:00 p.m. in their respective areas of Hama—Tarmanini in the Hadir quarter, and Qawuqji in the Suq quarter. Gerbail was forced to stay with Qawuqji and his men as a prisoner.

HAMA EST RÉVOLTÉ

For historians, beginnings are tricky. If we base our narrative on Qawuqji's and Tarmanini's accounts, the revolt in Hama began with the capture of Gerbail on the morning of October 3, 1925. If we use the French military documents as our primary source, the revolt began in the early evening of October 4. Here is the opening line of an account of the night of October 4, drafted on the morning of October 5 by the commander of the French forces in Damascus: "A 20h.10 le Capitaine Marthot de Hums téléphone. Hama est révolté. [At 8:10 p.m. Captain Marthot from Homs telephoned. Hama is rebelling.]" The French documents show only French officers' reactions to events that they are trying to control. For these officers the revolt begins when Qawuqji and his men enter their realm of responsibility as adversaries. The French military logs are very precise. For example, they record the exact times of events as they unfolded on the night of October 4. But the French documents seem distant from developments on the rebel side. Historians who foreground documentary sources from colonial archives when telling a story about anticolonial rebels are only able to narrate a shadow play. The account of the revolt that follows here is based primarily on rebel accounts.

In the early evening of October 4, the *adhan*, or call to prayer, filled the sky above Hama. This was the signal for the rebels to launch the attack. Tarmanini led his small group of men to the police station located at the entrance to the Khish quarter. They seized it without any resistance and took possession of eight German rifles and some ammunition. Tarmanini distributed these rifles among his men. Tarmanini knew one of the guards at the police station, al-Sayyid 'Abid al-Hiraki, who had a reputation in the town as a man of science and an astrologer. Hiraki begged Tarmanini to be allowed to keep his rifle, but Tarmanini refused and threatened Hiraki with violence. Hiraki, who was quite a bit older than Tarmanini, gave up his gun to this young man intent on rebellion. At the same moment, another group of rebels successfully acquired rifles from the police station at Bab al-Balad. Rumors spread among the rebels that some policemen, in particular 'Izz al-Din al-Turk and Khalid Murad Agha, both of whom were well-known in the town, were joining the revolt. Tarmanini and his men, along with the group that attacked the police station at Bab al-Balad, then made their way together toward the Serail, the French government building, in the center of town.

A bright moon lit up the night, and the men could easily see their way through the alleys and streets of Hama to the plaza in front of the Serail. When they arrived, they found Qawuqji (no longer in his Syrian Legion uniform) and a few dozen men battling for control of the building. Some of the men had defected from the Syrian Legion and joined Qawuqji; others were local townspeople. Here, in the open plaza in front of the building, the moonlight was a disadvantage. It shone on the rebels like a searchlight, while the French troops firing from the building from the inside were hidden in the darkness of the building's windows. Tarmanini saw many killed and wounded rebels as he entered the battle. The fighting lasted for several hours before the rebels finally managed to break into the building and seize weapons from the arsenal. They also freed prisoners, who immediately joined the rebels. Some rebels also set fires inside the building, forcing French soldiers to the top floor, where they would have been killed if they had not later escaped through an opening in the rear of the building that led to the rooftops of the adjacent 'Azm family compound.

Tribesmen watched the fire burn in the Serail from the hills above Hama. Qawuqji sent word to them to come into the city in the morning. As the sun rose, the tribesmen rode down from the hills and joined in the fight. Qawuqji gathered his forces in the Hadir quarter and commanded a group of men to spread out in the area of the main bridge over the Orontes. He also ordered an attack on the nearby barracks at Khan Sha'ba. French soldiers tried to ride out of their barracks to engage the rebels, but they were quickly pushed back inside. The defending soldiers then ran to the roof of the barracks and threw grenades down on the attacking rebels and onto the rooftops of nearby stores. The grenades started a fire in one of the stores that spread to the others in the densely packed homes and shops of the khan. A later report on the revolt in Hama describes how shopkeepers rushed toward their stores to save their provisions, which for most represented their only means of livelihood. As shopkeepers moved into the area of fighting, the French soldiers on the rooftop of the barracks threw grenades at them, killing several of them. One hundred and seventeen shops burned to the ground, along with the goods they contained.

The overall commander of French forces in Syria, Gen. Maurice Gustave Gamelin, ordered reinforcements to Hama. Many French soldiers were stationed on the Druze Mountain, where the Syrian-wide revolt had been fiercest up until that point. The first troops to reach Hama were made up of a Senegalese company that immediately started fighting the rebels both inside the city and in the surrounding orchards. The Senegalese were well trained, and the company commander called in the artillery, which had also arrived in Hama that day by train. Over one hundred rebels were killed in the fighting on October 5 and 6. Many more were wounded. The rebels were armed with old Ottoman rifles. In addition to well-trained soldiers of the French Army, they faced artillery barrages and bombardment from French aircraft. French soldiers terrorized many Hamawis, breaking into people's houses and making mass arrests. Tarmanini tells the story of Dr. Salih Qunbaz, who helped the wounded in the center of the town and then managed to return to his house late on October 5. As he entered his home, he heard cries for help coming from his neighbor's house. When he opened the door, he saw his neighbor standing over his son. The child had blood pouring from his head. Just as Dr. Qunbaz moved to enter the house, he was shot and killed by a Senegalese soldier. His corpse lay on the ground at the entrance to the house for two hours until the women of his family came out and carried him back to his home. The next morning, on October 6, the French soldiers entered his house and looted what they could find. They took over a thousand guineas and arrested Dr. Qunbaz's brothers, Muhammad and 'Abd al-Hamid, while the women watched in horror. Other incidents like this occurred all over Hama. When some citizens lodged an official complaint with the French commander of the Hama garrison, he replied that actions such as these were "natural" among soldiers who are triumphant in a rebellious city. Only a few French soldiers were killed in the fighting.

In the middle of the first hours of fighting, Qawuqji encountered Gerbail, the French officer whom he had kidnapped on October 3 and who had then become separated from his guards. This is Gerbail's official report:

> I found myself surrounded by a mob that was banging on the doors of the Serail. I continued on the main road toward the bridge and the Brazza quarter. At about thirty meters away, I saw a mob armed with revolvers and rifles heading toward the Serail firing gunshots. I turned and went up the side of the hospital and found myself with five cavalry-men and two gendarmes. After one hour we tried together to go back down toward the Serail, and there I saw Fawzi in civilian clothes. He commanded his men to dismount. Then he said to me: "This is going badly for you. I am no longer responsible for your safety." And then he assembled his men and made them put on their kaffiyehs. 'Abd al-Qadir al-Malishu, who was with Qawuqji, told me that he was going to take me to a civilian house. He gave me a kaffiyeh, and we went to the house of Sofi Hassan, who took me to his cousin Farid Bey's house, where they kept me until six the next morning. At that moment the city was a little calmer, and I was able to get back to the east bank of the river and reenter the area that was under French control.

The collective punishment that French soldiers imposed against Hama's residents, very few of whom actively participated in the revolt, led to the isolation of the rebels. French artillery bombardment, the de-struction of several houses and two bazaars by French troops, and the deaths of nearly 350 Hamawis were too much for the townspeople to bear. Najib al-Barazi, who had earlier claimed to support the revolt, con-tacted the French commander of the Hama garrison to say that most of the people of Hama were against Fawzi al-Qawuqji and his rebels and that he would cooperate with the French in trying to bring the rebellion under control. In Qawuqji's memoirs Barazi's action is cast as treasonous. Following his contact with the French commanding officer, Barazi arranged a meeting of the leading men of the town. Many of these men had pledged their support to Qawuqji before the outbreak of the revolt. Tarmanini and Qawuqji were present at the meeting, which took place in one of the houses of the Kaylani family. Qawuqji reminded them of their commitment to remain loyal to the revolt and urged them not to show weakness. He said that whatever the outcome, "the sword and justice" must come first. Farid al-Kaylani replied: "Fawzi, you have made an oath before God, and you have lived up to it; but as for us, we do not feel that we have the strength to endure this catastrophe for a single minute longer. You have kept your honor." Tarmanini watched the proceedings. He relates how all the men gathered in the room felt that Qawuqji and his men must leave the city quickly. They feared what the French were capable of doing to Hama if the revolt continued. Tarmanini noticed only one dissenting voice among the men. It came from a young man who was no older than fourteen. He stood up, begged the men to fight, and pleaded with Qawuqji and the other rebels present in the room not to quit the city. As Tarmanini left the meeting, heading home to prepare for his exile, he asked the people present who the boy was; the son of Shaykh Farid al-Kaylani, he was told.

From the French perspective, the city was much calmer on October 7 than it had been the previous three days. The commander of the Hama regiment, Colonel Martin, sent a telegram to the French military headquarters in Beirut, Damascus, and Aleppo reporting that "it is calm and we are able to move around the town." The telegram also shows that his focus had turned to tracking down and arresting the leading rebels:

ARRESTS THAT BEGAN YESTERDAY CONTINUE . . . ONE OF THE INSTIGATORS OF THE REVOLT APPEARS TO BE CAPTAIN FAWZI, COMMANDANT OF THE 2ND SYRIAN CAVALRY COMPANY. HE JOINED THE REBELS WITH 11 OF HIS MEN, AND IT APPEARS THAT HE ACTUALLY ORGANIZED THE BEDOUIN.

As Colonel Martin drafted his telegram, Qawuqji, Tarmanini, and most of the men who had fought with them prepared to leave the city. Many of those present at the meeting at the Kaylani house tried to persuade Tarmanini and Qawuqji that it was too dangerous for them to return to their homes before leaving the city. Tarmanini describes how he and Qawuqji separated at the Kaylani house. They agreed to meet at ten that night in the Asida neighborhood, at the house of Mustafa al-Dib, one of the rebels. Tarmanini and Qawuqji agreed that they would leave the city together. Tarmanini made it home only after dodging several of the French checkpoints that had been set up all over Hama. He managed to say goodbye to his grandmother and his brother 'Uthman— he had sent his wife and small sons out of the city before the revolt started—he took a little money and other supplies, and he then left for Mustafa al-Dib's house. He heard later that ten minutes after he left his home, French soldiers came to the house and arrested his brother 'Uthman. When Tarmanini arrived at Mustafa al-Dib's house, he discovered that Qawuqji had left the city three hours earlier because of reports that the French intended to track him down that day as the most high-profile leader of the revolt. Tarmanini and a couple of other rebels walked out of Hama, heading east. When Qawuqji left Hama on the night of October 7, he went to Shaykh Faris al-'Atur, who had been on his side during the fighting of the previous three days. With horsemen from 'Atur's tribe he continued to harass French positions outside Hama.

Historians debate about why the Hama rebellion failed. Some blame Qawuqji's leadership, arguing that he was reckless and failed to command enough support to execute such an ambitious plan. Others point to the huge disparity in weaponry. Qawuqji and his men were armed with rifles and hand grenades, whereas the French had field artillery and aerial bombers at their disposal. It also seems that Qawuqji relied on his training in the Ottoman Army to confront French troops. He organized the defense against the French counterattack by distributing men with rifles on the main roads into Hama, as he had been trained to do in the Ottoman Army. The French Army's overwhelming firepower meant that these exposed men took many more casualties than the French did.

Qawuqji would not make this mistake again during the other revolts that he participated in following Hama.

Tarmanini's assessment of what went wrong focuses on the false start of September 30, which signaled to the French that they should shore up their defenses and prepare for rebellion. He also blames those in Hama who broke their promises to Qawuqji and the rebels. He argues that without their support the revolt could never have succeeded. But he also points out that although Hama remained in French hands after the events of October 4–7, the revolt did achieve several objectives. Forcing Gamelin to withdraw troops from Hawran in order to deal with rebels in Hama took the pressure off Sultan al-Atrash and his Druze rebels. The events in Hama also extended the reach of the rebellion to an important Syrian city far from Hawran and in turn encouraged rebellion in Damascus. In the months that followed, Damascus became the new center of resistance to French colonial rule.

TO DAMASCUS

Qawuqji never forgave the leading families of Hama—especially the Barazis—for betraying him. He had risked everything at Hama. His actions there shaped the rest of his career as an itinerant anticolonial rebel, unable to return openly to Syria until the late 1940s, after Syria had been granted independence by the French. Qawuqji's tactics became uglier in the weeks and months that followed the failure of the revolt in Hama. French intelligence reports contain letters that he wrote to leading men in Hama, extorting money from them under threat of violence. One of these letters was addressed to Najib al-Barazi. Extortion became a common practice among rebels in Syria as the revolt intensified.

After fighting with the tribes around Hama in the days immediately following the revolt, Qawuqji evaded French attempts to capture him by traveling northeast, far into the deserts of eastern Syria. From this point on until he fled Syria for good in 1927, Qawuqji was an outlaw. He traveled with a small band of men, occasionally joining forces with other rebel groups led by other ex-Ottoman officers, such as Ramadan Shallash and Saʿid al-ʿAs. He spent late October and much of November among the tribes that grazed their livestock in the northeast corner of Syria and in northern Iraq. He knew this region well from his days serving as a young Ottoman officer in the Mosul garrison. He went to see Shaykh Najras al-Kaʿud, whose life he had saved over ten years before, and asked Kaʿud to help him get back to Damascus. He was eager to return to the revolt. Kaʿud gave Qawuqji and his men supplies and camels to make the long journey back across the desert to Damascus.

Rebel activity in and around Damascus intensified during the fall of 1925. A huge nationalist demonstration took place there on Mawlid al-Nabi, the day that Qawuqji had originally planned for the revolt in Hama. Attacks on the French Army came mainly from armed groups based in the Ghouta, the vast orchards and gardens to the south and east of the capital. In mid-October the French increased their efforts to keep the rebels under control. They sent locally recruited Circassian troops into the villages of the Ghouta to round up rebels. Circassians were a Sunni Muslim ethnic minority in Syria, originally from the Caucasus. About seventy thousand had immigrated to Syria in the late 1860s as a result of the Russian conquest of the Caucasus. During World War I and the period of the French mandate in Syria, Circassians served in large numbers in the French Army. On one day in the middle of October, Circassian troops brought 115 prisoners and 24 corpses to Marja Square in the middle of Damascus. They threw the corpses, along with a dead dog, into the square and forced the prisoners to march around the pile. Practices such as this became more and more common as the revolt progressed.

Damascene rebels, under the command of ʿAbd al-Rahman Shahbandar, Nasib al-Bakri, and Hassan al-Kharrat, among others, responded in kind. On the morning of October 17, 1925, rebels dumped the corpses of twelve Circassian soldiers, still in their French uniforms, outside Bab al-Sharqi, one of the entrances into the old city of Damascus. Full-scale revolt broke out in Damascus and in the villages of the Ghouta immediately afterward. Led by Bakri, Kharrat, and Shallash, rebels disarmed police stations and burned the ʿAzm Palace, which served as the French headquarters in Damascus. The French Army retaliated with a massive two-day aerial bombardment of the city, killing over fifteen hundred people. This was the first time that a colonial air force bombarded a major city in the Middle East in an attempt to put down a rebellion. The British used aerial bombardment to suppress revolt in Iraq in 1920, but there the bombing was restricted to villages and tribal grazing areas. In 1925 whole sections of Damascus were destroyed either by direct bombardment or by fires. The neighborhood of al-Hariqa ("the fire" in Arabic), which today lies just southwest of the Great Umayyad Mosque, was named for the fire that broke out there as a result of French bombing. During the assault on Damascus, Kharrat's son, Fakhri, was captured, tortured, and finally executed in early 1926. Other rebel leaders, including Bakri and Shallash, fled to the Ghouta and hid in the villages there. Although many nationalists from elite Damascene families capitulated to the French in the wake of the October events, the main rebel leaders, already condemned to death by the French, had nothing to lose by pursuing their revolutionary activities, so they continued to organize in the Ghouta.

Qawuqji did not establish himself in the Ghouta until the spring of 1926. His journey back from northeastern Syria took several weeks, and after he finally arrived in the general area of the Damascus–Homs corridor, he and his men roamed the area, attacking French troops wherever they could. He spent several weeks on Mount Qalamun near the town of al-Nabak, just fifty miles northwest of Damascus. In one incident Qawuqji and his men pursued a group of French soldiers into the small village of Jib'adin on Mount Qalamun. When Qawuqji discovered that the people of the village had hidden the French soldiers, he and his men set fire to the village. He says in his memoirs that this was in order "to teach those who had collaborated with the French a grave lesson." For many ordinary Syrians in 1926 Qawuqji was a hero and an anticolonial rebel, but for others he was a troublemaker and just one of several armed strongmen marauding the Syrian countryside, demanding food and lodging. In many villages Qawuqji's appearance created deep anxiety.

One symptom of the revolt's decline during its final few months was the fear of being accused of collaborating with the French. In early 1926, in the wake of Qawuqji's actions in the village of Jib'adin, Qawuqji set himself up in the village of Damir, also on Mount Qalamun. There he recruited more men and set up a court that tried several local men for spying for the French. Qawuqji's turn to intimidation and persecution characterizes many anticolonial rebellions. As the French colonial state began to crush the rebellion with better weapons, better-trained troops, better organization, and airpower, the rebels felt the pressure and made even hastier decisions. The most effective part of the French campaign was the fear it created among ordinary people, most of whom were keeping their heads down and trying to get on with their daily lives. These civilians began sealing themselves off from the rebels out of terror of French retribution. In order to reverse this trend, rebels used the accusation of "collaborator" as a way of frightening ordinary Syrians into supporting them. This logic, typical of anticolonial rebellions, put tremendous strain on the national ties that bound Syrians together across ethnic and religious differences. The French often accused Sunni villagers of supporting the rebels. In turn the rebels targeted minority communities, such as Syrian Christians and Jews, as well as minority Muslim Shi'a sects like the 'Alawis and the Isma'ilis. In the spring of 1926 Qawuqji sent a letter to the heads of the Isma'ili village of Salamiyya, near Hama:

Dear Brothers, Emir Tamir, Mirza, and Sulayman,
    May God guide you to the right way.
    I would never have believed that the Isma'ilis, our brothers in religion, nationality, and soil, would carry the arms of the enemy to fight their Syrian brothers and walk down the path of the Armenians, tyrants, despots, and imperialists. Know that the country belongs to its people. As long as oppression and usurpation carry on, the people will fight, and the country will be grateful to those who deserve it and will know how to take revenge against those who have done it wrong. It is indisputable that the revolt will succeed. With God's will, we have just become completely organized, and you will soon hear about our feats of arms and our brilliant campaigns.

I have many regrets, and I pity enormously those who will, in our country, have a fate similar to that of the Armenians in Turkey. We have agreed on very favorable conditions with Ibn Saʿud [ruler of the Kingdom of Hijaz and Sultanate of Nejd]. His troops, admirably supplied, are already making their entrance to the [Druze] Mountain. Our relations with the Turks are on the right track; they are starting to supply us with arms. The revolutionary government, which will be proclaimed shortly, has gathered serious assistance that will help it wage war for years to come. As for the enemy, you can observe its weakness with your own eyes. It has created fortifications in the interior of Damascus, while we have taken over all the exterior suburbs. Our current military operations are only a preparation for a complete takeover. So, have pity on your children. Remember them in their homes. If you don't want to join us, then at least be neutral. The reserve army that we have is on the verge of moving to take over several regions in Syria, including Salamiyya itself.

Accept our greetings, serve your country, and do not be seduced by the sweet talk of your enemies.

Your warrior brother in the holy cause,

Fawzy K., Leader of the Revolt in Hama

The reference to the fate of the Armenians in the letter is chilling. What has since become known as the Armenian Genocide occurred during World War I, when more than one million Armenians died. Accused of collaborating with the Allied forces, they were killed by Ottoman soldiers or died as a result of starvation and displacement. There is no evidence that Qawuqji acted on the threats he made in this letter, but his words convey the terrifying tactics sometimes used by the rebels. Other prominent rebels sent similar threatening letters to communities that were not showing enough loyalty to the revolt. But the revolt did enjoy real support from many Syrians because of the rebels' commitment to continuing the fight against the French in the face of increasingly brutal French reprisals. And even more Syrians supported the aims of the revolt—the end of French occupation and the establishment of an independent

Syria—even if they did not believe that the disruption to daily life was worth it. Some historians view the varying degrees of popular support for the revolt as corresponding to ethnic and religious differences in Syria. It is true that many Sunnis were prorevolt, particularly in the countryside and the more traditional urban areas. It is also true that support for the French could be found in minority communities. But the Druze, themselves a minority, were at the forefront of the revolt and worked in effective military alliances with Sunni merchants and ex-Ottoman officers. Christian communities were also split. Some Christian communities, in particular Orthodox Christians, openly supported the revolt. Catholic Christians, on the other hand, tended to support the French, although not uniformly. Class was generally a more important factor than religion or ethnicity. The revolt was most popular in the countryside and in lower- and lower-middle-class urban areas. These were the people who benefited the least from French rule. On the other hand, many members of the landed elite and some members of the professional class were doing quite well under French rule and had the most to lose from a rebel victory.

LEADERSHIP IN THE GHOUTA

After failing to expel the French from al-Nabak, even with the extra fighters he recruited in Damir, Qawuqji fled Qalamun with his men and traveled to the Ghouta, where other rebels fought on and where the supply lines to the rebel bases were much better. The leaders of these bands of fighters included ex-Ottoman officers like Ramadan Shallash, Sa'id al-'As, and Muhammad 'Izz al-Din al-Halabi, in addition to local strongmen such as Hassan al-Kharrat and the 'Akkash brothers. Merchants, like 'Abd al-Qadir Sukkar from the Maydan quarter, just south of Damascus, also led groups of fighters. Sukkar was a well-known grain merchant who had organized fighters during the battle of Maysalun in 1920. The participation of some merchant families in the revolt was important because it showed that the revolt had support not

just from ex-Ottoman soldiers and Syrian peasants but also from traditional urban classes that were important for the stability of the Syrian
economy. The big landowning families were not represented among the
rebels who continued to fight in the Ghouta, with the exception of
Nasib al-Bakri, who worked closely with Hassan al-Kharrat. In fact rebel
documents reveal that Kharrat and his men operated as a proxy army for
Bakri. Rebel letters to elite Damascene families asking for money and
support survive today in the French archives. It is not clear how these
requests were received.

Late 1925 and early 1926 saw emerging divisions between the leaders
of the rebel groups operating in the Ghouta. Rebels disagreed over the
tactics involved in gaining local support. In some cases rebels used
violence to coerce support from villagers. Some rebels also took food and
money from villagers who could not afford to give. This terrified the
villagers, who called on rebel leaders to impose order and discipline. Some
villagers accused the rebel leader Ramadan Shallash in particular of em-
ploying such coercion. This led to other rebel leaders' putting Shallash
on trial in a rebel court. Nasib al-Bakri was one of his accusers. Shallash
was expelled from the revolt and later surrendered to the French authorities. All this took place while the French were launching increasingly
successful attacks on the Ghouta, killing dozens of rebels every time they
moved into the orchards. From the rebel point of view, the most dreaded
French operation was aerial bombardment. By late spring of 1926, when
Qawuqji arrived in the Ghouta from Mount Qalamun, the situation
had become desperate. A few weeks after Qawuqji's arrival, the National
Council of the Ghouta appointed him the leader of the revolt there. This
appointment came because he was not implicated in any of the earlier
disputes between leaders of the revolt. Qawuqji was not present at
Ramadan Shallash's trial. The trial caused many rebels, including the
ex-Ottoman officer Sa'id al-'As, to accuse Bakri (Shallash's main perse-
cutor) of destroying rebel unity out of personal ambition and jealousy of
Shallash's popularity. The National Council of the Ghouta, the body
that coordinated the operations of the various rebel groups, began dis-

integrating as a result of these divisions. Here is part of the letter the council sent to Qawuqji, confirming his leadership of the Ghouta rebels:

> Yesterday afternoon, June 23, 1926 (on Wednesday), the National Council of the Ghouta and other areas in the north convened an extraordinary session. Owing to the seriousness of the situation and the resignation of the president of the council, some of the members suggested that you be entrusted with the job of being commander in chief of the Army of the Ghouta and that the council be dissolved so that you are entrusted with all the authority and responsibilities that were previously entrusted to the council.

In effect, Qawuqji was given responsibility for directing a revolt that had already started to fail. But he was determined to keep fighting. The first thing he did as leader of the rebels in the Ghouta was to organize the supply lines and food caches. He saw that dwindling supplies in the Ghouta were the main cause of the decrease in local support for the revolt. Qawuqji also imposed a "tax" on Syrians in the Ghouta area, arguing that they should pay taxes to the rebels and not to the French government. Again, this was a common practice among rebels, who needed money to pay the salaries of those who chose to fight on their side. Rebel soldiers would often ambush cars on the outskirts of Damascus and extort money from the drivers. A French intelligence report, entitled "On the Road to Douma," tells the story of one such incident. Douma is a suburb of Damascus near the Ghouta orchards, and the report is dated August 13, 1926. In the French documents, rebels are always referred to by the French word *bande*, meaning "gang":

> Yesterday morning at 7h, a gang stopped the Ford car of the driver Salim Hamada, close to the 'Arbin crossroad. They asked him for 15 gold pounds, and he replied that he didn't have that amount on him. They [the rebels] asked the travelers [in the car] to get out, and they drove the car, with the driver, to Zur to present him to their leader,

Fawzy K., but they didn't find him there. Then they left for Zamalka and Jubar. They met with Fawzy K. and told him the driver didn't pay the required sum. He asked the driver some questions concerning the taxes [the driver] paid to the government and told him: "You should pay just like you pay Damascus." The driver declined again, saying he didn't have that much money, and they let him go on condition that he pay that amount on another trip; otherwise they will burn his car. The driver was then able to return to Damascus.

In his memoirs Qawuqji castigates the leading families of Damascus for not supporting the revolt and choosing instead to negotiate with the French. This was not an option for him. Having mutinied against his commanding officer in the French Army in Hama, he knew that he would not be included in any kind of amnesty. In the summer of 1926 Syrian newspapers ran stories about possible pardons for many of those who had participated in the revolt. Qawuqji lists others who, by contrast, had stayed loyal to the goals of the revolt and thereby lessened or ruined their chances of amnesty: Sa'id al-'As, Shawkat al-'Adi, Fu'ad Salim, 'Abd al-Qadir al-Malishu, Zaki al-Halabi, Sadiq al-Daghistani, Subhi al-'Umari, and Zaki al-Durubi.

Qawuqji continued to use the Ghouta as a base for several months and fought a number of battles against the French as they tried to clear the area of rebels. On several occasions in the late summer and fall of 1926, French newspapers announced that the revolt was over. Qawuqji's response was to attack French soldiers or sabotage French installations as a way of demonstrating that the rebellion was still active. French intelligence reports dated toward the end of July 1926 say that Qawuqji, along with other rebels, was wounded in one of these actions. A photograph of Qawuqji (figure 17), one of the very few we have from this early period, shows him standing somewhere in the Ghouta. His right hand is in a bandage.

Many of the revolt's leaders, who had been active in the Druze Mountain in the summer of 1925, later fled French incursions there and moved their base of operations to Azraq, a small oasis town in the desert in north-

FIGURE 17

central Transjordan, then under British control. Azraq was just a two-day ride by horse from the Druze Mountain in Syria. In October 1926 'Abd al-Rahman Shahbandar, the Syrian nationalist who had pledged his allegiance to Sultan al-Atrash the year before, wrote Qawuqji a long letter from Azraq. Shahbandar was responding to a letter he had received from Qawuqji, in which Qawuqji claimed that he and his men were revitalizing the revolt in the Ghouta and bringing back some order to rebel ranks, which had collapsed as a result of the infighting that caused the dissolution of the Rebel Council in the Ghouta. Shahbandar thanked Qawuqji for his efforts and told him that he had read his letter to the exiled rebels in Azraq. Shahbandar reported that he and Sultan al-Atrash had begun setting up an organization that would include representatives of all the different parties to the revolt. This organization would raise money and acquire weapons in order to offer logistical support to the rebels still active in Syria. Shahbandar also told Qawuqji that the revolt was still alive on the Druze Mountain and mentioned examples of attacks on French troops. Shahbandar wrote about the importance of "the north" as a place that would welcome rebels and would make a good base for continuing the resistance. According to Shahbandar, rebels in the Zawiya Mountains, near Idlib, in the northwestern corner of Syria next to the Turkish border, were working tirelessly to organize resistance.

By the fall of 1926 the French blockade of the Ghouta had started to cause starvation. Memories of the famine of 1915 and 1916 were still fresh in the minds of the Ghouta's residents, who bore the brunt of supporting the rebels camped outside their villages. Dysentery spread in many of the villages and in the rebel camps. According to a report that Qawuqji wrote in late 1926, the French forced the villagers in the Ghouta to establish small guards of fifteen to twenty men, tasked with preventing the rebels from entering the villages. The French ordered these local village guards to shoot any rebels trying to enter the villages or risk being arrested themselves. Unusually heavy rains in the fall and winter of 1926 made it particularly difficult for the French to find rebels in the Ghouta, where traveling in the orchards had become extremely laborious. In one ominous line, Qawuqji reports that "we were forced to punish severely one of the villages so as to set an example for the other villages and thus prevent these village guards from accomplishing their aims."

Qawuqji left the Ghouta with just sixteen men sometime in the late fall of 1926. He went first to the Druze Mountain to regroup and then met with Sultan al-Atrash in Azraq, from where he journeyed to Amman, which by this time had filled with exiles from the Syrian Revolt, such as Saʿid al-ʿAs and Nasib al-Bakri. Qawuqji found Amman full of the old political divisions that had undermined the revolt in the Ghouta. Finding Amman stultifying, and annoyed by the prospect of endless rehashes of what had gone wrong and why, he returned to Syria with a small group of men and horses in December 1926. Over the next few months he moved around Syria, traveling at night and staying for a few days at a time with tribal shaykhs who he knew to be sympathetic to the goals of the revolt.

On the night of December 21, 1926, Qawuqji and eight other men entered Damascus in order to attack French soldiers and sabotage French lines of communication. The men wrote notes before entering the city and agreed that whoever survived the attack would pass these notes on to their families. Qawuqji's note read: "We are going on the road that leads to the highest honor and sacrifice. I am doing this so my country may live, and so that my mother may live, and so that my son Majdi may live an honorable life after I am gone." They spent a few days in Damascus and the Ghouta, sabotaging French installations, and then they left and eventually made their way back to Amman.

While politicians in Damascus were negotiating an end to the revolt, Qawuqji spent the first few months of 1927 trying to secure support for relaunching organized attacks against the French from the Zawiya Mountains in the northwest corner of Syria. The Center for Historical Documents in Damascus contains dozens of letters written by Qawuqji in early 1927 and submitted to the national councils of the revolt in Amman and in Jerusalem, asking for material support to rekindle the revolt in the Zawiya Mountains. In fact there are far more contemporaneous documents written by Qawuqji in these last few months of the revolt than there are from 1925 or 1926. Here the archive distorts the past. The very fact that these letters are extant gives the impression that Qawuqji was more active in 1927 than in the previous two years. But these long documents, full of forceful arguments about why the Zawiya Mountains were the perfect place to rekindle the revolt, as well as detailed lists of the weapons and money required to get the job done, carry a whiff of failure and inaction. When Qawuqji was fighting in Hama in October 1925 or organizing the revolt in the Ghouta in the summer of 1926, he had no time to draft long reports. Informal rebel groups in Syria and elsewhere in the Middle East in the early twentieth century did not issue many reports about their military actions because these groups were not regulated by the bureaucratic processes of state armies. By the time Qawuqji was fighting against the Israeli army in Palestine in 1948, the situation had changed. By then he was leading a modern mechanized army that produced official documentation, more or less in step with its actions on the ground.

Qawuqji believed that the Zawiya Mountains would prove to be a good location for rekindling the revolt because the mountains lay close to the border with Turkey. He claimed that he could draw on old contacts from his days in the Ottoman Army to secure Turkish support. This conviction took him to Turkey in the summer of 1927. He traveled with two close friends, a doctor named Amin al-Ruwayha who had fought with him in the Ghouta, and Sa'id Haydar, a prominent Syrian nationalist involved in promoting links with Turkey. In 1920 Haydar had participated in a delegation that traveled to Turkey to meet with Mustafa Kemal and other Turkish nationalists. At that meeting they drew up an agreement to present a united front to the Western powers from Ma'an (in present-day Jordan) to the Black Sea. According to the terms of the agreement, the Turkish and Arab armies would be placed under a unified command, and in the event of a successful outcome Arabs and Turks would have independent states federated the way Austria and Hungary had been in the prewar Austro-Hungarian Empire. Of course this never happened. But Haydar and Qawuqji clung to the Ottoman Turkish world in which they had been raised. Dozens of letters that they wrote to each other during this period attest to their desperate efforts in late 1927—with Qawuqji in Ankara and Haydar in Istanbul—to secure support from their Turkish friends. Qawuqji does not say so explicitly, but Turkey clearly served as a refuge when he could not safely remain in Syria.

The letters the two men sent to each other include references to contacts with the governor of 'Ayntab, a large Turkish town close to the Syrian border. In his memoirs Qawuqji also mentions a putative agreement with some Turkish army officers whereby Turkey would help the rebels in Syria in exchange for a share of power in Syria. All these attempts to resurrect the revolt failed. The Arabic documents contain no indication that Haydar, Qawuqji, and Ruwayha obtained any serious support from the Turks. In the old Arab provinces of the Ottoman Empire many still looked north to Istanbul for help, even as late as 1927. But the Turkish government under Ataturk's leadership focused on consolidating the borders of the new Republic of Turkey. The Turks (who had the resources of the disbanded Ottoman Army at their disposal) successfully fought off post–World War I attempts by Europeans to occupy Anatolia, and they emerged with an independent state. The same struggle by Syrian Arabs to the south, in many ways a continuation of the Ottoman war against European occupation during World War I, was excluded from the new world of the Turkish republic.

Qawuqji visited Istanbul on July 1, 1927, the same day that Ataturk made his first visit to the city as president of the Republic of Turkey. Ataturk sailed up the Bosphorus on the imperial yacht *Ertugrul*. The shoreline of the city was packed with people celebrating his return to Istanbul after eight years. Qawuqji entered the city with a false ID card. He traveled under the name 'Umar Fawzi 'Abd al-Majid and presented himself as a trader interested in setting up a textile business. He watched Ataturk's arrival from far back in the crowd: "The scenes of celebration really affected me. I couldn't help comparing our situation with the situation of the

Turks. I was struck by the opportunities that Ataturk had that allowed this success and by the obstacles that we had faced. If it hadn't been for these obstacles then, our victory would have been assured, and we would have had an even greater victory than the Turks were enjoying."

By the time Qawuqji was in Istanbul in the summer of 1927, the revolt in Syria was over. The British expelled Sultan al-Atrash and his followers from Azraq to Wadi al-Sirhan in the new Arabian sultanate of Ibn Saʻud. Other prominent rebels scattered to Amman, Jerusalem, and Cairo. Many of the lower-ranking rebels were pardoned by the French and returned to their farms and villages. Some rebels from elite landowning families, such as Nasib al-Bakri, were also pardoned. Bakri was even allowed to reclaim his landholdings from French confiscation. But most of the rebel leaders of the revolt remained in exile under sentence of death; these included Sultan al-Atrash, Muhammad al-Ashmar, Muhammad ʻIzz al-Din al-Halabi, Saʻid Haydar, Saʻid al-ʻAs, and Fawzi al-Qawuqji. Following the demise of the revolt, Qawuqji abandoned Turkey and relocated to the Hijaz, in what is today Saudi Arabia, to help train Ibn Saʻud's army. Qawuqji's time in the Hijaz is part of a little-known story of the late 1920s and early 1930s, when former Syrian rebels gathered in the new Arabian sultanate of Ibn Saʻud. These Syrians saw Ibn Saʻud as an independent Arab and Muslim ruler whose kingdom had not been colonized by the French and the British and was therefore free of foreign soldiers.

A SYRIAN IN THE KINGDOM OF IBN SAʻUD

Qawuqji left Istanbul for Jidda in the late summer of 1928. Jidda lies in the Hijaz region of western Saudi Arabia. Along with the two holy cities of Mecca and Medina, Jidda is today one of the major urban centers of the Hijaz. In 1928 it was a small trading town on the shores of the Red Sea, a stop along the trade routes between Arabia, Yemen, the Horn of Africa, and Egypt. As the home of Mecca and Medina the Hijaz remained a prize possession of the Ottoman Empire until World War I. Mecca was

the site of the hajj (pilgrimage), and the Hijaz garnered most of its revenues from the millions of pilgrims who came to Mecca every year from
all over the Muslim world.

During the Ottoman period the Hashemite family ruled the Hijaz in
their capacity as custodians of the two holy cities of Mecca and Medina.
Sharif Husayn bin 'Ali (King Faysal's father) was the last Hashemite to
rule there. In 1916 he declared the Hijaz an independent kingdom as a
result of his alliance with the British against the Ottomans in World
War I. After the war Sharif Husayn bin 'Ali was expelled from the Hijaz
by 'Abd al-'Aziz Al Sa'ud. Also known as Ibn Sa'ud, 'Abd al-'Aziz hailed
from a leading tribal family in the central Arabian province of Nejd. By
1926 the Hijaz was under Ibn Sa'ud's control. He ruled the Hijaz and
Nejd as two independent kingdoms until he united them in 1932, under
the new kingdom of Saudi Arabia.

The province of Nejd is well-known throughout the Arab world as
the home of Wahhabism, a Sunni Muslim religious movement known
for its austerity and strict adherence to the monotheistic principles of
Islam. The movement construes the core Islamic doctrine of *tawhid*
(the unity of God) as requiring the rejection of any form of saint wor-
ship or tomb visitation, which is seen as a form of *shirk* (polytheism).
Today Wahhabism is also associated with extreme forms of political
Islam preached by Usama Bin Laden and the leaders of radical Islamic
groups in Iraq and Syria. But in the 1920s and 1930s the Wahhabis
in Nejd were merely known for practicing a particularly austere form
of Sunnism that was, generally speaking, absent from the large urban
centers of Iraq and Syria.

Because of his conquest of the Hijaz, Ibn Sa'ud had become a famous
figure in the Arab world (and beyond) by the time Qawuqji arrived in
Jidda in 1928. European journalists flocked there to find out more about
this mysterious desert warrior. St. John Philby, a former British colonial
official, lived in Jidda in the 1920s and 1930s and served as a personal
adviser to Ibn Sa'ud. Many Syrians and Lebanese also traveled to Jidda to
try to find work in Ibn Sa'ud's growing kingdom. These included Fu'ad
Hamza, a Druze from Abey in Lebanon, and Yusuf al-Yasin, a Syrian

Sunni from Latakia. Both men gained prominence in Ibn Saʿud's government and devoted their careers to serving the Saudi state. They formed
the nucleus of a group of men within the Saudi government whom British
officials simply referred to as the Syrians.

Other Syrians traveled to the Hijaz in the wake of the failed Syrian
Revolt because they saw in Ibn Saʿud a potential patron who might help
them renew their struggle against the colonial powers. Here was a strong
leader whose kingdom was free of European soldiers. These men included Qawuqji, Munir al-Rayyis, the Syrian nationalist Nabih al-ʿAzma,
and the famous Druze Lebanese nationalist Shakib Arslan. In addition,
Ibn Saʿud provided refuge in Nejd for such prominent Syrian rebels as
Sultan al-Atrash, Muhammad al-Ashmar, and Saʿid al-ʿAs. These rebels
had been expelled from Transjordan by the British and for several months
lived in Wadi al-Sirhan, in the Nejdi desert, as guests of Ibn Saʿud. Unlike
Qawuqji, the Wadi al-Sirhan group never traveled to the Hijaz and were
not welcome at Ibn Saʿud's court. The photograph (figure 18), taken in
1929, shows Syrian rebels in Wadi al-Sirhan. Sultan al-Atrash is seated
in the middle, Muhammad al-Ashmar is on his left, and Saʿid al-ʿAs is
seated two to his right.

FIGURE 18

In the summer of 1928 Qawuqji traveled from Istanbul to Jidda by boat, first through the Mediterranean to Port Saʿid, on the coast of Egypt, and then through the Red Sea from Suez to Jidda. In his memoirs he describes the way he felt as the steamer approached the shores of the Hijaz and Jidda came into view:

> The sun was burning, and the sea quiet. The steamship carried the last load of pilgrims to the hajj, which was only a few days away. I concentrated my gaze on the horizon above the sea, and thoughts began swirling in my mind. I imagined the growing Saudi state, which had extended its influence to the area of the Hijaz and ʿAsir and Nejd, and I felt happy and optimistic when I thought that I could be a soldier serving this state. As the boat approached Jidda, my fascination increased and my hopes and dreams were great.

When Qawuqji arrived in Jidda, he stayed in the center of the town in the house of Fuʾad Hamza, a Lebanese Druze who was one of Ibn Saʿud's closest advisers. Shakib Arslan was also staying with Hamza. Arslan came from a very prominent Druze family in Lebanon. He was a poet, a historian, a politician, and an advocate of Pan-Islamism, believing that it was the most effective way to challenge British and French imperialism. Qawuqji, in his first few days in Jidda, also met a number of Syrians already working in Ibn Saʿud's new kingdom. These included the king's personal doctor, Midhat al-Ard, and Rushdi Milhis, the editor of *Umm al-Qura*, the most important newspaper in the Hijaz.

Because of his connection to Fuʾad Hamza, Qawuqji had several opportunities to meet Ibn Saʿud by attending the regular public council meetings that Ibn Saʿud convened. Qawuqji and Shakib Arslan also traveled with Ibn Saʿud's entourage when Ibn Saʿud left Jidda to visit other towns across the kingdom. Qawuqji's account of this time notes the cultural difference between the visiting Syrians and the Hijazis and Nejdis. This cultural difference was particularly stark in Nejd, the home of Ibn Saʿud and his family and the birthplace of Wahhabism. In an account of one meeting with some leading figures from Nejd, Qawuqji vividly describes how the Nejdis drew their cloaks around themselves at the sight of Qawuqji, in order to (in his words) "protect themselves from the smell of polytheism [*shirk*]." In his memoirs, Qawuqji also comments on the strangeness of the Nejdi Arabic dialect, spoken by the king himself and most of his advisers. In one meeting with Ibn Saʿud, at which Shakib Arslan was also present, the two men listened for some time to Ibn Saʿud's theories of world politics. While he was speaking, Qawuqji noticed the way Arslan was leaning forward and concentrating. Qawuqji was sure that Arslan, who came from a distinguished family and was proficient in Arabic, Ottoman Turkish, and French, simply could not understand the king's Arabic. Like Qawuqji, Arslan had spent his life in the cities of Greater Syria, such as Beirut and Damascus, where the spoken Arabic was very different from that of the Arabian Peninsula.

The fact that Qawuqji was light skinned and fair-haired also raised eyebrows in the king's circles. A few months after Qawuqji's arrival the king was preparing to fight the powerful Nejdi tribal shaykh Faysal al-Duwaish, who was gathering his forces to mount a challenge to Ibn Saʿud's authority. Shakib Arslan suggested that the king use Qawuqji's help because of Qawuqji's long experience fighting in the Ottoman Army and in the rebellion against the French in Syria. The king refused, fearing that if Duwaish's tribesmen saw such a fair officer in the king's army, they would accuse the king of collaborating with the British to suppress Duwaish's challenge. Qawuqji was dismissive of this concern, particularly given that the king was so close to St. John Philby, his British adviser, who was allowed much more access to the king than were most of the visiting Syrians.

St. John Philby (the father of the famous British double agent Kim Philby) was an eccentric figure and the object of almost obsessive suspicion from Qawuqji. Philby had started his professional life as a British colonial official, working in India, Iraq, and the Arabian Peninsula during the 1910s and 1920s. In 1924 he was forced to resign any official role in the British government because of suspicions that he had passed secret British information to Ibn Saʿud. From the mid-1920s onward, Philby lived in Jidda, working as a partner in a trading company and acting as one of Ibn Saʿud's advisers. Philby also converted to Islam in the summer of 1930 and took on a Muslim name, 'Abdullah Philby. The photograph of Philby (figure 19) was taken in Riyadh, the capital of Nejd, sometime in the 1930s.

Qawuqji, who met Philby on several occasions, never trusted him and saw him as a bad influence on the king, who was becoming increasingly pro-British. Qawuqji's suspicion was shared by many of the Syrians with whom he associated in Jidda, with the exception of Fu'ad Hamza, who had great influence over the king and who was himself very close to Philby. (In fact it was Hamza who arranged the logistics of Philby's conversion to Islam.) Nabih al-'Azma, a prominent Syrian nationalist who spent 1929 and 1930 in Jidda trying to reform Ibn Sa'ud's army (with

FIGURE 19

Qawuqji's assistance), was horrified by the influence that Philby appeared to exert over the king. Toward the end of 1930, 'Azma wrote a letter to Ibn Sa'ud after 'Azma had discovered that Philby had secured a British loan of two hundred thousand pounds for the king. In the letter 'Azma warned against Philby's influence, claiming that the Briton's assistance to the king was just the beginning of a British imperial land grab in the Arabian Peninsula. 'Azma included in the letter a long quote from a book published ten years before by an American, the Harvard-trained historian Lothrop Stoddard. The book, entitled *The New World of Islam* (Stoddard was better known in America for his white supremacist jeremiad *The Rising Tide of Color Against White World-Supremacy*), included an account of the way in which the British and the French had laid the ground for their empires by issuing loans. As 'Azma conveyed it to the king, after the loans came political influence, and after the political influence came imperial conquest.

REFORMING THE KING'S ARMY

In 1930 Ibn Sa'ud's kingdom was in financial trouble. It was not until 1933 that he granted Standard Oil of California the right to prospect for oil. Once the prospecting began it took a further five years before vast reserves of oil were discovered in the Dammam dome in eastern Saudi Arabia near the Arabian Gulf. But in 1930 Ibn Sa'ud still relied mainly on the revenues from the hajj, which were in decline. This forced him into debt, which in turn led to the deferral of government salaries and created a general sense of economic instability. Ibn Sa'ud always worried about challenges to his rule, but the financial situation made these worries even more acute. It was in this context that Ibn Sa'ud granted permission to 'Azma and Qawuqji to take steps to transform the king's small guard into an organized army. 'Azma was given the official title of director of military affairs, with Qawuqji as his deputy. Nabih al-'Azma had long connections with the Hijaz. He had visited the Hijaz in the early 1920s and even acted briefly as a negotiator between Ibn Sa'ud and

Sharif Husayn bin ʿAli, before Ibn Saʿud finally expelled Sharif Husayn from the Hijaz. ʿAzma had also traveled to the Hijaz in 1927 to try to secure Ibn Saʿud's support for the rebels in Syria. In letters to his brother ʿAdil and to his fellow nationalists, ʿAzma spoke of his great hope that Ibn Saʿud could play a leading role in uniting the Arabs against the imperialist powers. ʿAzma and many others, such as Shakib Arslan and Qawuqji, regarded Ibn Saʿud as an alternative to Transjordan's Hashemite amir ʿAbdullah, who had come to collaborate too closely with the British.

More prosaically, ʿAzma was also looking for a job when he showed up in Jidda in the spring of 1930. After his appointment as director of military affairs in the summer of 1930, ʿAzma wrote proudly to his brother ʿAdil, who was then in Amman: "This time I went to the Hijaz intending to stay a long time if events allow it, and I will work to obtain the trust of the king in order to benefit from his power by way of continuing our work against colonialism, and I will make the country a refuge for nationalists. He appointed me to the War Ministry and made me the commander of his organized army. This made me extremely happy." ʿAzma and Qawuqji had some strong supporters in Ibn Saʿud's government. Fuʾad Hamza, the Lebanese Druze who acted as Ibn Saʿud's main foreign policy adviser, was the most prominent. But ʿAzma and Qawuqji also had enemies, in particular ʿAbdullah Sulayman, the minister of finance, who resented these Syrian interlopers and feared their influence over the king and Prince Faysal, one of the king's sons. The first task facing ʿAzma and Qawuqji was to inspect the king's soldiers and armaments in order to determine what needed to be changed. But just gaining access to the king's weapons supplies proved to be a challenge. In his memoirs Qawuqji describes being denied permission to view the arms stored in Medina, in spite of his having been authorized by the king to inspect everything. It became clear to Qawuqji and ʿAzma that Sulayman was placing obstacles in their path. In September 1930 the two men wrote a letter of complaint to Prince Faysal's deputy. The letter describes the numerous occasions when they had been blocked from accessing weapons depots. They also asked for the office space that they had been promised in order to set up their administration. In addition, they requested the official decree confirming Qawuqji's appointment as 'Azma's deputy, paperwork that had not yet been issued. Most important, they asked Prince Faysal to write officially to the Ministry of Finance granting 'Azma and Qawuqji permission to inspect all weapons in the kingdom.

The letter of complaint proved effective because two months later, in November 1930, 'Azma submitted a long report to Ibn Sa'ud on the condition of the king's army. The report makes fascinating reading. It criticizes the deplorable living conditions of the soldiers and officers and the state of their uniforms and weapons. 'Azma and Qawuqji also stated that as far as structure was concerned, all they could see was "chaos." According to them, Ibn Sa'ud's army had "no organization, no method, and no shared goal around which soldiers and officers could unite." The report also said that there were hardly any worthy officers and that only the ordinary soldiers should be valued because they showed a "readiness to be trained."

The report is strikingly arrogant. After all, Ibn Sa'ud had recently conquered Nejd and the Hijaz. In 1930 the king had succeeded in putting down a revolt of Nejdi tribesmen led by Faysal al-Duwaish, who attempted to usurp Ibn Sa'ud's control of Nejd. By contrast, Qawuqji and 'Azma had fled to the Hijaz in the wake of the failure of the Syrian Revolt. As Syrians and as veterans of the Ottoman Army they saw themselves as being more advanced than the Hijazis and the Nejdis. When they looked at Ibn Sa'ud's desert army, they saw only backwardness. The tone of the report and of other letters that 'Azma sent to Ibn Sa'ud that year echoes the supercilious tone of French and British reports about the state of Syrian institutions in the 1920s and 1930s. It is impossible to know exactly how Ibn Sa'ud reacted to this report. What we do know is that 'Azma left the Hijaz for good in early 1931, leaving Qawuqji in charge of reforming the king's army. From his letters to his brother and friends, it seems 'Azma left because he was frustrated by the slow pace of decision making in the kingdom and the fact that he was not given the resources to make the reforms he saw as necessary.

In his memoirs Qawuqji claims that things improved for a while after 'Azma's departure. Qawuqji centralized the king's army in Jidda and initiated a training program for officers. He deepened his relationship with Prince Faysal and began to believe that he could rely on the prince's support against Sulayman. He even organized a military parade that was attended by the king and many of his ministers, as well as by foreign consuls. Sir Andrew Ryan, the first British envoy and minister plenipotentiary to the court of Ibn Sa'ud, was present at the parade. He wrote a dispatch back to London concerning the state of the king's new army. Ryan was not a British Arabist. He had spent most of his service in Istanbul during both the Ottoman and republican periods. He spoke excellent Turkish and, according to Philby, "was thoroughly versed in the elaborate etiquette of the Ottoman Court and the roundabout ways of polite and diplomatic conversation in vogue at the Sublime Porte." This led Ryan to be somewhat disparaging about politics in the Arabian Peninsula. Ryan's account of Qawuqji's parade was included in his regular report to London on the king's activities:

The review held by Emir Feisal at Kandara on the afternoon of the 8th of January presents features of interest. King Ibn Saud not long ago appointed a certain Nabi Bey al-Adhma to be director of Military Organization. This gentleman resigned after a very short time and was replaced by one Faudhi Bey al-Kawokji, a Syrian officer, who formerly served in the Turkish Army and took part, apparently with some distinction, in the Palestine campaign. He would appear to have been German trained, judging by his excellent knowledge of German. During the last Syrian Revolt he went over to the rebels and came to this country as a fugitive from the French. The review afforded an opportunity for displaying the meager results so far achieved in the direction of creating a regular army. The march past was headed by two detachments of infantry, about 500 men in all, rather ragged in formation but workmanlike and to some extent disciplined. Then followed a string of pack animals with various equipment and about 100 men in charge. Then came two armored cars, which were followed by the "cavalry" consisting of less than forty horsemen, ill-mounted and variously equipped, nothing more, in fact than a disorderly rout of tribesmen who indulged in wild shouts as they passed. The camelry, who came after them, were distinctly more impressive and numbered at least 320, perhaps more. This force, though also wild and composed of heterogeneous types, had a certain air of efficiency. Towards the end of the review three aeroplanes of the Hejaz Air Force swept round in great circles, while the "cavalry" again appeared to display their prowess in galloping, firing comic pistols and emitting war cries.

Its sneering tone set aside, this report is important because the very fact of having a military parade indicated Qawuqji's influence on Prince Faysal. The Wahhabi religious scholars frowned upon parades of any kind. Their devotion to the strictest understanding of God's unity led them to judge parades as idolatrous distractions, hence examples of polytheism. Immediately after the parade, when Qawuqji tried to persuade Ibn Sa'ud to sanction a repeat performance in Nejd, it emerged that leading Wahhabi scholars had spoken to the king and persuaded him to cancel plans for any further displays of this kind.

Qawuqji's success with the nascent Saudi army was short-lived. Because of the economic crisis of 1930 and 1931, Sulayman cut off salary payments to all government officials, including officers and soldiers, and Qawuqji faced increasing complaints from below. He went to his main supporter, Prince Faysal, and told him that unless things changed, he would have to resign. On the advice of Prince Faysal, Qawuqji wrote to Ibn Sa'ud detailing all the problems he faced and in particular the way in which Sulayman's actions prevented him from doing his job effectively. He handed the letter to Ibn Sa'ud personally. The king immediately called Sulayman into his chamber, handed him Qawuqji's letter, and told him to comply with Qawuqji's requests. But the situation did not improve, and again Qawuqji threatened to resign and to tell the world that Ibn Sa'ud was unwilling to do what it took to build up a strong Arab army and serve as a leader in the cause of Arab nationalism. The Syrians at Ibn Sa'ud's court—Fu'ad Hamza, Yusuf al-Yasin, Rushdi Milhis, and Midhat al-Ard—begged Qawuqji to stay. Qawuqji even received a letter from the king himself asking him to remain in the kingdom. Qawuqji kept this letter carefully in his private papers long into his retirement as evidence of the fact that the king had not rejected him. Qawuqji agreed to stay on in the Hijaz and became for a brief time an important member of Ibn Saʿud's close entourage, traveling with him regularly, particularly to Taʾif in the hills near Jidda, where the king often went to escape the stultifying heat of the coast. Qawuqji even had a house in Taʾif, organized for him by the king's secretaries. Qawuqji was also offered a wife by the shaykh of the Banu Thaqif, a prominent Hijazi tribe. Qawuqji agreed to take a second wife as a sign of the formal allegiance between him and the Banu Thaqif. From that marriage was born the daughter whom he named Suriya (Arabic for Syria).

ARRESTED

The economic crisis was not the only challenge the king faced in the early 1930s. Ibn Saʿud's rival, the Hashemite Amir ʿAbdullah of Transjordan (Sharif Husayn bin ʿAli's son and King Faysal of Iraq's brother), was rumored to be funneling support to certain Hijazi tribes, which might be persuaded to rise up against Ibn Saʿud's rule. A British report, drafted by Ryan in the summer of 1932, describes the paranoia in Ibn Saʿud's court around the possibility of a Hashemite conspiracy. Tribal leaders in Taʾif and Mecca, along with dozens of leading merchants in Jidda, were arrested. Even the king's son Prince Faysal fell under suspicion because of what Ryan describes as "his penchant for modern-minded Syrians." It was clear that the minister of finance, Sulayman, had instigated many of these arrests.

Qawuqji was of course no friend of Sulayman's and found himself caught up in this atmosphere of suspicion. One day in the early summer of 1932 police came to Qawuqji's house in Taʾif and took him to the main government building in Mecca. They kept him in a room inside the building, interrogating him daily about his loyalty to the kingdom. They also went through all of Qawuqji's belongings in his home. There they found a copy of the letter that Qawuqji had sent to Ibn Sa'ud complaining about Sulayman's obstructionism. After fifteen days Qawuqji began to sense that the police officer in charge of his interrogations was convinced by Qawuqji's denials of any wrongdoing. He felt that he was close to being freed. But then Sulayman himself arrived with a small unit of guards. He took Qawuqji to Mina, a small town just outside Mecca. There Sulayman's men shackled Qawuqji and put him in a truck for the four-day journey across the desert to Riyadh, the capital of Nejd and seat of the king's principal palace. In Riyadh the king's elder son Prince Sa'ud questioned Qawuqji. The prince asked him about his loyalty to the kingdom and accused him of being in league with "the seven states," the Arabian Gulf principalities that lay to the east of Nejd. Again, Qawuqji denied the accusations. He told the prince that Sulayman was behind all the rumors about him. Qawuqji finally managed to convince the prince to set him free.

Although officials in Riyadh encouraged Qawuqji to stay in the kingdom, he no longer felt safe. He knew he had to leave. In addition, many of his Syrian friends, themselves in exile in Cairo and Baghdad, had written letters to Ibn Sa'ud on Qawuqji's behalf when they heard that he was in trouble. Qawuqji began to think about making a life for himself in Iraq, where he had many contacts from his time serving in Faysal's Arab Army in Damascus in 1920. He made his way back to Ta'if from Riyadh, and in spite of Prince Faysal's attempts to persuade him to remain, he left the Hijaz in the summer of 1932. His Saudi wife and daughter Suriya remained with the Banu Thaqif in the Hijaz. It was not until many years later, when Suriya was in her early teens, that she joined him in Iraq. She then remained under Qawuqji's guardianship until the 1950s, when she married a British national and settled in London.

As the steamer pulled away from the port of Jidda to begin its voyage north through the Red Sea to Suez, on the coast of Egypt, Qawuqji thought back to the optimism he had felt when he first arrived in Jidda:

> I boarded the steamer that was going to Egypt. As Jidda and the Hijaz receded from view, I began to think at that moment of the dreams and hopes that I had had as I was approaching Jidda. I reviewed all

the things that had happened to me and that I had seen over the previous years. And I reviewed the position of the Arab nation in its entirety, and the external threats that surrounded it, and how its peoples were burdened by internal problems. I felt keenly the hopes and dreams that I had put into this patch of the Arabian Peninsula.

Qawuqji spent a few weeks in Cairo meeting with friends. Then he made his way to Iraq, which was to be his home for the next nine years. It was from Iraq that he traveled to Palestine in 1936 to fight the British army, the episode in his life that catapulted him from relative obscurity to becoming a household name in the Arab world.

3

■

PALESTINE 1936

Hajj Amin—Journey to Palestine—A rebel court—Battle in
Bal'a—Truce—Return to Baghdad

The story of Qawuqji's role in the Palestine Revolt of 1936 begins in
Iraq. Qawuqji arrived in Baghdad from Cairo toward the end of 1932.
Iraq had just been granted formal independence by Britain and had been
admitted to the League of Nations as a sovereign state under the leadership of King Faysal. However, the British retained military bases in the
country and remained as advisers to the king and to the government.
Immediately following independence, Faysal faced internal challenges
from some ex-Ottoman officers who had distanced themselves from pro-
British circles revolving around Iraqi prime minister Nuri al-Sa'id. As a
result, Sa'id resigned after Iraqi independence, and King Faysal invited
the more radical nationalist Naji Shawkat to form a government. Baghdad was alive with political controversy in the winter of 1932.

Qawuqji could not return to French-controlled Syria or Lebanon
because a warrant for his arrest on charges relating to his role in the Syrian
Revolt remained active. In Baghdad he still had friends from an earlier
time in Syria, when he had fought with Faysal's Arab Army against the

French advance. When Faysal fled Syria for Iraq in the late summer of 1920, Qawuqji had stayed on in Syria and had joined the French Army, but many of his old friends from the Ottoman Army, including Salah al-Din al-Sabbagh and Taha al-Hashimi, had accompanied Faysal to Baghdad. It was through these contacts that Qawuqji was able to obtain a position in the Iraqi Military Academy in Baghdad as an instructor in horsemanship and topography.

King Faysal drew most of his support from the ex-Ottoman officers in Iraq. He relied not only on those who had fought with him from the days of the Arab Revolt in 1916 but also on the men who had joined his forces later, in Damascus in 1918, after the collapse of the Ottoman Army. Many of these men drew their legitimacy as army commanders and high-ranking politicians in Baghdad from their association with Faysal's brief rule in Syria. Not only were they connected to one another through their shared experience of having been trained in the Ottoman military school system, but in some cases they were related to one another either through blood or through marriage. For example, Ja'far al-'Askari and Nuri al-Sa'id, both of whom served as prime minister of Iraq under Faysal's rule, were married to each other's sisters.

In his memoirs Qawuqji describes conversations that he had with King Faysal from late 1932 to the summer of 1933. Faysal wanted to know all about Qawuqji's exploits in Syria during the revolt. He was also particularly interested in Qawuqji's time in Saudi Arabia because of the rivalry between Faysal's family (the Hashemites) and the Sa'ud family. Sa'ud's forces had expelled Faysal's elder brother 'Ali from the Hijaz in 1924, and 'Ali had also fled to Baghdad. In spite of the fact that Faysal was considered too pro-British by many of the Iraqi nationalists with whom Qawuqji associated at the Iraqi Military Academy, Qawuqji had felt loyal to him from his time fighting in Faysal's army in Syria. He also respected Faysal's pan-Arab vision for the Levant. Faysal had never given up on his father's dream of a unified Arab kingdom that would stretch from the Mediterranean to the Euphrates. In this Faysal was supported by his brother Amir 'Abdullah in Transjordan. 'Abdullah believed in a reunited Syria, with no borders between Syria, Lebanon, Transjordan, and Palestine, that could federate with Iraq under Hashemite rule. The Hashemites' dynastic ambitions worried other Arab leaders, such as Ibn Sa'ud, along with politicians in Lebanon and Palestine who by the early 1930s were committed to Lebanese and Palestinian independence. Qawuqji was not particularly pro-Hashemite, but he was a staunch Arab nationalist and a Syrianist. He opposed the division of Greater Syria into separate states, and in this respect his vision for the region complemented Faysal's.

Qawuqji's connection to Faysal himself and to some of the ex-Ottoman officers in Baghdad, such as Yasin and Taha al-Hashimi and Salah al-Din al-Sabbagh, gave him access to the world of power brokers in Baghdad in the early 1930s. But unlike most of the ex-Ottoman officers in Baghdad, Qawuqji was not an Iraqi. Nor was he as important a figure as he sometimes presents himself as being in his memoirs. He did enjoy some prestige from his reputation as a rebel fighter, a reputation that had been forged in the Syrian Revolt. It was understandably difficult for Qawuqji simply to settle for being a cavalry instructor in the Military Academy in Baghdad. Already restless within weeks of starting his new job, he went to see Faysal to discuss plans to try to resurrect revolt in Syria. He asked for permission to contact his old friends in Syria and to start gathering arms and organizing men. Qawuqji gave Faysal a map detailing exactly where in Syria he would try to rekindle revolt. Faysal put the map carefully in his pocket and told him to wait for approval before he took any action. Qawuqji never saw him again after that meeting. Faysal died suddenly of a heart attack in a clinic in Switzerland in September 1933. His body was brought back to Baghdad for a huge state funeral. His body first landed on Arab soil at the port (figure 20) of Haifa in Palestine, from where it traveled by road to Iraq. Thousands of Palestinians came out to the port to pay their respects to the king who had briefly ruled in Syria at the end of World War I and had been such an important figure for pan-Arab politics.

In Qawuqji's memoirs there is a faded reproduction of a photograph of him saluting Faysal's coffin during the funeral procession through

FIGURE 20

Baghdad. The importance of Faysal's death was not lost on Qawuqji. He describes how it marked a moment of rupture for the pan-Arab movement, and he laments the power vacuum that followed Faysal's death in Iraq, which led to infighting and political chaos.

Faysal's death did allow Qawuqji the freedom to organize his contacts in Syria and Transjordan for a resurrection of revolt there. He was energized by the worsening relations between the National Bloc in Syria and the French mandate authorities. Founded in 1928, after the end of the Syrian Revolt, the National Bloc was a coalition of political parties in Syria, led by landowners, merchants, and professionals who wanted to bring an end to French rule through political pressure. Qawuqji's plans for revolt in Palestine were a natural extension of his goal of resurrecting revolt in Syria. It was difficult for him to travel to French territory at that time for fear of being arrested for mutiny. In British Palestine, by contrast, he was relatively safe. He made two trips to Jerusalem in this period, one in 1934 and one in 1935. In an interview published by *The Times* (London) in 1937, Qawuqji describes those two trips. The first trip was to meet with

Palestinian leaders and establish the broad contours of the planned revolt; the second was to prepare the logistical details, including organizing money and arms. The plan was to mount a double-pronged revolt
in Syria and Palestine, using Syria as a launching pad, thereby reunify-
ing the two areas within what Qawuqji saw as the natural borders of
Syria.

Developments in Syria toward the end of 1935 and into the spring of
1936 served as a catalyst for Qawuqji's actions in Palestine later in 1936.
The Syrian National Bloc increasingly confronted the French mandate
authorities, and in January 1936 the bloc declared a general strike. The
strike was accompanied by widespread protests. Pro-Syrian Palestinians
became involved in this movement, sending money to the Syrian Strike
Committee and calling on Palestinians to join their Syrian brothers in
revolution. In addition, an Iraqi parliamentary commission visited Palestine in early 1936 and promised to support the Palestinians if they
mounted a full-scale revolt. But then something happened that focused
Qawuqji's attention on Palestine alone. The French, under pressure from
the strike action in Syria and nervous about a resurgent Germany, agreed
to meet with the leaders of the bloc in Paris to discuss an agreement that
was shortly to result in France's signing a treaty granting Syria independence, a treaty that was never actually ratified by the French parliament.
In his memoirs Qawuqji admits that he was given a clear message from
his contacts in Syria not to initiate an armed rebellion in Syria while the
negotiations in Paris were ongoing. Completely sidelined by the bloc, his
role as a rebel fighter in Syria no longer needed, Qawuqji realized that he
had no future in a semi-independent Syria that might emerge from a
negotiated agreement with the French. Palestine thus became the sole
focus of his attention.

Toward the end of April 1936 a nationwide strike began in Palestine.
The newly formed Arab National Committee in Nablus in northern Palestine first organized the strike, which quickly gained support from
other national committees in all the major Palestinian towns. Strike
leaders made it clear to the British government in Palestine that they

would not call an end to the strike until Jewish immigration to Palestine was halted. Support for the strike quickly grew. Palestinian shopkeepers closed their stores. Schoolteachers and students refused to participate in classes. Palestinian laborers in the important citrus industry and in the oil refineries at Haifa refused to go to work. Lawyers and other professionals closed their offices. And most Palestinians refused to pay taxes to the British government. Qawuqji had only just returned to Baghdad after making a third visit to Palestine in early April 1936. He says in his memoirs that he was surprised by the news of the strike. This remark tells us something important about Qawuqji's connection with Palestine. As an Ottoman officer in World War I, he had fought in Palestine against the British advance. He had visited Palestine during the Syrian Revolt in order to procure money and support. He had also visited Palestine on the three occasions just mentioned, in 1934, 1935, and April 1936. But his friendships and his networks of contacts were mostly among men based in Damascus and Baghdad or in exile in Amman. These had been his comrades in the 1920 fight against the French and, more important, in the 1925–1927 Syrian Revolt. Qawuqji's tenuous connection to Palestinian affairs was through Palestinians from the north of Palestine, such as the writer and political activist 'Izzat Darwaza, who in the 1930s continued to view the political future of Palestine as part of Greater Syria. But Qawuqji remained remote from the complexities of local Palestinian politics, which had developed quite independently from Syrian politics after the separation of Palestine and Syria, the former a British mandate state and the latter a French mandate state.

During his visits to Palestine in 1934, 1935, and 1936, Qawuqji met with the Palestinian leader Hajj Amin al-Husayni, the mufti of Jerusalem. Qawuqji's relationship with the mufti, forged in the mid-1930s during the preparations for revolt in Palestine, came to dominate Qawuqji's career. Twelve years later, when Qawuqji served as field commander of the Arab Liberation Army in the 1948 War, the two men came to detest each other, and each worked to undermine the other's authority. The origins of this animosity lie somewhere in the mid-1930s, when Qawuqji turned toward Palestine as a venue for rebellion.

HAJJ AMIN

Hajj Amin al-Husayni and Qawuqji were of the same generation but came from very different backgrounds. The Husayni family were well-to-do landowners in central Palestine, where they held orchards and property mainly in Jerusalem and the surrounding area. Amin's father, Tahir al-Husayni, was the mufti of Jerusalem, and Amin was educated not through the Ottoman military system but through the more elite Ottoman civil system. He also studied at Al-Azhar in Cairo, at the time the most prestigious university in the Arab world. Upon the collapse of the Ottoman Empire, Husayni's and Qawuqji's worlds intersected in 1919 when both found themselves in Damascus as supporters of Faysal's claim to Syria. It is not clear from the memoirs of either man whether they met in Damascus during that time. By the time the French pushed Faysal out of Syria in the late summer of 1920, Husayni had returned to Jerusalem. Qawuqji, as we know, had stayed on in Syria and joined the French Army. But their careers overlapped from that point on through Arab nationalist circles and through their common struggle against colonialism. Qawuqji had traveled to Jerusalem in late 1927 to garner support for the rebellion in Syria. By that time Husayni had become prominent in Palestinian nationalist circles, and Qawuqji may well have met him during this visit. Husayni was an ardent Palestinian nationalist, but in the early days of the British mandate he was promoted and supported by the British government. The British appointed him mufti of Jerusalem in 1921 and also made him head of the newly established Supreme Muslim Council in Palestine. This early support from the British is something that Qawuqji brought up later as a way to undermine Husayni's nationalist credentials. Because of Husayni's appointment as mufti, many British colonial bureaucrats and Arab nationalists called him simply the Mufti. Qawuqji himself always referred to him this way, perhaps as a reminder of the British origins of Husayni's official status.

By the early 1930s the Mufti was a key player in Palestinian national-ist politics. Palestinian nationalists faced two enemies: the British and the Jewish settlers coming from Europe, whose numbers were rising in the 1930s. Persecution of Jews in Europe was beginning to change the demographic balance in Palestine. In 1931 the Jewish population of Palestine was around 180,000, and the Palestinian Arab population was around 850,000. By 1941 the Jewish population in Palestine had risen to around 475,000, and the Palestinian Arab population was just over 1 million. So in that ten-year period—between 1931 and 1941—the Jewish proportion of the total population of Palestine rose from around 17 percent to around 30 percent. Palestinian anger at Zionist claims to Palestine had broken out sporadically during the early mandate period, most notably in 1929, when there were widespread attacks on British soldiers and Jewish settlers. In addition to elite Palestinian leaders, such as the Mufti, more popular grassroots leaders were starting to mobilize Palestinians around the struggle against British colonialism and Zionism. The most famous of these was 'Izz al-Din al-Qassam, a popular imam from a prominent mosque in Haifa. His death at the hands of the British in 1935 is widely cited by historians as the spark that lit the Palestine Revolt. Qawuqji played no part in these developments in Palestine. In fact he does not even mention 'Izz al-Din al-Qassam in his memoirs, despite the fact that Qassam became a national icon for many Palestinians.

According to Qawuqji, the Mufti visited Baghdad in the early summer of 1936 to secure Qawuqji's help in expanding the rebellion that had broken out in Palestine in April 1936. Their meeting was arranged by 'Adil al-'Azma, a mutual friend who was living in Amman. 'Azma and his brother Nabih, with whom Qawuqji had worked in the Hijaz, came from a prominent Damascene family. Both were very active in nationalist circles in the 1930s. 'Adil had been educated through the civil system in Istanbul and become a lawyer in Syria in the early 1920s. Qawuqji remained friends with the two brothers throughout his life. 'Adil had been active during the days of the Syrian Revolt, particularly in recruiting money for the rebels. He met the Mufti in Jerusalem in 1927 because the Mufti headed one of the Palestinian committees that collected money on behalf of the revolt. Both 'Adil and Nabih al-'Azma worked closely with Qawuqji on plans to rekindle the revolt in Syria in the late fall of 1935 and winter of 1936. Nabih's activities attracted the attention of the British government, and he was imprisoned for several weeks in Sarafand Prison before being allowed to leave Palestine for Egypt.

Both 'Adil and Nabih al-'Azma maintained connections with Palestinians such as 'Izzat Darwaza and Akram Zu'aytir, who were founding members of the Istiqlal Party in Palestine. Palestinian members of the Istiqlal Party had been associated with Syrian politics from the days when Faysal briefly ruled Syria. They were sympathetic to the idea that Palestine was an integral part of Syria. Like Qawuqji, the 'Azma brothers—along with many other Syrian nationalists—believed that Palestine was part of Greater Syria and that the only real hope for Palestine was through the struggle for Syrian independence. For this reason 'Adil al-'Azma thought it was a good idea to promote Qawuqji as a rebel leader in Palestine because he wanted, as he put it, to "give the revolt [in Palestine] the color of a general Arab movement and extract it from being just a local phenomenon."

It was thus because of 'Adil al-'Azma that the Mufti approached Qawuqji in Baghdad in the early summer of 1936. Qawuqji and the Mufti had a long talk in the back of the Mufti's car, while the driver drove around the streets of Baghdad. During that conversation Qawuqji committed himself to recruiting a group of men in Baghdad and leading them to Palestine. He also agreed to help the newly formed Arab Higher Committee in Jerusalem organize and execute the rebellion against the British. Qawuqji is careful to say in his memoirs that at that moment he considered the Mufti the leader of the Palestine Revolt. He talks of the bond that formed between them during that conversation in Baghdad.

But by the middle of the 1930s the Mufti did not believe that Palestine was part of Greater Syria. From the moment Faysal's state in Syria failed, the Mufti, as well as many other Palestinians, had worked to build a Palestinian national movement that was independent of Syrian nationalism. One expression of this independence from Syria was the Mufti's project to renovate the Dome of the Rock and al-Aqsa Mosque in Jerusalem in the 1920s and 1930s. The photograph (figure 21) shows the Mufti (sixth from the right in the front row) standing with various Palestinian dignitaries outside the Dome of the Rock while renovations were under way.

FIGURE 21

These renovations were part of the Mufti's attempt to elevate Jerusalem's political importance to that of Damascus. The tension between the Mufti's vision of Palestine as independent of the surrounding Arab states and Qawuqji's vision of Palestine as part of Greater Syria—a Greater Syria that, if realized, would erase the borders imposed by the mandate system, including those drawn around Palestine—was to play a role in opening a rift between the two men in the years that followed their conversation in Baghdad.

After his meeting with the Mufti, Qawuqji spent several weeks in Baghdad organizing a company of around three hundred fighters to go to Palestine under his leadership. In addition to maintaining the strike, some Palestinians had shown that they were willing to fight the British to achieve their goals. Small rebel groups, drawn mainly from the countryside, attacked British soldiers and British installations in the summer of 1936. According to his memoirs, Qawuqji received the support of Yasin al-Hashimi, who had become prime minister of Iraq in March 1935. He also had the support of leading military figures in Baghdad, such as Subhi al-ʿUmari and Mahmud al-Hindi. Qawuqji's networks from the Syrian Revolt were still strong. Munir al-Rayyis, who was in Damascus, and ʿAdil al-ʿAzma, who was in Amman, helped recruit former comrades from the Syrian Revolt. A Druze from Mount Lebanon, Hamad Saʿab, who had fought with Qawuqji in the Ghouta, helped recruit men from the Druze areas. Muhammad al-Ashmar, hero of the Syrian Revolt in the Maydan area of Damascus, started organizing his own Damascene group, which was to join Qawuqji's men in Palestine. Qawuqji also recruited secretly from the Iraqi Military Academy in Baghdad. He stole documents about British military tactics, particularly manuals about the British aircraft and tanks that he knew he would come up against in Palestine. He also procured uniforms and other supplies from the academy and hid them in the orchards around Baghdad. He started socializing with British officers and frequenting cafés and clubs in Baghdad that were popular with the British community, pretending—as he claims in his memoirs—to be a bon vivant and a drinker. This was in order to blind senior British officers to his activities. In those days in the Baghdad of the early summer of 1936, Qawuqji befriended a British intelligence officer, who warned him that rumors were circulating in British circles about his plans to go to Palestine.

Qawuqji's casual mention of his connection with the British in Baghdad is interesting. A few years later, in Berlin, the Mufti circulated a document to the German Foreign Ministry accusing Qawuqji of being a British spy. Much of the evidence came from an Iraqi officer who was living in Baghdad at the time. The Iraqi officer told the Mufti that Qawuqji had close relations with the British and that he associated in particular with a British intelligence officer by the name of J. P. Domvile. The story of the Mufti's accusation belongs to the next chapter, but Qawuqji's open account in his memoirs of his deliberate courting of the British in 1936 may have been his way of countering this accusation.

JOURNEY TO PALESTINE

Qawuqji dispatched the first group of Iraqi fighters to Palestine under the leadership of two fellow officers in the Military Academy, Khalid al-Qanawati and Jasim al-Karadi. They set off with about one hundred men from the town of Karbala on August 6, 1936. Best known for its significance as a Shiite pilgrimage site, Karbala lies southwest of Baghdad in the fertile plains surrounding the Euphrates River. Karbala was about five hundred miles due east of Amman in Transjordan, where the rebels planned to meet with 'Adil al-'Azma in order to pick up arms and other supplies that he had been collecting for them. Once they left the river, the rebels would have to cross hundreds of miles of desert to reach Amman. It was the middle of the summer. Qawuqji had made contact with the Shammar tribe, so that he was able to help Qanawati and Karadi map out routes through the desert that would pass by water wells. Qawuqji stayed in Baghdad under British surveillance. By early August he had resigned his position as a cavalry instructor in the Military Academy. Yasin al-Hashimi was putting pressure on him to abandon his plans for Palestine out of fear of British detection. But Qawuqji was defiant. After just a few more days of preparation in Baghdad he slipped out of the city at night, with the help of one of his brothers, who had joined him in Baghdad. The two men traveled to a meeting point on the western outskirts of the town of Najaf, which lies just south of Karbala. Qawuqji took the small group of men who were waiting for him in Najaf and made the same journey across the desert that Qanawati and Karadi had made. He arrived in the hills of Palestine just west of the Jordan River in the last week of August. The photograph of Qawuqji outside his tent (figure 22) was probably taken during this journey.

While Qawuqji was in Baghdad mobilizing the Iraqi unit, Munir al-Rayyis had been organizing the Syrian and Lebanese units in Damascus. With the help of Sa'id al-'As, Qawuqji's old friend from the days of the Syrian Revolt, Rayyis succeeded in recruiting men from Homs and Hama. Hamad Sa'ab brought men from the Druze areas of Mount Leb-

FIGURE 22

anon, and Muhammad al-Ashmar gathered others from Damascus. The various groups met in the middle of August in the village of Sama al-Sarhan, near the Jordanian town of al-Mafraq, just south of the Syrian border. From there scouts traveled to various Bedouin camps, where they bought up old Ottoman rifles and other supplies. Then they traveled southwest, following the line of the British oil pipeline, until they were able to cross the Jordan River near the town of Baysan. In his memoirs Rayyis describes his concern about Muhammad al-Ashmar's attitude toward serving under Qawuqji's command. Ashmar was anxious about fighting alongside Iraqi soldiers whom he did not know, and he worried that many of the Iraqis whom Qawuqji had recruited were Shiites. Ashmar was a Sunni shaykh from a conservative area of Damascus. Rayyis, who was part of a younger generation of more secular intellectuals in Syria, reprimanded Ashmar for his prejudice. He reminded him that the Shiites were their brothers in 'Uruba (Arabism) and that without the Shiite Druze of the Hawran, the Syrian Revolt would never have happened.

By August 24 all the rebels had arrived in Palestine. That same day

Qawuqji met with the leaders of the various units on Jabal Jarish. There was much rejoicing, and rounds were fired into the air. Qawuqji then ensured that the various units spread themselves out in camps in the valleys around the town of Tubas. The Palestinian countryside around Tubas, Nablus, and Jenin was already in some turmoil. Local Palestinian rebel groups led by Farhan al-Saʿadi, ʿAbd al-Rahim al-Hajj Muhammad, and Fakhri ʿAbd al-Hadi, among others, had started sabotaging railway lines, telephone lines, and the oil pipeline as early as May 1936, and these rebel groups controlled many of the roads and villages in northern Palestine. In Jerusalem ʿAbd al-Qadir al-Husayni, the Mufti's nephew, had carried out attacks on British installations. But battles between the British army and the armed Iraqis, Syrians, and Lebanese, who came with military experience from the Syrian Revolt or from the Iraqi Army, marked a new phase of the anti-British revolt. Here is how the September issue of the monthly newsletter of the Second Battalion of the Lincolnshire Regiment describes Qawuqji's presence in the Tubas area a few weeks after his arrival:

> A new factor has been introduced by the arrival in Palestine of Fawzi Kawkagi [sic] with a band of about 200–300 armed bandits from Syria and Trans-Jordania; Fawzi, who is well-educated, and who has served in the French Army in Syria and in the Irak Army is now the recognized leader of an Arab "Army" consisting of the Syrian and Trans-Jordanian bandits above mentioned and local armed Palestinian Arabs who are reputed to have joined him in fairly large numbers.

Qawuqji considered the local Palestinian rebel groups fragmented and in need of coordination. Immediately after arriving in Palestine, he organized his own units around a central military command. He also invited Fahkri ʿAbd al-Hadi, one of the most prominent Palestinian rebel leaders, to come under his command. Qawuqji's aim was to consolidate what he regarded as a scattered resistance into a well-coordinated rebel army. He divided his forces into four units: an Iraqi company under the command of Jasim al-Karadi; a Syrian company under the command of Muhammad al-Ashmar; a Druze company under the command of Hamad Saʿab; and a Palestinian company under the command of ʿAbd al-Hadi. Munir al-Rayyis was assigned to head a unit that would deal with information, intelligence, and the issuing of *bayanat*, or communiqués. A formal photograph (figure 23), which was taken at the end of August 1936, shows Qawuqji surrounded by leaders of the units of his rebel army. The much taller Fakhri ʿAbd al-Hadi stands beside Qawuqji. Parts of their uniforms—the Sam Browne belts and jodhpur trousers— were British army style, taken from the Iraqi Military Academy in Baghdad. Every one of the leaders carried a relatively new British-made Enfield pistol. But the man standing in the left of the photograph is holding an old Ottoman Mauser rifle from World War I; this was the gun that most of the ordinary soldiers carried. They are all wearing the kaffiyeh, the Arab headdress, which was a marker of anticolonial rebellion across the Middle East.

Qawuqji's bayanat appeared in local Arabic newspapers, such as *Al-Difaʿ* and *Al-Jamiʿa al-Islamiyya*, and they were pasted up on the walls of villages and towns in the Jenin region. Probably written by Munir al-Rayyis himself, they were the official, public face of the foreign rebels

FIGURE 23

in Palestine. The first bayan was issued on August 28, 1936. Three pages long, it was a call to arms against the British, the Zionist project, and those Arabs who had cooperated with the British in implementing the Balfour Declaration. The bayan called on Palestinians and other Arabs to come out to fight until Jewish immigration was stopped and the British were expelled from the land. The bayan states that once this is achieved, the rebel soldiers will set up a temporary government of the Arab Revolution, which will construct a constitution and hold free and fair elections. The bayan uses the word "Palestine" many times, but it also states clearly that the "Arab nation is one nation" and that Palestine "is an indivisible part of that nation." Particularly striking is that this first bayan is signed in Qawuqji's name as "commander in chief of the Arab Revolt in Southern Syria."

In August 1936, it seemed natural for Qawuqji to call himself the commander in chief of the Arab Revolt in Southern Syria. In his mind the revolt had originally been planned as a double revolt in Syria and Palestine. He was also a Greater Syrianist, who had spent most of his adult life in Syria and Iraq. He was out of touch with the developments in Palestine, where Palestinian elites had consciously developed a particular Palestinian nationalism since the time of Faysal's expulsion from Syria. Or perhaps Qawuqji knew of these developments and was opposing them by explicitly laying claim to Palestine as part of Syria. The fact that many of the bayanat insist on the indivisibility of Palestine from Syria indicates that the latter explanation may be more likely. It is also possible that Qawuqji was deliberately allying himself with some Palestinian members of the Istiqlal Party, such as 'Izzat Darwaza, who still clung to the indivisibility of Palestine and Syria as late as 1935 and 1936. The popularity of Syrianism among rural communities in Palestine may also have played a role. Qawuqji was a populist throughout his career. Often shut out of elite politics, he drew political capital from his popularity with ordinary people. Calling himself commander in chief of the Arab Revolt in Southern Syria may well have been a tactic designed to mobilize support from the villages in northern Palestine.

Many Palestinians saw Qawuqji as a hero. Popular songs and poems were written about him. His arrival in Palestine in the summer of 1936 was a moment of hope: Arab fighters had come from afar to aid Palestine in its struggle against British rule. Fadwa Tuqan, who later became a famous Palestinian poet, was a young woman in the summer of 1936. She had traveled from the Palestinian town of Nablus to her brother's house in Amman that summer to be a companion for her brother's new wife. When she heard of Qawuqji's arrival in Palestine, she wrote one of her earliest poems:

> Hero of heroes, flower of all young men
> Come and tell us about your wondrous exploits

For some middle-class Palestinians, Qawuqji's involvement in the armed resistance against the British gave the revolt an air of respectability. Until his arrival in Palestine, Palestinian peasants had carried out most of the violent attacks against the British. Few elite Palestinians had taken part in violent operations against the British or the Jewish community, the most notable exception being ʿAbd al-Qadir al-Husayni. Qawuqji was known to have come from an urban background. He had served as an officer in the Ottoman Army and had come to Palestine to create an organized military campaign out of sporadic attacks and acts of sabotage by small groups of villagers. Some urban middle-class Palestinians, who had not fought during the revolt, were better able to show solidarity for it through asserting a connection to Qawuqji. They often did this by giving money to his army through their local revolt committee. Donating money to Qawuqji was seen as more respectable than donating money to local Palestinian peasant rebel leaders whom some urbanites regarded as riffraff.

By contrast, members of the Palestinian political elite loyal to the Mufti regarded Qawuqji's description of Palestine as Southern Syria as an act of aggression. When Qawuqji arrived in Palestine, he did not make any public gestures of support toward the Mufti, and he included only one Palestinian in his commanders' circle, Fakhri ʿAbd al-Hadi, who was associated with opposition to the Mufti's leadership. Nor did Qawuqji seek to coordinate his actions with the Mufti's nephew 'Abd al-Qadir al-Husayni, who was leading his own group of rebels a little farther to the south.

Some Palestinians traveled long distances to fight under Qawuqji's banner. One of them was Bahjat Abu Gharbiyya, who later became well-known as a fighter in 1948 and then as an important member of the Palestine Liberation Organization (PLO). In 1936 he was a young man teaching at the Rashidiyya School in Jerusalem. Like many of the other teachers and students there, Abu Gharbiyya participated in Palestinian nationalist circles. He had been arrested and briefly imprisoned by the British for his nationalist activities, and he had seen one of his closest friends killed by British soldiers. In the summer of 1936 he took part in the revolt in Jerusalem and helped attack British patrols. He fled north to evade capture by British forces, traveling to Tulkaram, where he had a close friend who worked as a pharmacist and was in contact with some of the Palestinian rebel leaders in the north. Through his friend, Abu Ghar-biyya managed to arrange a brief meeting with Qawuqji in the village of Bal'a, where Qawuqji gave him permission to join the revolt in the north. Abu Gharbiyya carried only a small pistol. He asked if there was any chance of his being given a rifle, but Qawuqji only laughed at this request and said that even if the whole valley below Bal'a was filled with rifles, it would still not be enough for all the young men who were coming to him and asking to join his forces. Qawuqji assigned Abu Gharbiyya to the Palestinian unit.

In the rebel camps Abu Gharbiyya was amazed by his first encounter with the Iraqi and Syrian soldiers. Some of the Iraqis had submachine guns, guns that he had never handled before. The way they wore their clothes and the food they ate were also strange to him. Many of them were much older than he was, with years of experience fighting in the rebellions in Syria and Iraq. Some were famous, such as Ashmar of the Maydan and of course Qawuqji himself from the rebellions in Hama and the Ghouta. These were names and places that Abu Gharbiyya had heard stories about as a teenager. To this young Palestinian, Qawuqji exuded confidence and manliness. In his memoirs Abu Gharbiyya tells us that after the revolt, he always kept a photograph of Qawuqji in his house with the words "The Commander, Fawzi al-Qawuqji, Symbol of Arab Unity." But he took it down after 1948, when it became clear that the Arab armies had failed to deliver on their promise to save Palestine from the Jewish forces.

A REBEL COURT

More complicated by far was the impact that Qawuqji's arrival had on those villagers he called upon to supply fighters, food, and water. For some of the young men of the villages it was an exciting opportunity to fight under Qawuqji's banner. Many families, however, felt the burden of having to give up precious food stocks and transport them to the supply dumps that Qawuqji set up in the hills. Some of the *mukhtar*s (village heads) had worked hard to maintain good relations with the British army, and it was difficult to show solidarity with Qawuqji while at the same time preventing British reprisal raids into their villages. This situation was made more precarious by the fact that a few days after his arrival Qawuqji set up a court that was assigned the tasks of maintaining order and security in the Jenin area and of trying collaborators. He chose as fellow judges 'Abd al-Hadi, Rayyis, Ashmar, and Khidr al-'Ali Mahfuz, a Syrian soldier from Hama who had traveled to Palestine with Qawuqji.

On September 2, 1936, a leaflet announcing the establishment of the court was issued:

> The Arab Higher Revolutionary Council in Southern Syria, "Palestine"
> announces that it has formed a court, the first task of which shall be
> ensuring justice and extending security and order in the country. It shall
> also rid the country of treachery, spying, and corruption.

In his memoir of fighting alongside Qawuqji in Palestine in 1936, Mahfuz describes the activities of the court in detail. According to Mahfuz, the court acted as more than just a vehicle of retribution against those accused of collaboration. It was also an attempt to impose the rule of law on those areas of Palestine where the rebels enjoyed control. The court resolved disputes between villagers and imposed punishments—in the form of fines or whippings—for ordinary petty crimes, such as theft. It thus served as a non-British alternative to which villagers could bring their grievances. The court also tried to guide the mukhtars by issuing rulings on how individual mukhtars behaved toward the British. In one case the villagers of Sayda accused their mukhtar of collaborating with the British. The court ruled in the mukhtar's favor, taking into account his reputation for having been loyal to the revolt up until that point. But the court made it clear that if similar accusations were leveled again, the punishment would be severe.

The fact remains that the court did execute some of the men tried for collaboration. Mahfuz narrates the case of Rushdi al-Barmaki from Tul-karam. Barmaki was brought before the court and accused of having been paid by the British to assassinate the commanders of the foreign rebels who had entered Palestine in August 1936, including Qawuqji. According to Mahfuz, the court deliberated for some time before it declared Barmaki guilty. Qawuqji then ordered his execution by firing squad. Abu Gharbiyya, the young Palestinian who had joined Qawuqji's forces, has a somewhat different account of the same incident. He says that Barmaki was brought before Qawuqji one evening, interrogated briefly, and executed the next morning. Abu Gharbiyya was so shocked by this event that he left Qawuqji's forces and returned to Jerusalem to reconnect with Palestinian rebels in Jerusalem who were engaged in attacks on British targets.

The specter of being accused of collaboration with the British created a climate of fear in the Palestinian community in 1936. Anyone could be accused on the barest of evidence or just because someone wanted to discredit a neighbor he happened to dislike. During the Syrian Revolt of 1925–1927 accusations of collaboration with the French had also dominated the final months of the revolt. And as we shall see, in the early 1940s the Mufti even accused Qawuqji himself of collaborating with the British. The atmosphere of suspicion around whose side people were really on was one of the most destructive legacies of the British and French colonial occupation of the Middle East.

BATTLE IN BAL'A

During the few weeks Qawuqji was in Palestine, his rebel army fought three major battles with British forces. These battles are known by the names of the three villages in which they were fought, Bal'a, Jab'a, and Bayt Amrayn. Bal'a was the first battle and the best known because the rebels shot down two British planes. (Even today you can see pieces of the sheet metal that the villagers took from the British planes and used to reinforce the roofs of their houses.) In 1936 Bal'a was a large village of about fifteen hundred people. Six miles northeast of Tulkaram, the village lay very close to the road that connected Tulkaram to Nablus. The villagers lived off the revenues from the olive oil that was produced from olive groves surrounding the village. Wheat and barley were also grown in the winter, and tomatoes, marrows, and green peppers in the summer. Villagers lived in simple domed buildings, where families slept on raised wooden platforms above areas where the livestock was kept.

Months before Qawuqji arrived in Palestine, many of Bal'a's residents had actively participated in the strikes that marked the beginning of the Palestine Revolt in 1936. Bal'a's school was closed because teachers and students had gone on strike in solidarity with the national strike. Villagers had formed a strike committee, which was tasked with liaising with other village strike committees in northern Palestine. The village also had rebel connections. One of the leading men in the village, Muhammad Ibrahim Shuhaybir, was a close friend of the famous Palestinian rebel leader 'Abd al-Rahim al-Hajj Muhammad. Shuhaybir's wife, Umm Rmaih, who was also the village midwife, was well-known by the children of the village for storing rebel weapons in her house. Bal'a had already witnessed confrontation with the British when one of the villagers was arrested and taken to prison in Tulkaram for being in possession of an old Turkish mortar shell. When the villagers heard of the arrest, they marched on the jail and were driven back by British soldiers. This was often the way violence broke out between Palestinians and the occupying forces. British tactics, including arbitrary searches and arrests for possession of weapons, fueled Palestinian anger. Most Palestinian villagers kept pistols or rifles in their homes; they had done so since World War I.

When news reached Bal'a that Qawuqji and his men had arrived in the area, the villagers began preparing to receive the foreign rebels. Each family was charged with storing coffee, tea, and tobacco to supply the men. When the rebels, led by Muhammad al-Ashmar, first rode into the village, the villagers prepared meals for them and found places for them to sleep. In some instances families gave up their only blankets so that a rebel could stay warm while sleeping in the orchards and groves that surrounded the village. Some of the young men rode with the rebels at night, acting as guides through the rocky terrain.

Qawuqji chose the Tulkaram to Nablus road that ran close to Bal'a as the site of his first major ambush of British troops. He placed small ambush units on both sides of the main road and also on a smaller dirt track that ran between Bal'a and the neighboring village of Silat al-Zahr. He planned to draw the British into an engagement with rebel forces. Before Qawuqji's arrival, rebel attacks in Palestine had been single strikes, done quickly and at night. What Qawuqji brought to the revolt was his expertise in longer-term strategies that he had learned as an officer in the Ottoman Army. In his memoirs Qawuqji describes how the ambush began on the morning of September 3, 1936:

> The dust of the convoy of cars coming from Tulkaram rose up at 8:15 a.m. The convoy was moving slowly, our soldiers waiting to fire and extremely nervous. At 8:40, the head of the convoy reached the appointed place, whereupon the ambush unit started its operation. The unit fired on the convoy from the north and from the south, and it was only a matter of seconds before machine guns and light arms exploded from the British cars and tanks. The soldiers started coming out, crawling under cover of the fire toward the ambush, which was continuing to fire at them. After that the ambush unit left its position and withdrew along

the prearranged line, and the British soldiers followed them, splitting up into two groups, one of them following the southern company and one of them following the northern company toward our lines, whereupon our units fired on them from close quarters.

A somewhat terser description of the same opening moments of the ambush also appeared in the September issue of the monthly newsletter of the Second Battalion of the Lincolnshire Regiment: "'C' Company (Striking Force) came under heavy and accurate fire in one place, from Arabs in prepared sangars at about 150 yards range; this resulted in the following casualties being sustained:—Killed, Corporal J. Wilkes, Dangerously Wounded, Capt J. V. Faviell, Comdg. 'C' Coy. (Shot through pelvis). Pte. J. Dinsdale (shattered wrist), Pte. R. Cudworth (hip)."

Once the British realized that the ambush was part of a coordinated attack and that there were additional rebel forces beyond those units that had been involved in the initial ambush, they called in reinforcements from the British military base in Nablus. These reinforcements included tanks, artillery—3.7-inch howitzers and naval pom-poms—and RAF planes equipped with bombs and machine guns. Qawuqji's attempts to engage the British army served only to provoke the full force of British military might, which far outweighed the capabilities of the rebels, who were fighting with old Ottoman Mauser rifles and some machine guns. Despite this, the rebels managed to shoot down two British aircraft. Qawuqji had organized a unit of men armed with machine guns and had placed them on a small hill to fire at aircraft. One plane crashed in flames on the Tulkaram road. The crash was accompanied by shouts of triumph from the rebel units scattered across the hills. Another plane came down in flames near where the Homs company and the Druze company were fighting. The rebels took the identity documents and the notebooks from the corpse of the British pilot, in addition to the airplane's Bren gun.

Rebels fought the British throughout the day. They were helped by some of the women from Bal'a, who brought them water and food in the field. But the intensity of the British artillery fire and the arrival of new

British troops from Nablus led Qawuqji to give the order to withdraw as dusk was falling. Munir al-Rayyis and his unit reached an orchard near the village, where he thought his men would be safe. But when Qawuqji arrived, they agreed that they should withdraw to the next valley because they could hear British firing in the village itself. Some unit commanders did not heed the order to withdraw. In his memoirs Rayyis describes hearing Mahmud Abu Yahya cursing when the withdrawal order reached him and urging the men from Hama and Homs to follow him into British lines. Abu Yahya was one of the nine rebels killed by British forces that day.

The day after the battle of Bal'a, Qawuqji issued a bayan describing the events of the battle and declaring a victory over the British. The text of the bayan is careful to name all the different units for their particular roles:

> The line of fighting stretched in the beginning for four kilometers and then quickly extended to the lines of the Palestinian units, which specialized in defending against the arrival of enemy reinforcements to the field of battle. They undertook this duty very well, and clashes with the enemy continued until dusk fell. The Iraqi units excelled in yesterday's battle in the soundness of their aim and the number of hits on their targets and in their organization. The Druze units and the units from Homs, Hama, and Damascus also excelled in their defense against the enemy, which lost three aircraft at the beginning of battle.

The bayan's mention of the role of the Palestinian fighters as defenders against the arrival of enemy reinforcements belies a controversy that emerged in the days after the battle. Some Syrian rebels claimed that the Palestinians had withdrawn from the field once the battle started to get intense. Khidr al-'Ali Mahfuz gives a number of reasons for this withdrawal. He cites the fact that the Palestinians were not used to fighting and were terrified of the British artillery and the bombardments from RAF planes. He claims that the Palestinians did not trust Qawuqji and the Syrian and Iraqi officers. The Palestinians mistakenly suspected that they were being led into a trap and that Qawuqji was working with Abu

Hunayk, the Arabic nickname for John Bagot Glubb, or Glubb Pasha, the British army officer responsible for running the army in Transjordan. Rayyis in his memoirs confirms this story about the Palestinians' concern that Qawuqji was working with Glubb Pasha to entrap the Palestinian rebel groups.

Whatever the truth may be, postbattle recriminations flew about between the Palestinian rebels and the Iraqis, Syrians, and Lebanese. Some historians of the revolt blame Qawuqji for creating a shadow of bad feeling that extended beyond the battle. In particular, the historian Mustafa Kabha accuses Qawuqji of generating the controversy by drawing attention to the Palestinian withdrawal. But this is not borne out by the bayan cited above. In it, Qawuqji is careful to include the Palestinians and point to their role as defenders against the British reinforcements. And in his memoirs, compiled much later, Qawuqji addresses the issue of the Palestinian participation in the battle head-on: "Because the Palestinians were not used to this kind of battle they had left the field in the first hour. This departure was not as a result of cowardice but because they were not experienced. The bravery, valor, and sacrifices they showed later on in battles, and that record their glory in this great national struggle, are the biggest evidence and the clearest proof of what I say."

Some Palestinian rebels, interviewed years later by the historian Sonia Nimr, disputed Qawuqji's claim that they had withdrawn from the battle because they were not used to facing aircraft and artillery. Bashir Ibrahim was one of the rebels Nimr interviewed. According to his account, the Palestinians did not trust Qawuqji. Bal'a was the first battle in which the Palestinians joined Qawuqji and his men. The Palestinians fell back after only a short while in order to watch the fighting and be sure of the genuineness of Qawuqji's claims to be on their side. They were convinced only when they saw the ferocity of the fighting and the deaths of several foreign rebels. In subsequent battles led by Qawuqji in 1936, Palestinians fought in large numbers and, in the words of Bashir Ibrahim, "proved to him that they were not afraid of planes."

A number of villagers from Bal'a joined the fighting and were killed.

The British army subjected the village to collective punishment for its participation. The day after the battle, the British army moved into the village. They arrested the better-educated villagers, in particular three teachers, who were taken to the nearby prison of Sarafand. After gathering all the women and children in the mosque and the men on the outskirts of the village, the army entered all the houses in the village, looting and destroying everything inside. As one villager described it, "They broke all the ceramic food containers and spilled out onto the dirt floor the meager stores of flour, grain, bulgur, lentils, and onions, emptying over it the stored animal feed, and pouring over the mix the family's olive oil. They broke down home doors, mixed sugar with oil, salt with sugar, sugar with lentils, poured oil on the mattresses and the quilts, stole every valuable thing they could find. I can never forget the scene that I saw with my eyes. I saw a British soldier catch two chickens and asphyxiate them by pressing on the chickens' necks with his army boot, before stuffing them into his bag."

FIGURE 24

The British also brought in dynamite and completely demolished six houses belonging to Ibrahim Hajj Khadir, Hassan al-Wawi, Hajj 'Abd Wannan, Tawfik al-Wannan, 'Abd al-Fattah Abu Ma'in, and the Abu Yunus family. This type of house demolition was normal practice for the British army during the Palestine Revolt. The most famous incident of British demolition of houses was in the Palestinian port city of Jaffa (figure 24).

The British military archives are full of accounts of the destruction of Palestinian villages, mass arrests, and executions. British actions were particularly brutal in 1937 and 1938, long after Qawuqji and his men had left Palestine but while the revolt was still active.

TRUCE

In the weeks that followed Bal'a, Qawuqji and his men went on to fight more battles against the British, in and around the villages of Jab'a and Bayt Amrayn. But by late September and early October the Arab Higher Committee, under the Mufti's leadership, had helped broker a truce between Palestinian rebels and the British and tried to bring an end to the nationwide strike. Pressure to call off the strike was coming from Palestinian citrus farmers, who needed to begin their harvest at the end of September. Pro-British Arab leaders, such as Nuri al-Sa'id in Iraq (who by this time was back in the Iraqi government as foreign minister) and Ibn Sa'ud in Saudi Arabia, also worked with the Arab Higher Committee in Palestine and with the British to conclude a truce. Most of the Palestinian rebel groups had dispersed by the middle of October, and the Arab Higher Committee began to pressure Qawuqji to leave Palestine. According to Rayyis, Qawuqji and his men tentatively agreed to the truce because they understood it to be temporary. They assumed that it had been agreed to only in order to enable the Arab Higher Committee to negotiate concessions from the British. The British, however, argued that they could not negotiate a truce while there were still armed foreign rebels in Palestine. The British backed up their stance by moving some army units into the hills around Bal'a and surrounding a large contingent of Qawuqji's forces.

British sources portray Qawuqji's rebel army as a ragtag group of bandits, who were little more than a nuisance to both the British and the Palestinian leadership. According to Qawuqji, his forces posed a significant enough challenge to the British army in Palestine that the British had been forced to the negotiating table. Also, according to Qawuqji, by conceding to the truce, he was only agreeing to put down arms while the negotiations were under way, but he was ready to take them up again should the British not agree to withdraw from Palestine and to allow the establishment of an independent Arab state there. This all was happening in mid-October 1936, just weeks after Syrian negotiators in Paris had extracted just such a promise from the French about the future of Syria. Qawuqji believed that the British might be willing to offer the same kind of deal on Palestine because of the pressure that his forces and the Palestinian rebel forces had put on the British army. The bayan that he issued on October 20, 1936, reflects this confidence. It takes the form of a series of instructions to the people of Palestine about how they should conduct themselves while the negotiations were ongoing. The bayan also details the procedures for disarming the rebels—again, only while the negotiations were ongoing—in such a way that the rebels could immediately take up arms again if the British did not deliver on the demand for independence. Here is the full text of the bayan:

1. There should be no retaliations against the Jews. They attack not out of bravery or chivalry—two traits that are missing from their nature—but with the intention of causing intrigue and bad relations between the Army of the Revolution and the British army in order to bring back disputes and conflict and to unsettle the negotiations and make tricks that are not in the interests of the country. I appeal to the Arabs to have patience and to wait for what the British authorities will give by way of rights for the Arabs. And if the British are remiss then, the Jews will see how the defense can be, how revenge can be, and they will see our strength, which they are

not ignorant of. I ask the Arabs to cut off all contact with the Jews and any kind of dealings with them, just as I ask the Arabs to cut off contact with any Arabs who have dealings with the Jews, whether it be an individual or a village. This is even more important than cutting off [contact with] the Jews themselves, so that these dissenters are not able to find among the people anyone who will greet them.

2. The people of the villages in all the regions should persist in solving their small disputes among themselves, as they have done up to now. As for the bigger disputes, they should bring these to the revolutionary court, which will take care of everyday issues that are put before it and which will not leave an issue until there is a solution based on clear justice.

3. The local committees in the villages and their leaders will become responsible for the safety of the weapons of the mujahideen present in their villages and will look after them all so that they are ready for use when needed. The [army] leadership is keeping an inventory of the weapons belonging to the mujahideen in all regions for verification and checking when necessary. In making this request on this occasion, I would appeal to you not to forget the dead and the wounded and those whose homes were blown up because of their sympathy. All the support and the volunteering for their families help them. We must always remember our dead, for they are the ones who have given al-Umma (the nation) victory, and we must mark October 27 every year as the day of the fallen and of the victory. For what glorifies our dead is the bravery and the welcome of the coming caravans of those who are ready to die in the name of defending the holy nation when schemes and dangers have it in its grip.

The tone of this bayan is both logistical and triumphalist. It is full of expectation that the negotiations will bring serious results. It is also striking that the British army appears as the only formidable enemy. The Jewish communities are portrayed as less important, a factor that can be easily dealt with in the event of the failure of negotiations and resumption of fighting. At this point, on October 20, there is no mention of the withdrawal of the rebel forces from Palestine. But just over a week later the newspaper *Al-Ayyam* published Qawuqji's formal announcement of withdrawal, an announcement sent to the newspaper even earlier, on October 23. Alarmed by the possibility that the truce that it had brokered could flounder if fighting broke out between Qawuqji's forces and the British, the Arab Higher Committee persuaded the British to allow Qawuqji and his men to leave Palestine unimpeded. The rebels crossed into Transjordan on October 28.

Qawuqji had miscalculated British aims and underestimated the British commitment to the Jewish presence in Palestine. By 1936, out of a total population of 1.3 million, approximately 30 percent were Jewish. At this stage the British had no intention of handing over Palestine to the Arabs. For the leadership of the Yishuv, establishing something more than simply a "national home" for the Jews in Palestine was becoming urgent. The year 1935 had seen increasing persecution of Jews in Germany with the passing of the Reich Citizenship Law, which stripped German Jews of their citizenship. In 1936 all German Jews were banned from being employed in any profession. The British dealt with growing tensions in Palestine not by negotiating a treaty but by sending a royal commission to investigate the causes of the revolt. The commission, under the leadership of Lord Peel, arrived in November 1936. After taking testimony from prominent figures in both the Jewish and the Palestinian communities, the commission drafted a four-hundred-page report, which laid out the reasons for the revolt and recommended a solution to what the British were starting to call the Palestine Problem. The Peel Commission's solution was to divide Palestine into two states, one Jewish and one Arab. Outraged by the suggestion that they should give up half their land to European settlers, Palestinians discarded the truce, and the revolt broke out again in September 1937, when Palestinian rebels assassinated the British acting district commissioner for the Galilee, Lewis Andrews. This second phase of the revolt lasted until 1939.

In later years Qawuqji blamed the Mufti for forcing him to withdraw from Palestine in late October 1936. In Qawuqji's private archive there is a letter to him from his cousin 'Adil al-Hamadi, dated October 14, 1936. The letter is Hamadi's response to Qawuqji's attempts to sound out the Mufti on whether he supported Qawuqji's staying in Palestine. Hamadi conveyed the Mufti's message that Qawuqji should withdraw, for the sake of the negotiated truce. Hamadi said of the Mufti: "It appeared to me, on the basis of the firm way he spoke, that from the bottom of his heart he wants you to leave the land." Years later, when he was going through his own archive, Qawuqji wrote a note at the top of the letter: "Here again the Mufti asks us to withdraw, but he does not dare to announce it publicly."

In another letter to Qawuqji written by 'Adil al-'Azma, 'Azma uses careful language to convey the information that the Palestinians who are asking for Qawuqji to leave Palestine are in fact voicing the Mufti's own wishes. In 'Azma's view, it would be a mistake for Qawuqji to leave Palestine:

> The enemies should believe and be convinced that the rebels have not abandoned their weapons but rather suspended the attack in anticipation of the results that will crown your victory. But if you withdraw from Palestine, even withdrawing just to Transjordan, such a belief by the enemies will be undermined and will give them proof that the revolution has come to an end and that there is nothing to be afraid of . . . He tries, through his followers, to keep you away from Palestine and to make you leave it, not just to Transjordan but to Iraq, to cage you there so that you are unable to return to Palestine. I believe that those who told you of the necessity of withdrawing are these followers of his. And the claim that your presence in Palestine interrupts the course of the negotiations with the British is a red herring.

Again, Qawuqji scribbled some notes at the top of the letter, making it clear that the "he" to whom 'Azma refers is the Mufti: "The persons who insisted that I withdraw are the Mufti's people, and they spoke on his behalf. There is no doubt that the Mufti wanted us to leave, pressured as he was by the British."

Qawuqji always believed that it had been a mistake to leave Palestine in 1936. He was convinced that if he had stayed, the British would have been under sufficient pressure to concede to Palestinian rebel demands. This perception colored his view of subsequent cease-fires during wartime, particularly in 1948. For example, he was against the Arab agreement to sign on to what became known as the 1948 War's first truce, which was put into place on June 11, 1948. Most historians of 1948 believe that by agreeing to the first truce, the Arab armies allowed the Jewish forces, who were under serious pressure in early June 1948, to regroup and rearm. But in 1936 Qawuqji overestimated the role that this group of two to three hundred men was capable of playing in forcing the British government to make serious concessions. By the fall of 1936 the British army had twenty thousand troops in Palestine. Qawuqji was little more than a thorn in the flank of British military power.

RETURN TO BAGHDAD

Many of those who came to Palestine under Qawuqji's leadership in August 1936 had already made their way home by late October 1936. Accompanied by only about a hundred men, Qawuqji left Palestine the same way that he had entered, by crossing the Jordan River near Baysan. The Palestinian rebel leaders Fakhri 'Abd al-Hadi and 'Arif 'Abd al-Raziq traveled with him. The waters of the river were unusually high for that time of year, and the men rested on the eastern bank to make tea and dry their clothes. From there they took refuge with the tribes that were grazing their flocks just east of the river.

Amir 'Abdullah was out of the country when Qawuqji's forces entered Transjordan. The amir's eldest son, Talal, visited Qawuqji in the tribal areas as a way of showing support for him. But when 'Abdullah returned, he immediately set about getting Qawuqji out of Transjordan as quickly as possible. 'Abdullah worked very closely with the British, and as Qawuqji says in his memoirs, the British wanted him out of Jordan so badly that they were almost willing to escort him to Iraq. Qawuqji insisted that a unit of the Transjordanian army travel with him to the Iraqi border so that British forces would not attack him. 'Abdullah agreed. The men traveled east along the route of the pipeline and crossed into Iraq close to the Rutba Fort, where Qawuqji was to fight the British again in the summer of 1941. By the time they crossed the border, Qawuqji was traveling only with the Iraqi unit, along with 'Abd al-Hadi and Hamad Sa'ab. The Syrian units had separated from the group earlier and returned to Homs, Hama, and Damascus.

Qawuqji's small group stayed the night in the town of Ramadi on the Euphrates before moving on eastward to Baghdad. There Qawuqji was treated as a returning hero. Delegations came to see him in his house in the Karada district, and journalists wrote in the Iraqi press articles about his heroism in Palestine. In November 1936 he published a manifesto in the Damascus newspaper *Alif Ba'*. The manifesto was a direct appeal to the British people to support the Palestinians in their struggle against the Zionists. This is how Qawuqji concludes his appeal, in the archly exotic English translation contained in a contemporaneous U.K. Foreign Office report:

> Oh Britishers! I am enemy No. 1 of great despair to those who serve the Zionists, and friend No. 1 of great faithfulness to any just and honourable Englishman, who values Great Britain and her noble ally the Arab People. I beg you to shout in the faces of some of your politicians to give justice to the Palestinian Arabs and grant them their demands. You will find, then, on the part of this Arab people of glorious history, nothing but friendship, devotion and assistance, which you will never find amongst the Zionists. I send my faithful *salaams* to every noble Britisher who is on the side of right and justice and helps the heroic Arabs of Palestine.

He also continued to maintain his links with Palestinians, traveling to Basra in December 1936 to meet a touring delegation, led by 'Izzat

Darwaza of the Palestinian Arab Higher Committee. Darwaza's memoirs contain a photograph of Qawuqji standing on the banks of the Shatt al-'Arab in Basra with Darwaza and two other leading Palestinians, Mu'in al-Madi and 'Awni 'Abd al-Hadi. The delegation was touring Iraq and Saudi Arabia to garner support for the Palestinian position in the ongoing negotiations with the British over the future of Palestine.

4

■

BAGHDAD TO BERLIN

Exile in Kirkuk—Plotting against Amir ʿAbdullah—Fritz
Grobba—The Rutba Fort—Back to the Euphrates—Attacked
from the air—Berlin—Captured by the Russians

The timing of Qawuqji's return to Baghdad was unlucky. The Iraqi
prime minister, Yasin al-Hashimi, had been ousted from power just a
few days before Qawuqji's arrival. He was replaced by Hikmat Sulayman,
as part of a coup engineered by the army chief of staff Bakr al-Sidqi.
This coup marked the beginning of the end of constitutional order in Iraq.
Qawuqji's fate for the next five years was closely tied to the political
upheaval that followed the Bakr al-Sidqi coup.

In the wake of the coup, prominent figures associated with the previous regime no longer stood at the center of power. These included not
only the ex–prime minister Hashimi but also his brother Taha al-Hashimi,
who had been minister of defense. Taha al-Hashimi was in Turkey when
the coup took place. Yasin al-Hashimi fled to Damascus, where he died
two months after the coup. The ascendance of Bakr al-Sidqi resulted
from a struggle for power between top Iraqi military officers. But there
were also ideological differences at play, both in the Iraqi Army and in
civilian political circles. These differences centered on the question of

which direction Iraq should take as far as its relationship with the rest of the Arab world was concerned. The Hashimi brothers represented the staunchly pan-Arab camp, which believed that Iraq was not only an integral part of the Arab world but that Iraq should be the leader in pan-Arab politics. Sidqi and Sulayman, on the other hand, believed that Iraqi identity should be built first and foremost around the idea of its ethnic and religious diversity. Both Sidqi (a Kurd) and Sulayman (a Turkoman) came from Iraqi minority groups. Their Iraqi nationalism was more locally focused, and they aimed to minimize Iraqi involvement in Pan-Arabism.

By 1936 the struggle for Palestine had emerged as a central tenet of Pan-Arabism. The Hashimi brothers had supported Qawuqji's campaign in Palestine as part of their pan-Arab outlook, and Qawuqji had relied on their patronage. For this reason, the new regime led by Sidqi and Sulayman did not look with favor on Qawuqji. The fact that he was feted in Baghdad upon his return from Palestine and that journalists took intense interest in him made him even less popular with the new government. There is also evidence in the British archives that London was pressuring the Iraqi government to bring Qawuqji under control. A series of telegrams sent back and forth between the Foreign Office and Archibald Clark Kerr, the British ambassador in Iraq, shows that Clark Kerr met regularly with Hikmat Sulayman to request that the Iraqi government prevent Qawuqji from talking to the press about his imminent return to the fight in Palestine. On January 23, 1937, Qawuqji was forced into exile in Kirkuk. On January 25, Clark Kerr sent a telegram to London informing the Foreign Office of Qawuqji's exile. He reported that Kirkuk was a good choice because there "the people are Turks and Kurds and unlikely to join in any mischief with him."

EXILE IN KIRKUK

In the 1930s Kirkuk was indeed a mainly Kurdish and Turcoman town. It lay sixty miles south of Mosul and about two hundred miles north of Baghdad. It was considered physically and politically remote from

Baghdad, which was the hub of Iraqi politics. Kirkuk was most famous for its oil, which had been discovered there in 1927. In 1935 the British-owned Iraq Petroleum Company started pumping oil through the pipeline (figure 25) that it had built between Kirkuk and the city of Haifa in Palestine, on the Mediterranean, some six hundred miles to the southwest.

Although Qawuqji lived quietly in Kirkuk, he still drew the attention of journalists and other visitors because of his growing fame as the hero of the Palestine Revolt. Journalists became particularly concerned with Palestine in late 1936, after the British announced that they were dispatching a royal commission, under the leadership of Lord Peel, to look into the causes of the Palestine Revolt and to recommend a solution to the growing conflict between the Palestinians and the Jews. Shortly after Qawuqji's arrival in Kirkuk he received a visit from Daniel Oliver, a British Quaker mediator and also the principal of the Friends' School in Beirut. Oliver was traveling all over the Middle East in the wake of the Palestine Revolt, gathering opinions on the events in Palestine. In early

FIGURE 25

1937 Oliver conducted interviews with leading Iraqi politicians and foreign ambassadors in Baghdad. He sent reports on those interviews to the British Colonial Office. Here is his account of his meeting with Qawuqji in Kirkuk:

> One of the principal visits to Baghdad was to see Fawzi Bey Kawakji, the brilliant leader of the Revolution in Palestine. He is called by the [British] Palestine Government, "Enemy no. 1." That is surely an American title borrowed from Chicago. He had been indiscreet in his talk and the Government of Iraq has, for the present, banished him to Kirkuk about 200 miles north of Baghdad. I asked the Foreign Minister if I might see Fawzi Bey. "Oh yes," he said, "you are free to see him and anyone else." So I started by train at nine o'clock at night and reached Kirkuk early in the morning. One of our old boys, now the City Engineer at Kirkuk, met me at the train station, which is about three miles from the town (of 40,000 inhabitants) . . .
> After breakfast I was taken across the courtyard, and there face to face I saw "Enemy no. 1." Fawzi Bey is a man of about forty-three, good-looking, blond in color with blue eyes and fair skin, inclined to be a little stout. His manner is very cordial, and I almost immediately sized him up as being good hearted, a man of action and decision, accustomed to command and be obeyed. He is a leader undoubtedly . . . and I said "I wanted to see you and spend the night with you in the hills of Palestine, but your outposts made it difficult for me to get to you. They told me your men would shoot me." "No," he said "no follower of mine would ever shoot Mr. Oliver." "Well" I said, "I tried to catch up with you in Transjordan but you moved so quickly. Then I tried to meet you in Baghdad and when I got there I find you in Kirkuk. Now at last I stand face to face with Fawzi Bey."

The two men discussed many issues. Qawuqji made it clear to Oliver that if the result of the British royal commission to Palestine was what Qawuqji called a poor compromise, the struggle in Palestine would begin all over again, and the Arabs would fight "until the end" for their rights.

Oliver urged Qawuqji to follow the Quaker way and bring about a settlement through peaceful means. He concluded his report by saying that Qawuqji had a "heart of pure gold" and that he was brave and commanded a large following. He said that it was foolish to belittle Qawuqji, as some of the British papers had done.

Iraqi journalists also turned their attention toward Qawuqji in this period. Qawuqji kept the clippings of some of the articles written about him in 1937 in his private archive. In early 1937 the pro-German newspaper *Al-'Alam al-'Arabi* published a long critique of the new Sulayman government in Baghdad. The article mocked the government for two things: being too timid to bring Yasin al-Hashimi's body from Damascus for burial in Baghdad and exiling Fawzi al-Qawuqji to Kirkuk. The article carried a photograph of Qawuqji from his days as an officer in the Ottoman Army. It called on him not to despair in his exile, telling him that the people regarded him as a hero and fighter. Another newspaper clipping, kept carefully by Qawuqji, told of his exploits up until that point. The article vividly described his heroic actions at Hama and the Ghouta, in Nejd, and in Palestine just the year before. The article's author compared him with the famous Turkish leader Ataturk, for both his statuesque physique and his leadership skills. The attention that Qawuqji received from the Iraqi press while he was in Kirkuk was a direct result of the time he had spent fighting in Palestine. Up until 1936 Qawuqji's name had been one of many associated with the 1925–1927 Syrian Revolt. But his actions in Palestine in 1936, especially his battles with the British army, had made him stand out from the crowd. His popularity also grew as Palestine emerged as the central symbol of Pan-Arabism in the wake of the first phase of the Palestine Revolt at the end of 1936. Qawuqji was thus caught up in the ideological struggles taking place in the Iraqi military in the mid-1930s. As a Sunni and a pan-Arabist he was associated with the mainly Sunni Arab Iraqi officers who wanted Iraq to take the lead in the pan-Arab project of building a single unified state encompassing all Arabs. At the same time, Qawuqji was himself not an Iraqi, so he remained outside the inner circle of Sunni Iraqi army officers who were intent on trying to reverse the Bakr al-Sidqi coup.

Qawuqji received a different kind of attention in the Western press as a result of his actions in Palestine. The year 1937 saw several articles about him in British and American newspapers. The focus on him was provoked by rumors that he was going to return to Palestine to fight again against the British. Perhaps the most interesting of these were the sensationalist articles published in small American and Canadian newspapers—*The Salt Lake Tribune, Portsmouth Daily Times* (Ohio), *The Morning Herald* (Hagerstown, Md.), *The Winnipeg Tribune*—in which he was described as a swashbuckling Arab adventurer complete with robe and turban. The headlines of these articles read: "British Plan to Split Holy Land Inspired by the Terroristic Acts of Palestine's Public Enemy No. 1" and "Fawzi Bey Kaukji Called Public Enemy No. 1 Awaits Ripe Hour" and "New Saladin Leads 'Holy War' for the Holy Land." All the articles have the same photograph of him as a young officer in the Ottoman Army (although unlike Arab readers, most American readers would not have recognized this uniform). These feature articles also contained photographs of Arab soldiers marching in the desert and exotic veiled girls. The articles evoke a world that is closer to Rudolf Valentino and the Hollywood movies of the 1930s than to the realities of the Middle East (figure 26).

A comparison of the English and Arabic articles about Qawuqji shows the distance of the American and Canadian journalists from what was happening on the ground in the Middle East. None of these English articles are in Qawuqji's private archive. He probably never knew that for a brief moment he was famous in Salt Lake City and Winnipeg.

Qawuqji was best known in Palestine itself. At the annual festival of Nabi Musa in 1937 farmers held up banners with Qawuqji's image, much to the annoyance of the Mufti, who was used to being the most prominent figure in the festival. Since the 1920s the Nabi Musa festival had been an important Palestinian nationalist event. Postcards of Qawuqji were also sold in the markets in Palestine in 1937. After the negotiations between the British and the Palestinian leadership collapsed following the decision of the Peel Commission to divide Palestine into an Arab and a Jewish state, many Palestinians expected him to return to Palestine to fight.

FIGURE 26

In keeping with his new status as an anticolonial hero, it was also in Kirkuk that Qawuqji began to compile a memoir of his life up until that moment. These are the same memoirs that provide such an important source for this book. Here is how he relates his decision to start recording his memories:

> Many of my friends, upon the annual celebration of the Syrian Revolt, requested that I publish my memoirs. Their urging increased as

events piled up, and I was always refusing them because of the belief that our work was not yet done and that publishing memoirs about past revolutions would reveal weaknesses and secrets that the enemy would spend effort and money to know about. Thus I forced myself to keep them to myself as a lantern for my approaching activities. Except that, after my return from the Palestine Revolt, my brothers implored me to publish these memoirs. At the same time the offices of Arab and Western newspapers and magazines began to request their publication. When they put the pressure on a second time, I started to review the events that I had been engaged in during the Great War and the events of the Syrian Revolt and the last Palestinian Revolt of 1936. I found myself in front of realities, and recording them would require volumes. And the idea came to me to record the most important events that had had the greatest influence on our contemporary history. And so I decided at that time to edit these memoirs with the title *My Adventures*. I informed one of my friends that I had decided this, and he promised that he himself would undertake to transcribe what I would dictate to him. We made an appointment for four o'clock in the afternoon on Saturday, January 23, 1937, in my house in Karada, Baghdad. But at exactly the time that had been set to record these adventures, I found myself in a car between two police officers, being escorted by two cars equipped with machine guns, taking me quickly down the road toward Kirkuk—to exile—where I arrived in a snowstorm the like of which Kirkuk had not seen for decades. I arrived in Kirkuk on January 24, 1937. My secretary, Hamid Sulayman, had arrived before me, carrying my belongings, just as my mujahid friend Baha al-Din Taba'a joined me the following day in order to be at my side. The tranquillity and quietness to which I had become a prisoner in my room, and which I had not been used to in my life, began to grate on my nerves and fill me with boredom. How could I overcome this boredom and inactivity? Through *My Adventures*.

PLOTTING AGAINST AMIR 'ABDULLAH

The Peel Commission's recommendation to partition Palestine into a Jewish and an Arab state sent shock waves throughout the Arab world. The gravity and apparent irrevocability of this decision were not lost on Qawuqji and his friends. It brought home the fact that time was running out for Palestine. In the late summer and early fall of 1937 Qawuqji, still in Kirkuk, received several letters from Munir al-Rayyis, who was at that time based in Damascus and working for the daily newspaper *Al-Qabas*. By 1937 he and Qawuqji were old friends. Rayyis had fought alongside Qawuqji in 1925–1927 during the Great Syrian Revolt and then in Palestine in 1936. Rayyis was later to fight alongside Qawuqji in Iraq in 1941, during the Rashid 'Ali al-Kaylani coup against the pro-British government there. In a letter that he wrote to Qawuqji in the summer of 1937, Rayyis described what was going on in Syria that summer and informed his old friend that Qawuqji had been appointed honorary president of the Arab Club.

The Arab Club, on Fu'ad Street in Damascus, was one of several pan-Arabist organizations operating in Damascus in the late 1930s as a response to what was perceived as the National Bloc's weakness toward the French. The club's letterhead, on which Rayyis's subsequent letters were written, carried the second article of its bylaws, which summarized the aims of the organization. These aims were, among other things, to "revive the history and glory of the Arabs, strengthen the links between all Arab countries, and spread and unify Arab culture." Considered subversive and pro-German, the Arab Club was shut down by the French authorities in 1939 after the Allied declaration of war against Germany and the concomitant French imposition of martial law in Syria. While the club was still in operation, its members, particularly Rayyis and Qawuqji himself, came to be involved in plans to launch a new revolt by overthrowing Amir 'Abdullah in Transjordan and then using Transjordan as a bridgehead for the liberation of Palestine and Syria. Rayyis wrote again to Qawuqji in October 1937 concerning the plans for this revolt. The letter is an account of Rayyis's meeting with an officer in the Jordanian army named Muhammad al-'Ajaluni, who was charged with launching the rebellion in Jordan and with whom, according to the plan, Qawuqji, accompanied by troops from Syria and Iraq, would later join. The plan was that Qawuqji would then take over the leadership of the entire revolt. Rayyis informed Qawuqji that the first and most important job that 'Ajaluni should carry out was ensuring that the shaykhs of the tribes in Transjordan would support the revolt. In his letter he also talked about the fact that Qawuqji's "friend in the Hijaz" was opposed to Qawuqji's involvement in the plan and wished instead to see 'Ajaluni remain the leader of the revolt. From the context of the correspondence, Qawuqji's "friend in the Hijaz" was probably the Mufti. This is supported by two letters sent by 'Umar al-'Umari to his brother Subhi toward the end of 1937. Subhi al-'Umari had fought alongside T. E. Lawrence in the 1916 Arab Revolt and also at the battle of Maysalun in 1920. He later went on to become prominent in Syrian politics. 'Umar al-'Umari was a businessman who lived most of his life in Amman. Both brothers were friends of Qawuqji's. The letters contain details of plans for the 'Ajaluni rebellion that 'Umar, who was in Amman, wanted Subhi to pass on to Qawuqji. Qawuqji scribbled the following words at the top of one of the letters:

> The Mufti insists that 'Ajaluni should be the commander in chief instead of me. This will not work. Jordan follows only its tribal shaykhs. He who can bring the tribal shaykhs to his side can dominate all of Jordan.

Qawuqji's note echoes 'Umar al-'Umari's concerns about 'Ajaluni's suitability as the leader of the rebellion in Jordan. 'Umar al-'Umari expressed these concerns to his brother and asked Subhi to warn Qawuqji about involving himself in a plan that had no chance of success because, as 'Umar put it, "Transjordan as a country will not be agitated by 'Ajaluni, who is just a simple villager, but rather by the heads of its tribes." He also wrote that the time was not right for a revolution in Transjordan, that if Qawuqji came to Transjordan, he would not receive the support that he was being promised by people in Damascus, and that he should ignore the "honeyed words" of 'Ajaluni:

> If dear Fawzi is still in Baghdad, then you have to convince him that this is not a good time for any movement he intends to set up, as luck will not be on his side owing to the fact that precautionary measures have been taken [by the British] on the borders, and even if he managed to penetrate the 'Ajlun woodlands, he will find no one to support him . . . and would only be able to stay for a few days. Any other theory is just wild fantasy.

The archive that Qawuqji has left us indicates that he ignored these pleas and remained committed to launching a revolution in Transjordan, at least until the onset of war in Europe made it effectively impossible. He continued to believe that the key to this revolt lay with the tribes. He gave a detailed account of the history of these plans in a long letter that he wrote to Ibn Sa'ud in February 1939. By the time Qawuqji wrote this letter, he had lived in Baghdad for over a year after having been freed from his exile in Kirkuk. 'Adil al-'Azma took the letter to Ibn Sa'ud. It appears to have been a last-ditch attempt to secure funding and supplies in order to implement the operation in Transjordan. Qawuqji asked for these supplies and money to support the revolt and went into detail about what would be gained if the revolt were successful:

> Transjordan will be saved from the control of Amir 'Abdullah, who has turned out to be a deaf tool in the hands of the British and who tries to kill the Arab spirit there as a means of spreading hatred against Saudi Arabia and other neighboring countries, including Palestine, and as a means to isolate Transjordan from the Arabs and make it easier for him to sell its lands to the Zionists and open the door for the colonial British and Zionist project. Transjordan is a connecting point and a bridge linking all Arab countries together. To lose it means that all parts will be disunited, and thus it will become very difficult to set up any Arab solidarity between the Arab countries, whether it be eco-

nomic, military, or political solidarity. This separation will also allow
the foreigners to colonize each territory separately, and thus all of the
Arabs' dreams will be weakened and will vanish away. Should the financial aid and the sympathy of Ibn Saʻud become available to us, we
guarantee to achieve all the said targets through the campaign. We
are in particular need of this campaign at a time when the smell of
gunfire reaches us from all the countries of Europe.

Qawuqji concluded his letter to Ibn Saʻud by assuring him that there
were tribes in Jordan that would join the revolt the moment it was
launched and that Qawuqji was waiting for his contacts in Jordan to
give him the names of the shaykhs who would aid him in uniting their
forces. Attached to this letter in Qawuqji's archive—although it is difficult to know whether this attachment was sent to Ibn Saʻud or not—is a
list of the tribes of Jordan. Qawuqji scribbled on this list: "the revolution
in Jordan." The list is divided into three categories: tribes that would be
inclined to fight against them, tribes that would be neutral, and tribes
that could be relied on for support.

Ibn Saʻud sent a polite letter back to Qawuqji saying that he would
consider the situation. But by the late spring of 1939 Qawuqji's contacts
in Transjordan were sending him news that everyone there was talking
about the operation and that the British were prepared to repel any attempt
at revolt. Plans for revolt in Transjordan had withered by the fall of 1939,
which saw the outbreak of war in Europe.

FRITZ GROBBA

Qawuqji's military service with German officers during World War I,
combined with his pan-Arab, anticolonial politics, had always inclined
him to the idea of seeking German support for fighting the British and the
French in the Middle East. In the summer of 1936, before he left for
Palestine, Qawuqji met for the first time the German ambassador to
Baghdad, Fritz Grobba. From that moment until the Russian occupation

of Berlin in the summer of 1945, Qawuqji's fate was linked to that of this German diplomat.

Grobba, sometimes referred to as the German Lawrence of Arabia, had studied law and Oriental languages at the University of Berlin before World War I. As an officer in the Imperial German Army Grobba had fought on the Turkish front during the war. After the war he worked for the German Foreign Ministry and became an expert on the Muslim world and one of the leading architects of Germany's foreign policy in the Middle East. After his appointment as ambassador to Iraq, he persuaded the Iraqi government to accept German officers in Iraq as advisers. He also made connections with the pan-Arab radicals living in Baghdad in the late 1930s, including Qawuqji. In the summer of 1936, according to a report that Grobba sent back to the German Foreign Ministry, Qawuqji asked for German support for his campaign in Palestine. Grobba was sympathetic but refused material support because Germany was still trying to maintain good relations with the British. Qawuqji visited Grobba again after returning from Palestine in late 1936 as well as several times in 1938, after he had been allowed to return from Kirkuk to Baghdad following the fall of the Hikmat Sulayman government and the installation of Jamil al-Madfa'i as the new prime minister.

According to Qawuqji's memoirs, by the summer of 1938 Grobba had made it clear that the German Foreign Ministry was now willing to support Arab organizations involved in anti-British activities. Grobba apparently promised Qawuqji substantial material support. It was also in the summer of 1938 that Qawuqji first made contact with German counterintelligence. He had a meeting in Baghdad with Helmuth Groscurth, who was then the director of the Second Counterintelligence Division of the Department for Foreign News and Counterintelligence. But the British discovery of Qawuqji's plans for revolt in Transjordan and the fact that Grobba was forced to leave Baghdad because of his connection to an incident of Iraqi sabotage of the oil pipeline brought a lull in Qawuqji's contacts with German officials.

By 1939 Grobba was back in Germany, serving in the Foreign Ministry. After the fall of Paris to the Germans in June 1940, he became part of the German Foreign Ministry's efforts to recruit Arab nationalists in the Middle East to the German side. German foreign policy makers, including Grobba, planned for a postwar pan-Arab union that would be dependent on Italy and Germany. They also supported the idea of a Muslim jihad against the British, French, and Russians. German officials focused on the Mufti as someone who could help bring this about. Grobba himself drafted several policy plans for the Middle East in 1940 and 1941. He was also affiliated with a unit within the German Army, Special Staff F, which had been assigned the task of supporting the Iraqi coup against the pro-British regime in Baghdad.

THE RUTBA FORT

On April 1, 1941, four Iraqi army officers, known as the Golden Square, overthrew the pro-British Iraqi government in Baghdad and installed as prime minister Rashid 'Ali al-Kaylani, an anti-British, pro-Axis Iraqi lawyer. In spite of Iraq's nominal independence from Britain, British troops invaded Iraq in order to restore the old regime and to protect British troops already stationed there. Procoup Iraqi troops surrounded and laid siege to the British air force base at Habaniyya, just west of Baghdad. The fighting lasted for several weeks before the British were able to regain control of Iraq; the leaders of the coup fled to Iran. The Mufti, then in exile in Baghdad, supported the coup. Qawuqji fought as the commander of the Desert Forces, which were set up to defend Iraq against the British-led Arab Legion, which invaded Iraq from Transjordan and Kingcol, a British army flying column. Both the Arab Legion and Kingcol were mobilized in order to break the Iraqi siege of Habaniyya.

Qawuqji's memoirs do not contain many details about how he came to be involved in the coup. But the memoirs of Salah al-Din al-Sabbagh, who was one of the four Iraqi officers of the Golden Square, describe how Qawuqji had been secretly in contact with him in the years leading up to the coup. Sabbagh had helped Qawuqji procure uniforms and arms for his campaign in Palestine in 1936. He had also met with Qawuqji several times after Qawuqji's return to Baghdad in the fall of 1936, and he had helped support Qawuqji's plans for revolt in Transjordan and Palestine. It was through Sabbagh and his circles and through Qawuqji's connection to the Mufti, albeit an uneasy one, that Qawuqji was recruited to fight in the coup. Many of the men who served in the Desert Forces under Qawuqji's leadership were Syrians and Palestinians living in exile in Baghdad. Some of the Palestinians were loyal to the Mufti, who acted as a civilian liaison in Baghdad for the Desert Forces. Some accounts of the Mufti's connection to the Desert Forces claim that he wanted to be sure of having some control over the large amounts of money that Germany was giving to support the campaign in the desert against the British. Grobba, by this time back in Berlin, was involved in funneling this money (which was said to amount to thousands of dinars) to Iraq. The Mufti made it clear that he did not trust Qawuqji with the money.

Rayyis, still in Damascus when the coup took place, traveled to Baghdad to support the new Iraqi government's struggle to consolidate its power in the wake of the coup. On the day he arrived in Baghdad he went to Qawuqji's house in the Karada district, where he found Qawuqji getting ready to move out with his soldiers to the desert. Qawuqji's first objective was to secure the Rutba Fort. Rutba was a large stone fort built over a well in the Iraqi desert about eighty miles east of the Transjordanian border. It lay on the desert road to Baghdad. The fort was surrounded by high masonry walls with a single gate, which was guarded by a garrison of the Iraqi police. Before the war it had also served as a hostel for passengers of the transdesert car service that ran between Damascus and Baghdad and as a refueling point for the British-run Imperial Airways. An RAF pilot took the aerial photograph of Rutba during a bombing raid on May 10, 1941 (figure 27).

Rayyis agreed with Qawuqji that he would join Qawuqji's forces in the desert after a week or so, when he had had time to rest from his journey from Damascus and visit a few friends in Baghdad. He did not join

FIGURE 27

Qawuqji's forces until after the fighting at Rutba, but his memoirs provide a detailed account of later battles between Qawuqji's unit and the British army. Most of these battles took place in small towns along the Euphrates on both the Iraqi and Syrian sides of the border.

In his memoirs Qawuqji is terse about the events at Rutba. They are covered by just a few diary entries mainly dated from the days immediately following the fighting at the fort. From the memoirs of Glubb Pasha, who commanded the Arab Legion unit sent to occupy Rutba after the pro-Axis coup, we know that Qawuqji and his men did enter the Rutba Fort on the evening of May 9, 1941, following a successful battle against

British troops, who were waiting for them in the sand dunes around the fort. Qawuqji and his men left the fort after only one day, to travel due east through the desert to the town of Hit, which lay on the Euphrates. The Arab Legion and Kingcol then moved in and occupied the Rutba Fort, where they found that the dining room and kitchen had been partially looted. The British forces also stayed for a short time, leaving on May 13 in order to travel east to break the siege of Habaniyya. According to Qawuqji's own memoirs, he was forced to leave Rutba because many of his men mutinied and wanted to return to Baghdad. He also could not persuade the Iraqi police in Rutba to provide his men with food and petrol. His diary entries for the days immediately following Rutba are full of concerns about supplies, cars getting stuck in the sand, and the difficulty of recharging the wireless sets in the desert.

In the years following 1941 and the collapse of the pro-Axis coup in Iraq, Qawuqji was blamed for his actions at Rutba. The fact that he had left the fort so quickly, thereby making it possible for British forces to take his place, led to accusations of treachery. Most of these accusations came from people affiliated with the Mufti. Kemal Haddad, the Mufti's private secretary, accompanied the Mufti during the events in Iraq in the summer of 1941. He also fled to Iran with the Mufti at the end of May 1941, when it was clear that the coup had failed. In his memoirs, Haddad blames Qawuqji's actions at Rutba for the British victory in Iraq. Two years later, in Berlin, the Mufti circulated a document to members of the German Foreign Ministry in Berlin, accusing Qawuqji of being a British spy. The document was supposedly written by Badri Qadah, an Iraqi army officer who served in the Desert Forces with Qawuqji in 1941. The document is a long and detailed character assassination of Qawuqji, intended to offer evidence of treachery across the span of Qawuqji's career. A full account of this document belongs in the final section of this chapter, which is devoted to Qawuqji's time in Berlin. But there is a short segment that questions Qawuqji's actions at Rutba: Why, when Qawuqji left Rutba, did he not destroy the fort and poison the well so that the British could not use it? Why did he disappear for a few hours while the fighting was ongoing? Was it because he was contacted by Jamil al-Midfaʿi, an old supporter of Qawuqji's and a pro-British Iraqi politician, who persuaded him to withdraw? Why did he not arrest Abu George, the well-known spy from among the Iraqi police at the fort? After Qawuqji left the fort for the Euphrates, he came close to a British patrol in the desert; why did he not attack it?

The Mufti's efforts to destroy Qawuqji's reputation have made it difficult to get at the truth of what happened at Rutba. This is because later accounts, particularly the Arabic memoirs, tend either to support the Mufti's version or to defend Qawuqji against the Mufti's accusations. What we do know for sure is that Qawuqji fought against British forces in the desert for several weeks after Rutba, long after the coup had failed and the Mufti was safely in Tehran under the protection of the Italian Legation. Qawuqji did not leave the field until he was seriously wounded when the RAF bombed his convoy in the Syrian Desert, near Palmyra, in late June 1941.

BACK TO THE EUPHRATES

After he left Rutba, Qawuqji headed east toward Hit, passing through the town of Kabisa, which lay to the west of Hit. In his memoirs Qawuqji mentions that he came very close to a British convoy but that he decided not to attack it because of the low morale of his men and their eagerness to reach the Euphrates. In fact, in this section of his memoirs, Qawuqji often refers to problems with his men and the fact that they were irregular volunteers, not trained soldiers. Given that he compiled his memoirs in the 1970s, Qawuqji's explanation of why he declined to attack the British convoy could have been a direct response to the accusations that Badri Qadah later leveled against him in Berlin. To make matters worse, some of the volunteers in Qawuqji's forces were Palestinians affiliated with the Mufti. According to Rayyis, the Palestinians proposed by the Mufti for service in the Desert Forces were rough troublemakers, whom the Mufti was keen to remove from his circles in Baghdad.

One factor that is not explicitly mentioned in Qawuqji's memoirs or in the memoirs of others involved in the rebellion against the British in Iraq in the summer of 1941 is the role that looting played as an incentive for men to join Qawuqji's Desert Forces. The desert track that ran due west from the Euphrates to Rutba lay along the Kirkuk–Haifa oil pipeline. This was the same pipeline that Qawuqji and his men had sabotaged in northern Palestine in the summer of 1936. In both the English and the Arabic accounts of the fighting in Iraq in 1941, the geography of the desert is described in relation to the pumping stations along the pipeline. The Iraqi pumping stations were labeled "H1," "H2," and "H3." The pumping stations of H4 and H5 lay in Transjordan, in the desert west of the Iraqi border. Each pumping station contained a small settlement of workers, who, along with their families, lived there to maintain the pumps. When the revolt erupted, the Iraqi Army took control over the Kirkuk oil fields from the British, and after April 1941 oil no longer flowed through the pipeline. As a result, the British army evacuated all the pumping stations. Here is how Glubb Pasha describes the scene at the H4 pumping station, when he and the Arab Legion arrived there in the first week of May 1941, on their way to Rutba:

The desert at H4 is monotonously flat, and the arrival of military forces and vehicles had churned the surface into deep powdery dust. Soft yellow dust filled one's clothes, covered faces and hands, lay thick on the food, and drifted perpetually through the air. Since the declaration of war by the usurping Government of Baghdad, the Kirkuk oil-fields has been occupied by the enemy, and oil was no longer being pumped down the pipeline. Most of the oil company personnel had been evacuated, and their formerly green cheerful gardens had been trampled down and covered with dust. A child's teddy bear was lying in a flowerbed, forgotten perhaps in the hurry of evacuation.

British military documents show that by mid-June 1941 all the pumping stations along the Iraqi section of the pipeline had been looted. The employees of the Iraq Petroleum Company refused to return to their pumping station compounds unless the British army gave them proper protection. It is likely that Qawuqji's men, who would have traveled close to the pipeline to reach Rutba, had looted the pumping stations, given that they certainly looted supplies at the Rutba Fort itself. It is also likely that without this incentive of further looting, it was hard for Qawuqji to keep his men in Rutba, isolated as it was in the middle of the desert. Perhaps his only choice was to leave the desert and Rutba behind and return to the towns along the banks of the Euphrates, where supplies were plentiful.

After staying for a few days on the outskirts of Hit, Qawuqji and his men moved north up the Euphrates, stopping at the towns of Haditha, 'Aana, and al-Husayba. Al-Husayba lay right on the Syrian border. Qawuqji arrived there at the end of May. These were a crucial few weeks of World War II in the Levant. The Vichy French government, which had been in power for a year since the German occupation of France in June 1940, controlled both Syria and Lebanon. Under an agreement with the Vichy regime, Germany had access to military installations in Syria and had provided German aircraft to Vichy French forces to help them defend Syria and Lebanon against an anticipated Allied offensive. The Allies began their invasion of Syria on June 8 and completed it on July 12, when the Vichy forces surrendered. Qawuqji, who in early June was operating just miles from the Syrian border, found himself caught up in the battles between the Vichy French and the British.

But at the end of May he was still on the Iraqi side of the border. On May 31, just before he and his men arrived at Haditha, news reached them that the coup had failed. The Golden Square officers had fled Iraq, along with Rashid 'Ali al-Kaylani and the Mufti. Remarkably, Qawuqji decided to fight on, engaging in a firefight with a British unit in al-Husayba in the first week of June. He also sent his adjutant, Hamad Sa'ab, to put out feelers to German officers in Dayr al-Zur, on the Syrian side of the border, trying to secure their support in the war against the British. The German officers had arrived in Dayr al-Zur after fleeing Baghdad in the wake of the failed coup. Munir al-Rayyis, who had been trying to reach Qawuqji and his men, finally met up with them in early June in their camp on the outskirts of 'Aana, just south of al-Husayba.

In his memoirs Rayyis marked this meeting as the moment that the real battle against the British began: "By joining my brothers, I was sure that our real role began when the role of the Iraqi government in its war against the British had ended."

After the fall of Kaylani's government and the entrance of British troops into Baghdad, the pro-British Iraqi regent Prince 'Abd al-Ilah returned to the throne, and a new Iraqi government was formed under Jamil al-Midfa'i. He had served as prime minister of Iraq several times in the 1930s, including right after the fall of the Sulayman government, which had sent Qawuqji into exile in Kirkuk. It was Midfa'i's government that had allowed Qawuqji to return to Baghdad in 1939. Right after he took office on June 2, Midfa'i sent a message to Qawuqji, through the governor of Ramadi. In the message Midfa'i sent Qawuqji formal greetings and reminded him of the bond between them. Midfa'i asked Qawuqji not to take any action until he, Midfa'i, was able to talk directly to him on the telephone. Qawuqji went to the house of the governor of 'Aana, who had the only telephone nearby, and called Midfa'i, who begged him to give up his fight against the British and come to Baghdad. Qawuqji refused because he had Syrian and Palestinian fighters in his group who were under threat of arrest or execution by either the British government in Palestine or the French government in Damascus, and he feared the British authorities in Baghdad might seize them. Qawuqji told Midfa'i that he had promised them safe passage to Syria. When Midfa'i promised his personal protection for these fighters in Baghdad, Qawuqji stressed that his men did not trust the British and would not travel into British-controlled territory. Midfa'i asked him at least to hand over all the weapons in his unit to the governor in 'Aana, but Qawuqji refused to do this either until he had his men safely over the Syrian border. This conversation happened on the same day that Hamad Sa'ab returned to the camp at 'Aana from Dayr al-Zur, carrying the news that the German officers in Dayr al-Zur were willing to help Qawuqji acquire arms and other supplies.

It was also in the first week of June that Qawuqji made contact with the German diplomat Rudolf Rahn, probably with the help of Fritz

Grobba, who was by this time in Mosul trying to coordinate German support for the Iraqi rebels. Rahn had been sent to Syria in May 1941 as a "political officer" in order to help the Vichy French in the same effort. It seems that Qawuqji seriously considered Midfa'i's request to return to Baghdad, given that Qawuqji remained under sentence of death in French-controlled Syria because of his role in the Syrian Revolt against the French from 1925 to 1927. On June 10 Rahn reported back to Berlin that he had succeeded in persuading the Vichy French to annul Qawuqji's death sentence, and this in turn enabled Qawuqji to cooperate with Vichy French forces in Syria close to the Iraqi border.

In his memoirs Qawuqji briefly mentions his contact with Rahn, but he does not elaborate on his decision to join the Vichy French. He made this choice at the same moment that Allied troops were marching into Syria to expel the Vichy government. Rayyis was present at Qawuqji's first meeting with Vichy French officers in al-Husayba, in Iraq. The French officers had traveled across the border from Al-Bukamal, which lay just on the Syrian side of the border. When the French officers first saw Qawuqji, they saluted him and spoke with him in French, saying that they were messengers from Gen. Henri Dentz, the French high commissioner in Beirut. They said that they were proud to shake the hand of Fawzi al-Qawuqji, the Syrian officer whom the French government had put under sentence of death. Qawuqji and the French officers discussed plans to cooperate in repelling the Allied invasion of Syria. Qawuqji insisted on complete amnesty for the Syrian fighters in his unit, who were also under sentences of death because of their participation in the Syrian Revolt. Qawuqji's loyalty toward the men who fought with him characterizes his career. A few weeks later, after he had been wounded and flown to Berlin, he continued to pressure his contacts within the German Foreign Ministry to secure the well-being and safety of the men he had left behind. In contrast with Badri Qadah's testimony against him in Berlin, the memoirs of the men who actually served with Qawuqji are generally positive about his leadership and loyal to the memory of his role in the various rebellions in which they fought alongside him.

ATTACKED FROM THE AIR

Qawuqji and his men spent the next weeks moving west and north along the Euphrates between 'Aana in Iraq and the Syrian town of Dayr al-Zur, which was controlled by a Vichy French garrison. Qawuqji engaged in skirmishes with British forces on several occasions during this time: at Husayba, in Iraq, where he captured two British armored cars, and at Al-Bukamal and Mayadin, just a few miles south of Dayr al-Zur, in Syria. Qawuqji's actions in those few weeks of fighting along the Euphrates show up in the reports of the Special Operations Executive (SOE), the organization set up by the British government in World War II to conduct espionage, sabotage, and reconnaissance in Axis-occupied areas. On June 14, after Qawuqji had met with Rudolf Rahn, but while he was still in Iraqi territory, a British intelligence officer reported that Qawuqji was active in the area of the pipeline near the H1 pumping station. H1 was the first pumping station after the pipeline left the Euphrates and headed west into the desert. The report stated that Iraqi soldiers guarding the pumping station were threatening to leave their posts out of fear of attack by Qawuqji and his men. Obviously unaware of Qawuqji's meeting with Rahn or of Qawuqji's new alliance with the Vichy French officers now in control of southern Syria, the British intelligence officer wrongly believed that Qawuqji was trapped between the pipeline and the Syrian border.

> The Fawzi referred to above is a well-known scallywag leader of considerable cunning. He cannot escape into French territory, as the French are quite desirous of hanging him. It is therefore likely that he will soon be caught in a trap just north of the Pipe Line. Force headquarters have requested that DPX be held in readiness to assist in operations should definite action be taken to liquidate Fawzi's party.

"DPX" was probably a Royal Air Force unit, closely coordinated with the SOE, that would have been able to respond quickly in a combat air support role. On July 2 another British intelligence report said that the same DPX had been involved in operations on June 19 to occupy the al-Ghaim pumping station near Al-Bukamal in Syria, just north of the Iraq border. This pumping station lay on the northern pipeline that ran from Haditha to Tripoli, north of Haifa, on the Lebanese coast of the Mediterranean. The memo stated that the occupation of al-Ghaim was necessary because of the actions of "Fawzi, who was proved to be in greater force than had been anticipated." Given that Qawuqji's convoy was bombed by the RAF just a few days later, it may well be the case that Qawuqji's effectiveness in threatening the infrastructure of the Iraq Petroleum Company in the summer of 1941 did indeed lead to a British military decision to "liquidate him and his party."

Sometime in mid-June he set up camp in Mayadin about twenty miles south of Dayr al-Zur. Today Dayr al-Zur is Syria's sixth-largest city, and even in the 1940s it was a sizable Syrian town on the banks of the Euphrates, about 280 miles northeast of Damascus (figure 28).

By the time Qawuqji set up camp in Mayadin, some of his close Syrian and Palestinian friends from Baghdad had also arrived in eastern Syria, fleeing Iraq after the coup failed and the British regained control. They included ʿAdil al-ʿAzma, Akram Zuʿaytar, and Qawuqji's cousin ʿAdil

FIGURE 28

al-Hamadi. Qawuqji was reunited with them in mid-June. Because of Qawuqji's agreement with the Vichy French he could reassure them that they need not fear the French army, and he negotiated for them to remain in Dayr al-Zur. Qawuqji's cousin 'Adil also brought Qawuqji's two teenage children, Majdi and Haifa, to visit him in the camp. Majdi and Haifa were Qawuqji's children by his first wife, Ruhaifa, whom he had married in Tripoli in 1918. It is not clear how Majdi and Haifa arrived in eastern Syria, although Majdi, who was in his late teens, may well have traveled with some of Qawuqji's men throughout the Iraq campaign. Rayyis is the only source for Qawuqji's stay in Mayadin and for his children's visit. Qawuqji does not mention any of this in his own memoirs, but the reunion with Majdi and Haifa and with his close friends must have been emotional for him, particularly as it took place in his beloved Syria, from which he had been exiled for so long.

Qawuqji dined regularly with the Vichy French officers who were serving in the garrison in Dayr al-Zur. During one of these dinners the French officers asked Qawuqji to help defend the T3 pumping station from British occupation. T3 lay along the Haditha–Tripoli pipeline just a few miles from Palmyra. Palmyra is an oasis town 150 miles due west of Dayr al-Zur, in the middle of the Syrian Desert. Qawuqji agreed to help. A couple of days later he set out at night with a small unit of men to travel in convoy from Dayr al-Zur into the desert toward Palmyra. The Vichy French unit traveled a few miles ahead of Qawuqji's convoy. Qawuqji was in a car with Raji, his driver; Hamid Karrada, his servant; and Hamad Sa'ab, his loyal adjutant, who had fought with him in Syria from 1925 to 1927 and again in Palestine in 1936. Rayyis was traveling in a car behind Qawuqji's car. Here is how Rayyis describes what happened after a few hours of traveling:

> Suddenly, and without prior warning, we were fired on. It wasn't clear where the fire was coming from, and in the moment that I looked out of the window of the car toward the ground, bullets came from the sky and formed a line to the right of my car of explosions of dust on the ground. I looked up at the sky, and there were two airplanes at a

height of tens of meters flying like arrows from back to front above the convoy, and I turned by instinct to the left and shouted to the driver, "Go left, go left," and he gripped the wheel hard and drove the car quickly to the left of the roads tens of meters, when I shouted to him, "Stop!" The three of us got out of the car to get away from it, and we hit the ground in preparation for the return of the planes. The planes returned, circling high above our stopped convoy. After ensuring that they had hit their target and probably having photographed the situation, they left the place quickly until they were no longer in view. I saw the door of Qawuqji's car opening, and I saw Qawuqji get out leaning on his servant Hamid. Two soldiers rushed to help him, and he asked to be laid down on the earth. I realized that he had been hit with machine-gun fire, and I was with the soldiers firing our rifles at the planes when they returned until they disappeared. I rushed to the commander to see him drowning in blood that was coming from his head and flowing like a drain from the sleeve of his jacket.

Both Hamad Sa'ab and Qawuqji's driver, Raji, were killed in the attack on the convoy. Qawuqji's servant, Hamid Karrada, was also wounded, but not as severely as Qawuqji himself. The French convoy was miles ahead and did not return to help. What followed was a frantic attempt to get Qawuqji to the military hospital at Dayr al-Zur in order to save his life. He was laid down on the rear seat of one of the undamaged cars, and the whole convoy turned back to Dayr al-Zur. Once they arrived at the hospital Qawuqji was taken straight into an operating room. Rayyis called his friends in Dayr al-Zur to send Arab doctors to the hospital. He was convinced that the French officers at the garrison had betrayed them by colluding with the British to organize the attack on Qawuqji's convoy. He did not want French doctors operating on Qawuqji without someone whom Rayyis could trust also in the room. Muhammad 'Ali al-Qanawati, a Syrian doctor from Dayr al-Zur, arrived quickly and participated in operating on Qawuqji along with the French doctors. According to Rayyis, once the Free French troops occupied

Dayr al-Zur a few weeks later, it became clear that the Vichy French officers who had wined and dined Qawuqji and his men had in fact been working secretly for the Free French. According to Rayyis, they had informed the British about the exact time that Qawuqji's convoy would be traveling across the desert to Palmyra and the route that the convoy would take. This may have been what happened, but British intelligence documents show that Vichy wireless conversations were being carefully monitored during this period. It is just as likely that the British knew about Qawuqji's convoy because they had intercepted Vichy communications about his movements in the Syrian Desert.

After Qawuqji's emergency operation, funerals were held in Dayr al-Zur for Qawuqji's driver and for Hamad Saʿab. Qawuqji's injuries, multiple wounds in his back and head, were so serious that he was flown to a better-equipped hospital in Aleppo. Fighting in Syria, particularly in the north, still erupted between the Vichy French and the Allies, who were being helped by the Free French. On July 3, 1941, Qawuqji was flown from Aleppo to Berlin via Athens. His evacuation to Berlin was almost certainly organized by Rudolf Rahn with the help of Fritz Grobba. Qawuqji's son, Majdi, Qawuqji's brother Yumni, and his servant, Hamid Karrada, accompanied him. Upon arriving in Berlin, Qawuqji was transported directly to the main hospital in Hansaviertel, where he underwent another operation. During the surgery nineteen bullets and pieces of car metal were removed from his body. However, the surgeon left a bullet that had lodged in his head. Afraid that if he tried to remove the bullet he would cause brain damage, the surgeon described his body as a lead mine and told him that it was a miracle that he was alive. Qawuqji suffered from headaches for the rest of his life as a result of the bullet in his head. Years later, after he had retired from military life and was living in Beirut, friends and family remember that he always wore a hat inside on rainy winter days because the metal lodged in his skull would become cold. Yumni and Majdi stayed with Qawuqji in the hospital, and German officers from Special Staff F visited Qawuqji from time to time in order to debrief him about the state of the pro-Axis Arab forces in the Middle

FIGURE 29

East. They were intent on securing promises from him concerning his playing an active role in pro-German propaganda in the Middle East. After a few weeks he was able to walk around the grounds of the hospital and even venture out into the streets of Berlin (figure 29).

BERLIN

Qawuqji's time in Germany between 1941 and 1947 has been a subject of interest mainly among amateur historians dedicated to proving that the Arab nationalists who spent the war years in Nazi Germany were committed to the anti-Semitic goals of National Socialism. In the view of these commentators, the fact that Arab nationalists lived in Nazi Germany explains the subsequent struggle by those nationalists to prevent the establishment of a Jewish state in Palestine. It is not surprising that the most detailed work published on Qawuqji's life, an article written in

1995 by the German historian Gerhard Höpp, focuses on this period in Berlin between 1941 and 1947. But Höpp shows that at least in the case of Qawuqji, his interest in German power in this period came from his desire to rid the Middle East of the British and the French, not from anti-Semitism or some commitment to Nazi ideology. Höpp drew on materials contained in the German archives to produce a detailed account of the relations between Qawuqji and the other Berlin-based Arab soldiers and politicians, all of whom hoped that an Axis victory in the war would bring about Arab independence from French and British colonial rule and who spent the war years negotiating with the German and Italian foreign ministries in anticipation of this outcome. These included well-known figures such as the famous Arab pro-German propagandist Yunus Bahri, the Mufti himself, and the leader of the failed pro-German coup in Iraq, Rashid 'Ali al-Kaylani, but also lesser-known people like the Syrian journalist Munir al-Rayyis. Arab nationalists who spent the war years in Berlin were not the only anticolonial activists supported by the Nazis. It had long been part of Nazi foreign policy to nuture movements that were opposed to British and/or French rule. The Indian nationalist Subhas Chandra Bose and the Irish nationalist Sean Russell also spent time in Berlin during the war in the hope that a German victory would bring full independence to India and Ireland.

Qawuqji's contact with German officers in the first few weeks of his time in Berlin convinced him of their optimism concerning a German invasion of the Middle East. Erwin Rommel was dug in on the coast of North Africa, and the British had yet to defeat him at El Alamein. In addition, two weeks before Qawuqji's arrival at the hospital, Germany had invaded Russia. From Qawuqji's hospital bed German military power must have appeared to be invincible. Of course we now know that it was in the summer of 1941 that the Nazi government began to plan the extermination of all the Jews of Europe, six months before the basic logistics of the Final Solution were settled at the Wannsee Conference in January 1942. In his memoirs, compiled in the early 1970s, Qawuqji does not mention the Holocaust. This is in spite of the fact that he stayed in Germany until 1947. The few pages of his memoirs that speak about his time in Germany focus on the narrow world of negotiations between the Arab nationalist exiles in Berlin and their German supporters. These negotiations always revolved around the nature and scope of German support for an independent Arab state in the wake of a German victory in the Middle East.

Qawuqji experienced a personal tragedy in those first few weeks in the hospital in Hansaviertel. His son, Majdi, died after a gastrointestinal illness. There is nothing in the German sources that explains this death. Qawuqji always believed that German officers poisoned Majdi because during those early visits to his hospital bed Qawuqji had not been as cooperative as they wished him to be. The Foreign Ministry paid for Majdi to be buried with a full funeral in the Muslim cemetery at Columbiadamm. Convinced that Majdi had been poisoned, Qawuqji refused to attend the funeral. Whatever the cause of Majdi's death, Qawuqji was stricken by grief and from that moment on treated his German interlocutors at Special Staff F with suspicion. The blow of Majdi's death was softened, however, by another important event in his personal life. During his time in the hospital he met and fell in love with a young German woman who was a regular visitor to a patient in the bed next to Qawuqji's. Her name was Anneliese Müller, and she later became Qawuqji's wife and the mother of three sons still living today. This was the first time that Qawuqji married for love. His previous marriages were formal arrangements born of the social conventions of the time.

When Qawuqji was released from the hospital, he moved into an apartment on Cuxhavener Street near Hansa Square, where the hospital was located. It was a quiet bourgeois area with tree-lined streets and nineteenth-century apartment buildings. The flat was paid for by the German Foreign Ministry and came with a car and driver. Qawuqji used the flat to host many gatherings of Arab exiles in Berlin during the war, including some of his closest confidants such as his brother Yumni and his close friend Munir al-Rayyis. According to Rayyis's memoirs, it was Qawuqji who persuaded the Germans to bring him to Berlin in order to get him away from the threat of British arrest in Syria, after British and Free French troops had ousted the Vichy government in Damascus.

Rayyis spent long hours in Qawuqji's flat in Berlin, and in March 1942 the two men went on a twenty-two-day tour of Germany, paid for by the Foreign Ministry. Later that year Qawuqji and Rayyis also took a fully paid trip to Paris, where they stayed at the Bristol Hotel, on the Champs-Élysées. There they met with many young Syrians living in Paris during the war and also with German officials from the German Embassy in Paris. At one lunch in Paris, Qawuqji and Rayyis got into a fierce argument with a German official after the German casually announced that the eastern Mediterranean countries would fall under Italian rule in the wake of an Axis victory. Qawuqji and Rayyis told the German that they would fight just as hard against Italian rule as they had fought against French and British rule.

It was in his flat on Cuxhavener Street that Qawuqji wrote the long report for the German Foreign Ministry, entitled "The Customs and Traditions of the Tribes of Syria and Iraq," mentioned at the beginning of Chapter 2. In the report he drew on his participation in the Syrian Revolt of 1925–1927 to offer detailed information on the locations and political affiliations of the Syrian tribes whose support he had relied on during the revolt. He described the people and geography of what he calls "the beautiful mountainous regions of Syria," such as Jabal Druze, Jabal al-Zawiya, and Jabal Qalamun, focusing on the tribes that were most likely to support a German invasion, which, according to Qawuqji's reckoning, would lead to the end of British and French imperialism in the region and to the independence of Syria and Iraq. While in Berlin, he drafted other reports for the Germans. These were based on his fighting against the British in Iraq and contained accounts of battles, tactics, and topographical charts, in addition to his thoughts on the question of German propaganda in the Middle East. Qawuqj made it clear in the reports that Germany risked losing support in the Middle East because of its failure to help pro-Axis nationalists defeat the British in Iraq.

Qawuqji's early hopes of German help in the struggle for Arab independence are reflected in some of the letters that he was writing to his friends. He wrote to 'Adil al-'Azma, who by that time was in exile in Istanbul, at the end of October 1941. In the letter he spoke of the importance of setting up better communications between him and the Arab nationalist exiles in Istanbul. He suggested to 'Azma that they establish a committee to serve as the link between the nationalists in Berlin and the nationalists in Istanbul. Qawuqji claimed that Grobba could ensure that the German Embassy in Istanbul would provide support for such a committee. The letter is full of optimism about the future and the importance of getting the Germans to make a public declaration in support of Arab independence. Three months later, in early February 1942, he wrote to 'Azma again. Qawuqji's tone in this letter is completely different. Both the Mufti and Rashid 'Ali al-Kaylani had arrived in Berlin in November 1941, and they became the main focus of German interest. Qawuqji had been working hard to influence German policy in favor of Arab independence. He had also repeatedly tried to persuade the Germans to bring to Europe some of the men who had fought with him at Rutba. But in his letter to 'Azma he describes how the Mufti completely ignored him since arriving in Berlin and surrounded himself with his own men. The Mufti also refused to cooperate with Kaylani, who in turn was complaining bitterly to Qawuqji about the Mufti's actions.

This second letter shows that Qawuqji was a marginal player in German-Arab relations after the arrival of the Mufti and Kaylani in Berlin. As a consequence, Grobba's influence with Special Staff F was also reduced. Grobba fought back by supporting Kaylani (and by extension Qawuqji himself) against the Mufti. In the fall of 1942 Grobba spread rumors that the Mufti was showing German military secrets to his inner circle and cited Qawuqji and Rayyis as witnesses to this treachery. At the same time, the Mufti tried hard to undermine Grobba, Kaylani, and those, like Qawuqji, who were associated with them. As part of this campaign to undermine both Kaylani and Grobba, the Mufti sent a report to the German foreign minister accusing Qawuqji of being a British spy. The report was a twenty-two-page document entitled "The Life of the 'Hero' Fawzi al-Qawuqji Issued by the Office of the Mufti in Berlin." Written by Badri Qadah, who had been an officer in the Desert Forces in Iraq and who was acting in Berlin as the Mufti's main military adviser, the text offers evidence and arguments to support the charge that

Qawuqji was a spy for the British. Among the allegations were the "facts" that Qawuqji was associated with J. P. Domvile, who worked for British intelligence in Baghdad; that Qawuqji had meetings in the house of Emile Kourmi, "a well-known British spy"; and that Qawuqji had enough money to buy land in Baghdad. The report also mentioned Qawuqji's "abandoning" the Rutba Fort in May 1941. In addition to this list of evidence, Qadah also slandered Qawuqji's integrity on the basis of his name and his fair complexion, both of which implied, according to Qadah, that he was not a "real" Arab. Scholars writing about the Mufti have shown that accusing people of treachery was part of his standard repertoire and served as one of the many weapons he used to silence his opponents. There is no evidence in any of the hundreds of original sources used for this book to indicate that Qawuqji was a spy for the British.

Qawuqji knew that the Mufti was trying to damage his reputation. In the second letter to 'Azma, in February, he had complained that the Mufti was spreading rumors about his being a womanizer and a drinker and thus not a serious interlocutor for the Germans. We can be certain that Qawuqji knew about the Qadah report by the summer of 1946 because he says that it helped him convince the Russians, who had taken him prisoner in Berlin because of his close collaboration with the Germans, that the Germans mistrusted him. By mid-1943 the Mufti's efforts had paid off. Grobba had been dismissed from Special Staff F and sent to Paris to work as an archivist. With his wife Anneliese Müller, Qawuqji left Berlin for the German countryside, and stayed in a small house in the town of Altenberg in the mountainous Erzgebirge region.

Qawuqji's time in Berlin was the only significant period in his life up to that point when he was not fighting in or training an army. He thought of this period as his most intense encounter with what he termed politics. In March 1947 he gave an interview to the Lebanese newspaper *Al-Hayat*. In that interview he said: "I have been a military man since my child-hood. I don't understand anything about politics, and I don't want to understand anything about it." He must have had in mind this experience of being embroiled in the negotiations among the Germans, the Italians, Kaylani's camp, and the Mufti's camp. But Qawuqji's actions in Berlin show that he was not the politically naive soldier he claimed to be. According to German archival sources, Grobba himself was concerned about Qawuqji's political ambitions, in particular Qawuqji's insistence that he be the main Arab interlocutor for the German government in Berlin.

But Qawuqji's German period is not just a story of infighting between Arab nationalists and their German sponsors. Qawuqji had serious differences with the Mufti's approach to both the Germans and the Italians. According to Rayyis's memoirs, Qawuqji was involved in attempts to set up a military camp in Greece with the intention of training Arab soldiers for a future campaign in the Levant. Both Qawuqji and Rayyis soon quarreled with the Germans over the question of what exactly these future soldiers would be fighting for. Would it be to help install German or Italian rule or to establish an independent Arab state? According to Qawuqji, the Mufti was willing to help the Germans set up this unit, which was later called the Arab Free Corps, in spite of the fact that the Germans insisted that it be under their command and that it become an integral part of the German Army. For Qawuqji and Rayyis, this was unacceptable. In addition, neither the Mufti nor Kaylani was ever able to secure a public declaration from the Germans that they supported Arab independence. Qawuqji had pushed hard for this public declaration since arriving in Berlin. The Mufti and Kaylani did sign what was called a secret exchange of notes in April 1942. This secret document contained vague language from the Italians and the Germans about Arab independence. Qawuqji was furious at the nonbinding nature of the document and was very skeptical of German and Italian intentions.

One of the ways that Qawuqji discredits the Mufti in his memoirs is to mention the Mufti's involvement in Axis plans to revive the caliphate, the old Islamic state led by a supreme religio-political leader known as the caliph. After the German defeat at El Alamein and the retreat from Stalingrad, German plans for the Middle East became increasingly fanciful, and Arab nationalists in Berlin got caught up in these fantasies. Some members of Special Staff F began to concentrate on a plan to revive the caliphate, in order to persuade the Muslim world—particularly the huge Muslim population in British India—to support the Axis powers.

The Mufti was selected as the perfect candidate for caliph, and he was involved in the early planning to revive this thousand-year-old institution. Sultan Abdul Majid, the last surviving caliph from the Ottoman period, was still alive and living in exile in Paris. The Germans persuaded him to sign a document wherein he gave up all his rights to the caliphate and bestowed them on the Mufti. Qawuqji tells how he visited Rashid 'Ali al-Kaylani in his flat in Berlin sometime in 1944. Kaylani had just been visited by people whom Qawuqji describes as "leading members of the Nazi Party." Kaylani told Qawuqji that the men had come to tell him of the plan to revive the caliphate and to seek his support for bestowing this office on the Mufti. He also said that he had told the Germans that this was an absurd idea. First, the caliphate was a moribund and unimportant institution, and second, there were many people in the Muslim world more qualified for the post than the Mufti.

Qawuqji's intention in bringing up the issue of the Mufti and the caliphate in his memoirs no doubt stemmed from his personal animosity toward the Mufti. But it is also possible that he wished to distance himself from the Mufti's actions in Berlin during the war. In the histories that have been written about Arab nationalists in Berlin during this period, the Mufti always features as the most important and controversial character. This is because he had face-to-face meetings with both Himmler and Hitler. The official photographs taken at these meetings are well-known to Israeli schoolchildren from their history textbooks. Moreover, the Mufti is on record as having been an enthusiastic supporter of Nazi plans to exterminate the Jews and is known to have visited a concentration camp. In the last year of the war the Mufti was also involved in establishing a unit of Bosnian Muslims within the SS, the Thirteenth Waffen Mountain Division. The historian Ilan Pappe, in a recent biography of the Husayni family, describes the events surrounding the Mufti's support of Nazi ideology as being "highly important as an indication of al-Hajj Amin's transformation from a bright sensible leader of a movement into a hallucinatory figure losing touch with reality and assuming roles and capabilities far beyond those he actually possessed." One could argue that the Mufti's active and enthusiastic support of Nazi ideology has done more to discredit the Palestinian cause than any other actions by a Palestinian nationalist. Of course the Mufti's actions did not represent Palestinians as a whole. And yet some Israeli writers and politicians have cynically used his collaboration with the Nazis to discredit the goals of Palestinian nationalism today. Qawuqji, compiling his memoirs in the early 1970s, must have been acutely aware of the sensitive politics surrounding his time in Nazi Germany. By ridiculing the Mufti, as he does in his memoirs, he is attempting to distance himself from the stigma of those years in Berlin.

Apart from the description of his meeting with Kaylani sometime in Berlin in 1944, Qawuqji's memoirs contain no information about his life in Germany between the end of 1942, when Grobba was dismissed from Special Staff F, and 1945. Qawuqji shows up on a couple of occasions in the German sources during this period, but as a marginal character in German reports about the Mufti's active and ongoing lobbying of both the Germans and the Italians. It appears that Qawuqji withdrew into a private life and spent more and more time in Altenberg. This was particularly the case after the late fall of 1943, which saw intensified Allied bombing of Berlin. Many Arab nationalists left Germany altogether in the last two years of the war. Qawuqji does not explain why he decided to stay on, but at least part of the reason must have been his marriage to Anneliese Müller.

Qawuqji was used to being close to the action, and these relatively quiet years were difficult for him. It appears that he spent long hours brooding over how the Mufti had gotten the upper hand with the Germans involved in promoting Arabs in Berlin. The Mufti was a regular feature on Radio Berlin in 1943, 1944, and early 1945, and these broadcasts were a constant reminder to Qawuqji of his current distance from the center of German-Arab affairs.

Qawuqji's memoirs start up again in earnest in Berlin in the winter of 1945, after the Soviet army had occupied the city. Central Berlin was by then a devastated landscape, captured in a photograph taken for *Life* in the summer of 1945 (figure 30).

The impact of this devastation on Qawuqji caused him to see beyond

FIGURE 30

the small world of Arab nationalists in Berlin and their German and Italian interlocutors. Here is how he describes Berlin in the winter of 1945:

> A thick layer of snow lay over Berlin, and columns of smoke rose from the burning ruins that were left in the wake of the advancing armies on the eve of the Nazi defeat. The German people, who were reduced to a seminomadic existence, lived in damp, squalid and dingy shelters and pined away, hungry and frostbitten. They moaned and suffered underneath an ice roof. They fed on the morsels that were left over from the Red Army, and their bodies were nearly as bare as their homes, which had been looted and pillaged in a succession of raids.

CAPTURED BY THE RUSSIANS

Qawuqji stayed in his flat in Berlin with Anneliese and their baby son, Nizar, along with Qawuqji's adjutant, Hamid al-Safi. They remained hidden for several months until the Russians arrested them on a rainy day at the end of May 1946. Russian soldiers arrived at the flat and took everyone out of Berlin to a camp on the outskirts of the village of Basdorf. The baby must have been with them, although Qawuqji does not mention this in his memoirs. Qawuqji describes passing mounds of corpses in a small grove near a cemetery on the way to the camp. He had seen a great deal of death and violence in the rebellions in the Middle East and in the Ottoman Army during World War I. But the spectacle of mass killings on a European scale made a lasting impression on him. They were kept in the camp for a short time. After a few weeks a Russian officer arrived and, speaking to Qawuqji in Turkish, told him that he was to be taken away for questioning. He was kept in isolation for several weeks in a Russian prison in Berlin and interrogated about his collaboration with the Germans during the war. Qawuqji told them that he had indeed cooperated with the Germans in the early part of the war. And he told them of the reports that he had written for the Germans on the tribes in Syria and Iraq. But he said that ultimately his cooperation had been unsuccessful because some of his Arab compatriots had denounced him as a British spy. According to Qawuqji, the Russians were able to find the Badri Qadah report, which bore the Mufti's signature and was written on his official letterhead. It seems that this report, which came to haunt Qawuqji again in Damascus in the fall of 1947, probably saved his life in the fall of 1946.

After a month of interrogation he discovered that Anneliese and Hamid al-Safi had been taken to the same prison. They were put together in the same cell and spent a few weeks in the prison before being released to house arrest in a small house opposite a Russian military post in Berlin. This was one of the darkest periods of Qawuqji's life. He was hearing on the radio snippets of news about events back home, including the fact that Syria had been granted independence by France. He also heard about the mounting tension in Palestine between the Jewish and Palestinian populations and the emergence of American support for the establishment of a Jewish state in Palestine. But Qawuqji was stuck in Berlin under Russian surveillance, with few resources and no travel documents. He was also hit by another personal tragedy in this period. His baby son, Nizar, and his brother Yumni both died of the diphtheria epidemic that swept through Berlin in the summer and winter of 1946. He buried them in the Muslim cemetery at Columbiadamm, alongside the grave of his older son, Majdi.

In the late summer of 1946 he wrote to his friends 'Adil and Nabih al-'Azma in Damascus. In the letter he laid out the desperate situation that he was in and appealed to them for help on the basis of his long record of struggle for the goals of Arab nationalism. In particular he needed their assistance in his efforts to get passports for himself, his wife, and Safi. He asked them to contact the Syrian Legation in Paris for help in obtaining passports to travel to France. Qawuqji had acquaintances at the legation in Paris, and he thought that Paris would be his best route home to Tripoli. British documents reveal that in late 1946 Qawuqji also sent a message to the British military government in Berlin stating that his difficult circumstances had driven him to seek a reconciliation with the British and to ask for their help in escaping Russian-occupied Germany. The message was delivered by an Egyptian friend who had a contact in the political section of the British military government. The flurry of correspondence prompted by Qawuqji's request shows that British officials turned him down because they did not want him to return to the Middle East, citing "the possible repercussions that his return might have on the security situation in Palestine." British officials also worried that he might in fact be a Russian spy.

Eventually the passports to France were obtained, not through the 'Azma brothers (despite their efforts on Qawuqji's behalf) but through a contact who was working at the French military administration in Berlin. Qawuqji scared his Russian guards away from his home by pretending to fall ill with diphtheria and calling repeatedly for a doctor. Qawuqji, Anneliese, and Safi crossed from the Russian zone of Berlin over into the American zone on February 8, 1947. In the American zone they went to the house of a Lebanese friend, who helped them get to the railway station in Berlin and to board the train for Paris. On the train they sat with some Moroccan soldiers who had served in the French Army. It was the first time that Qawuqji had talked Arabic in public for many months.

When they reached Paris, they went straight to the Syrian Legation. Here is how Qawuqji describes his feelings upon arriving there:

> For the first time in many years I found myself enjoying the protection of an Arab flag, in an Arab government office, and all in the French capital. As I shook hands with Mr. Shakir al-ʿAs, the chargé d'affaires of the legation, a feeling of the happiest relaxation and relief and tranquillity came over me. It seemed to me as if I were shaking hands with every Arab in the world. After a while one of the officers of the legation accompanied us to the Hôtel Prince de Galles on the Champs-Élysées, where he was able to obtain a room for us.

After his arrival in Paris Qawuqji telegrammed many of his friends in the Middle East, including the ʿAzma brothers, telling them that he had come safely to Paris and was preparing for his return home to Tripoli.

5

■

PALESTINE 1948

Two narrow escapes—Conference at Aley—Struggle for
Jaysh al-Inqadh—War preparations—Crossing the Jordan—
Telegrams—Into Palestine—The battle for Mishmar
Haemek—Jaffa falls—Fighting for the north—Soldiers and
politicians

On February 9 and 10, 1998, the Lebanese newspaper *Al-Hayat* ran a
two-part feature on Fawzi al-Qawuqji. Written by the Lebanese journalist Jan Daya, the articles were occasioned by the release of British
government documents that had just been declassified under the fifty-
year declassification rules—fifty years rather than thirty because, as Daya
points out, the material contained in these documents was considered
particularly sensitive and secret. The documents refer to the events surrounding Qawuqji's return to Tripoli in March 1947, following his
escape from Russian-occupied Germany to Paris. After recovering in Paris
for several weeks, Qawuqji flew home to Lebanon via Cairo and arrived
in Tripoli on March 5 to a hero's welcome. Daya's article focuses on two
aspects of this return: the unexpected diversion of Qawuqji's plane to
Lod [Lydda] Airport in Mandate Palestine and the fact that the hero's
welcome in Tripoli quickly turned into a gun battle between supporters
of two prominent Tripolitan families, the Muqaddams and the Karamis.
Hence the titles of the two *Al-Hayat* articles: "Why Didn't the Mandate

Government Capture Him at Lod Airport?" and "Tripoli Receives Its Returning Son in a Family Bloodbath." Daya begins the piece by taking us back to the 1973 Arab-Israeli War, when he was a young journalist working in Beirut and looking for a subject for a feature that would be relevant to the conflict. On a whim he decided that it would be a good idea to interview one of the many aging Arab nationalist army officers then living in Beirut, to find out what he thought of the war and whether he had any strategic advice on what the Syrian and Egyptian armies should do. This all happened during the first few days of the war, when an Arab victory seemed possible.

Daya decided to interview Qawuqji, whom he had not met before. On his way to see Qawuqji, Daya was aware of having a preconceived image of him—based, he said, on stereotypes of this older generation of retired army officers—as a typical military adventurer who loved money and women and lived in a big villa and had servants and a new young wife. But when he arrived, he found Qawuqji living in a simple apartment, in a middle-class neighborhood of Beirut, and still married to his German wife, whom he had met when he was in the hospital in Berlin in 1941. Daya and Qawuqji sat and chatted for a while about the war, but Qawuqji did not seem to want to talk for long and really had only one important thing to say, that Egypt and Syria had to stay on the offensive and keep up the attack week after week, and that if they did this, they would have a chance of winning because Israel could not survive a prolonged Arab offensive. But if they stopped and then accepted a temporary cease-fire, the balance would tip in favor of the Israel Defense Forces. Daya left the apartment and returned to the office to write his article. A couple of days later the Egyptians suddenly stopped their offensive, and the war took a definitive turn in Israel's favor.

Having given us this introduction to his encounter with Qawuqji, Daya then changed the setting, from the small apartment in West Beirut to Kew Gardens in London, home to ornate Victorian greenhouses and what was then the British Public Records Office. From the documents housed there Daya told the story of Qawuqji's journey from Paris to Cairo in late February 1947. The British memos and letters are full of surprise and outrage over the fact that the plane that carried Qawuqji landed briefly at the small airstrip at Lod. Lod was in British-controlled Palestine, and Qawuqji had long been wanted by the British for his roles in both the 1936 rebellion in Palestine and the Rashid 'Ali al-Kaylani uprising in Iraq in 1941. According to the British documents, Qawuqji's brief footfall on British-controlled soil had been a rare chance to arrest him but one that had been missed.

TWO NARROW ESCAPES

The prospect of return to the Middle East after seven years in exile was momentous for Qawuqji. He was returning home to Tripoli and would see friends and family again and would have the opportunity to introduce them to his new German wife. He was also eager to play a role in the newly independent states of Syria and Lebanon and in the increasingly heated confrontation with the Jewish community in Palestine. Qawuqji gave several press conferences while he was in Paris; but the first interview that he gave was to an *Al-Hayat* reporter, and it was published on the front page of the newspaper. The journalist asked about his future plans, and Qawuqji replied as follows:

> It is extremely difficult for me to answer your question, but perhaps you will find the answer in my past. I have been a military man since my childhood. I don't understand anything about politics, and I don't want to understand anything about it. And those periods of my life that for one reason or another have been empty of soldiering have been the most barren. Now I am dedicating myself to the struggle to free the Arab lands from the yoke of foreigners. So I am a hostage to Arab events and interests, and when the struggle calls me to whichever area I am needed, I am ready to follow that call.

The plane took off on the morning of February 22 from a small airstrip outside Paris. Apart from the pilot and one stewardess it carried

Qawuqji, his wife, Anneliese, his aide, Hamid al-Safi, and five men who were members of the Jewish Agency, the central organization representing the Jewish community in Palestine. One of these men, David Horowitz, directed the Economics Department of the Jewish Agency. Horowitz was returning to Jerusalem after a meeting in London. It was snowing that morning in Paris; but as the plane flew south toward the Mediterranean, the weather cleared, and Qawuqji was able to look out the window and see the sea shining in the sunlight. Horowitz and the other Jewish Agency officials believed that the plane was taking them directly to Lod but were informed in midflight that the pilot had been ordered by the company to fly instead to Cairo first. They would have to spend the night in Cairo and fly to Lod the next day. Furious that this would cause him to miss a Jewish Agency meeting in Tel Aviv, Horowitz complained privately to the pilot and asked him to stop briefly in Lod before flying on to Cairo. When Qawuqji, who had assumed that the plane was flying directly from Paris to Cairo (where he would travel on to Lebanon), found out that they were to land in Lod, he was terrified. After surviving the Russian invasion of Berlin and his escape from Germany, he couldn't believe that he might suddenly find himself taken from the airplane to a British prison. He said nothing of these feelings to his young wife as the plane made its descent into Lod, telling her that there would just be a short delay to their arrival in Cairo. Hamid al-Safi, on the other hand, knew exactly the danger they were in. When the plane landed, Horowitz and the four other Jewish Agency executives, much relieved not to have to spend the night in Cairo, left the plane. A Palestinian working for the British army at the airport boarded the plane and approached Safi, who was sitting separately from Qawuqji and his wife. He spoke to Safi in Arabic. He said that the list of passengers that he had been given included the name Fawzi al-Qawuqji, and he asked if he was on the plane. Safi replied that he had never heard of him. Because Qawuqji had such a fair complexion and because he was sitting with a German woman, the Palestinian assumed that they were not connected to the name Fawzi al-Qawuqji. He did not even question them. A few moments later another man came onto the plane and asked the pilot if there were any other passengers on the plane; the pilot said that there were not. In his memoirs Qawuqji describes his thoughts at that moment: "I imagined that telephones were all busy communicating news to the authorities that we were in Lydda. I imagined that instructions had been issued and that these instructions were already on their way demanding my arrest. I stood at the door of the aircraft and lit a cigarette and began to try and think of a way out of this fix."

After an hour or so of refueling, the plane took off for the short flight to Cairo. Qawuqji did not feel relief until the plane started to descend and he saw the lights of Cairo below him.

In the following weeks the British press made much of the fact that Qawuqji had landed on British-controlled soil without being arrested. Newspapers such as *The Times* (London) accused the British government of incompetence in allowing Qawuqji to escape. Questions about the issue were also asked in the House of Commons. On February 27, Alan Cunningham, the British high commissioner in Palestine, sent a memo to the secretary of the colonies concerning the negative coverage. The memo does indeed reveal almost comic incompetence on the part of the British officials at the airport. Apparently Qawuqji and his wife were traveling with Syrian passports under the names Mr. and Mde. Kaouski Fouazzi. According to Cunningham, Qawuqji was on a special list for immediate arrest upon entering Palestine, but "owing to the disguised name, and in the absence of warning of his departure from Paris, he most regrettably escaped the vigilance of the frontier control personnel at the airport."

David Horowitz describes the aftermath of the plane journey in his memoirs. He had followed the press coverage about Qawuqji with some amusement:

> The British press went on for days conjecturing why the plane, ordered to Cairo, had gone instead to Lydda and not only precipitated a major scandal, but blemished the name of the Palestine Government. The newspapers tried to ferret out some highly mysterious and significant motive, and some of them advanced the most far-fetched theories. No one, of course, could stumble on the plain, unvarnished truth of the

matter; and even if it had been told at the time, few would have believed it, that in persuading the pilot to fly to Lydda, I had no idea that Fawzi Kaukji was aboard. The British authorities would no doubt have puzzled for days over why the Jews first contrived that Kaukji be brought to Lydda and then took no steps to get him arrested.

British documents show that the Egyptian government was itself op-posed to allowing Qawuqji to enter Egypt. When he landed at the Cairo airfield, the border guard refused him entry. The guard showed him a document from the Egyptian Foreign Ministry stating that under no cir-cumstances was Fawzi al-Qawuqji to be allowed to enter Egypt. Qawuqji immediately telephoned 'Azzam Pasha, the head of the Arab League, whom he knew personally. He also called Halim 'Izz al-Din, who was the head of the Lebanese Legation in Cairo and whom Qawuqji knew from when he had lived in Baghdad. Through the efforts of 'Azzam Pasha and 'Izz al-Din, the Egyptian government agreed reluctantly to let Qawuqji in on a twenty-four-hour visa.

Qawuqji's small entourage, exhausted from the stresses of the jour-ney, were taken by 'Izz al-Din to the comfort of the grand Continental Hotel in downtown Cairo (figure 31). They stayed there for about ten days, at the expense of the Lebanese government.

It was not difficult for Qawuqji to extend his stay at the Continental Hotel beyond the twenty-four hours his visa allowed. Once he was in Egypt, it was hard for the government to force him to leave. His seven years away from the Arab world and his dramatic return made a good story for the Egyptian press. On February 24, *Al-Ahram* carried a long front-page story about his arrival in Cairo, including an interview with him. The article listed all the revolts that Qawuqji had fought in and then described his wounding at Palmyra and his exile in Germany. In the interview he was asked what the worst hour of his life had been. He answered that the worst hour of his life was actually half an hour, and it was at Lod Airport right after his plane to Cairo landed there unexpect-edly. Qawuqji was also asked about his future plans. He replied that after taking some time to rest and visit with friends and to find out what

FIGURE 31

had changed in the Arab world since he had left seven years before, he would be ready to undertake any duty that was required of him. The implication that he expected a role in the impending war with the Jewish community in Palestine was clear. Just a few days previously Britain had announced that it would be withdrawing from Palestine and that it was handing over to the United Nations the question of how Palestine would be governed. Qawuqji was cast in the Egyptian press as a returning Arab nationalist hero who would play an important role in rescuing Palestine from becoming a Jewish state.

According to Qawuqji, the halls of the Continental Hotel were filled with visitors who came to congratulate him on his safe arrival in Egypt. Qawuqji's nemesis in Berlin, the Mufti of Jerusalem, Hajj Amin al-Husayni, was also in Cairo, trying to get support from the Arab League and the Egyptian government. Also, according to Qawuqji, the two men met twice during the ten days that Qawuqji was in Cairo, both times at Qawuqji's instigation. He describes how he offered to do anything he could to advance the struggle for Palestine, including being ready to fight. But the Mufti politely rebuffed him at both meetings. The only sources that we have on these meetings comes from Qawuqji's memoirs and British reports on his activities in Cairo. The Mufti does not mention them in his memoirs. Given the accusations the Mufti had leveled at him in Berlin, it seems odd that Qawuqji would have swallowed his injured pride by visiting him in Cairo. It is possible that Qawuqji had only heard about the Mufti's denunciation but had not actually read the text that Badri Qadah had written. (Qawuqji certainly read it a year later, in early 1948, when the Mufti circulated the text in the Middle East.) Maybe Qawuqji wanted to show that there were no ill feelings on his side and that he was ready to cooperate with the most important Palestinian leader during the run-up to war. It is hard to know. But in Qawuqji's memoirs his description of the way in which he was snubbed at these two meetings is part of a consistently negative portrayal of the Mufti's behavior toward him.

One of the reasons that the Egyptian government tolerated Qawuqji's presence in Cairo was that it was clear that he was in transit and intended to travel on to Lebanon once he was able to make the necessary arrangements. Again, British documents from the time show that Britain was putting pressure on Lebanon not to allow Qawuqji's return. The Lebanese government told the British through private channels that it was also concerned, but as one Lebanese official put it, "he was a Lebanese citizen; the government could not refuse him permission to return." Qawuqji's arrival in Lebanon came at a particularly sensitive time in Lebanese politics, just two months before the first national elections since Lebanon achieved official independence from the French. In Tripoli in particular, the election campaign was playing out as a competition for power between the Karamis and the Muqaddams. The previous few years had seen a series of violent confrontations between these two leading families. In the most recent of these a member of the Muqaddam family had tried to assassinate 'Abd al-Hamid Karami in the mid-1940s just before he became prime minister of Lebanon. The fact that Qawuqji had been away for seven years increased his status as an Arab nationalist hero. Supporting his return to his birthplace was a

way for both families to establish their Arab nationalist and anticolonial credentials.

Qawuqji flew from Cairo to Beirut on March 2. Interestingly, he was
on the same flight as Antun Saʿada, the well-known Lebanese intellectual and advocate of Syrianism. Like Qawuqji, Saʿada was returning to
Lebanon after many years in exile in Argentina. At the airport Qawuqji
was met by ʿAbd al-Hamid Karami and Saʿdi Munla, who was also from
a prominent Tripolitan family. The fact that Karami received Qawuqji
in Beirut was a clear indication that the Karami family hoped to use
Qawuqji's symbolic prominence as an Arab nationalist hero in their election campaign in Tripoli. Qawuqji stayed in Beirut for just two days, and
then, on March 4, he set off for Tripoli, in spite of the concerns of the
foreign minister, Henry Pharoun, that his visit might exacerbate an already
unstable situation in Tripoli between the Karamis and the Muqaddams.
When the small party left Beirut on the morning of March 4, it traveled
in a convoy for the three-hour drive to Tripoli. By the time it reached the
small coastal town of Qalamun, just four miles south of Tripoli, the
convoy had grown so large that Qawuqji could not see all the way to its
rear. People came from Qalamun itself and from Tripoli, as well as from
Homs and Hama, now located in the newly independent state of Syria.
When he finally reached Tripoli, Qawuqji was advised to get out of
the car and have coffee with representatives of both the Karamis and the
Muqaddams. This was to show that he was not favoring either side. He
describes in his memoirs what happened next:

> As soon as I descended from my car, I was carried against my will on
> the shoulders of the crowd. The shouts of the crowd were drowned out
> by the whizzing of bullets [fired in celebration], thumping in my ears.
> The visit concluded peacefully after much trouble. Then people from
> Hama and Homs joined the crowd, and I and my guard were carried
> on a human wave until we reached al-Taal Square in the middle of the
> city. The procession stopped, but the shooting continued without a
> break, and it seemed to me that the firing became more violent. No one
> was hurt in spite of the fact that people filled the streets and spectators

were crowded in the windows, on balconies, and on roofs. The distance to the house of Shaykh Fakhri al-Qawuqji [a relative], where it had been decided that I should stay, was just a short distance away. At that moment one group wanted to lead the procession, taking over from the group that had led it until that moment, and what happened then is something I will never forget in all my life. It had a terrible and painful impact on me when rifles and machine guns suddenly changed their targets, moving from vertical positions to horizontal ones. Bodies fell; blood flowed in the public square and the coffeehouses. It was like being on the battlefield.

The only way that the Lebanese government managed to calm the situation in Tripoli was by forcing Qawuqji to leave and to go into hiding in the nearby village of Qarnail. Sixteen people were killed and over seventy wounded that day in al-Taal Square. Qawuqji had not been the cause of the violence. But the excitement around his return to Tripoli and the fact that it brought Karamis and Muqaddams into direct conflict because both families wanted to claim Qawuqji as their ally had ignited an already volatile situation.

When Qawuqji left Syria for Berlin in the summer of 1941, he had already achieved a degree of fame from his fighting in Palestine in 1936. But he had not enjoyed anything like the kind of popularity that he witnessed on his return to Tripoli in March 1947. What explains this change? Unlike the many leading Arab nationalists, who came from elite landowning families, Qawuqji always possessed the ability to connect directly with common people, whom the elites claimed to speak in the name of but who in fact often represented a threat to their social and economic status. The fact that Qawuqji was able to convince the tribes outside Hama to revolt against the French in 1925 and the tribes in Iraq to revolt against the British in 1941 is a testament to this quality. Because of his record of sustained military action against colonialism from 1925 to 1927 in Syria, in 1941 in Iraq, and, most important, in 1936 in Palestine, Qawuqji commanded real respect from ordinary people and was able to tap into, although not always control, the "crowd" so feared by most elites. In 1940, however, Qawuqji's arrival in Tripoli would not have brought so many people out. In March 1947 many who could not make it to Tripoli (or who stayed away because of rumors that there might be trouble) sent him telegrams of welcome, which he kept in his private archive. These telegrams came mainly from men he had known during the days of the Syrian Revolt. The bulk of the telegrams were sent from Jabal Druze, Damascus, Ladhikiyya, Aleppo, and, of course, Hama. Sa'id al-Tarmanini, who had been his main collaborator in the Hama revolt and who was in 1947 the head of the municipal council in Hama, wrote "to the great mujahid Fazwi al-Qawuqji. In memory of the days of your heroism, I am so grateful that you have returned safely, and I am honored to invite you to visit us."

One reason for all this attention was his rather lengthy return from Europe to Tripoli. Qawuqji's stay in Paris and in Cairo and the drama of the flight between them had generated articles in the Lebanese and Egyptian press about the return of the great anticolonial fighter. In Lebanon people were also beginning to tire of the politicians who had managed the transition of power from French to Lebanese rule. Qawuqji had been in exile and was not implicated in any of the failed policies and compromises associated with the independence movement. He represented a period that was already being romanticized by many ordinary people as an era of heroic struggle against colonialism. Qawuqji's reputation was based on his prowess as a soldier and man of action rather than as a member of the political elite. The local politics of Tripoli at the time and the intensity of the election campaign also meant that young men were already mobilized. His return was a catalyst for action by the supporters of the two rival families, despite the fact that Qawuqji had very little to do with the dispute between the two families.

When Qawuqji reflected on the events in Tripoli, the power that the crowd represented was not lost on him. He started to think about what he called the enthusiasm of the masses and how it could be deployed in support of Palestine. Qawuqji's apparent ability to draw ordinary people out onto the streets was to have important ramifications over the next two years. His popularity meant that political leaders had to take him seriously as a soldier who could recruit troops and command support. But it was also exactly this capacity that made politicians wary of him. So a pattern began to emerge whereby politicians would support him in public but withhold real resources from him in private, out of fear that those resources might eventually be turned against them. This tension was the driving factor in the unfolding tragedy of the 1948 War.

CONFERENCE AT ALEY

Qawuqji spent the summer of 1947 in Damascus receiving delegations from various parts of the country. His old friend Munir al-Rayyis let him use the offices of the Arab Club for these meetings. Qawuqji lived with his wife for part of the summer in rooms in the Orient Palace Hotel, just steps from Marja Square, from which he had fled the British occupation of Damascus in October 1918. After leaving the Orient Palace Hotel, he stayed in a villa supplied to him at no cost by Ahmad Sharabati, the Syrian minister of defense. A member of the American Legation in Damascus, called only Mr. Meminger in the archives, went to see Qawuqji in this villa in the fall of 1947. The two men had a long conversation, which was then reported to the British Legation in Damascus. From there the information was passed on to the British Foreign Office in London. According to Meminger, Qawuqji was being paid a monthly stipend of a thousand Syrian liras. Qawuqji's villa was replete with offices and clerks helping him to lay the ground for what he called a people's army to fight in Palestine. Qawuqji was dismissive of the ability of the Arab armies to fight effectively in Palestine, and according to Meminger, he described the Mufti as "a danger to everyone and universally disliked." An official from the British Legation attached a handwritten note to the report about Meminger's conversation with Qawuqji: "This shows that Fawzi Qawuqji is completely at odds with the Mufti and therefore suggests the possibility of two independent and mutually antipathetic Arab guerilla gangs in Palestine when the situation deteriorates." This comment proved to be a prescient evaluation of what was to come.

Soon after he arrived in Damascus, Qawuqji also met with Shukri al-Quwatli, the president of Syria. He offered Quwatli his services in the struggle for Palestine. However, it was not until late September, when Britain declared that it would be withdrawing from Palestine within a few months, that Qawuqji became deeply involved in discussions among the leaders of the Arab states about how to handle the impending Palestine crisis. He was invited to the meeting of the Arab League in early October 1947 in Aley, a picturesque resort town in the mountains just a few miles north of Beirut (figure 32).

Britain's announcement of its impending withdrawal from Palestine gave a sense of urgency to the meeting. Both Quwatli and Salih Jabr (prime minister of Iraq) were present, and their agendas dominated the discussion. King 'Abdullah of Jordan did not attend but tried to exert his influence through the Iraqi delegation; he preferred to keep his distance from any joint plans for military cooperation among the Arab states in Palestine because he had ambitions of his own in Palestine. The Palestinians were noticeably absent from the guest list for the Aley meeting. The Mufti in particular was not invited.

One important outcome of the meeting was the submission of a long report on the situation in Palestine by a special military committee

FIGURE 32

established by the Arab League. The Iraqi assistant chief of staff, Gen. Isma'il Safwat, led this committee. The famous Palestinian historian 'Arif al-'Arif visited Safwat in Baghdad after the 1948 War while doing research for *Al-Nakba*, his multivolume history of 1948. During their meeting Safwat showed 'Arif the full text of the report that had been presented in October 1947 at the Aley meeting. The report laid out in detail the grave danger faced by the Palestinians in light of Britain's impending withdrawal. It included an analysis of Zionist institutions, stating that the Jewish Agency in Palestine was ready to field at least twenty thousand well-trained and well-armed troops, with many more in reserve. In addition, the Zionists had well-developed lines of communications and were recruiting volunteers and receiving other forms of financial and logistical support from Europe and America. The report stated that the Palestinians had nothing comparable to this level of preparation and it concluded with a number of recommendations, including the deployment of the Arab state armies (such as they were) on the borders of Mandate Palestine. It recommended the immediate dispatch of ten thousand rifles and other weapons and ammunition to the Palestinians and an allocation of one million dollars to the Military Committee so that it could buy more arms. The report also recommended the immediate recruitment and arming of volunteers from all over the Arab world.

Qawuqji had no official status at the meeting, but he was nevertheless consulted as the discussions unfolded. He was also present at many of the late-afternoon meals where the delegates gathered. In the wake of Safwat's report, informal discussions took place at Aley concerning the establishment of a trans-Arab volunteer army that would be run by the Arab League's special Military Committee. Qawuqji's name was one of those circulated as the possible field commander of such an army. In his memoirs Qawuqji recounts how during the first days of the Aley conference he was lunching with 'Azzam Pasha, the director general of the Arab League, when 'Azzam Pasha was called away to the telephone. When he came back to the lunch, he told Qawuqji that Riyad al-Sulh, the prime minister of Lebanon, had telephoned to warn him that the

Mufti had shown up in Beirut and was clearly intending to drive to Aley and attend the conference.

According to Qawuqji, as soon as the Mufti arrived at the conference, he voiced his strong opposition to Qawuqji's playing any role in the volunteer army. The Mufti was suspicious of Arab intentions in Palestine, and he feared Qawuqji's selection as leader of a joint Arab force. The Mufti tried to persuade the delegates that if anyone should be the leader of such an army, it should be he. But the Military Committee under the leadership of Isma'il Safwat felt strongly that Qawuqji's military experience made him much more suitable for the job. Like Qawuqji, Safwat had been trained in the Ottoman Army and had also served in the Iraqi Army. In Safwat's view, it was ridiculous to consider appointing someone like the Mufti, who did not have the same kind of military experience, to a position of control over a military force. Salih Jabr supported Safwat in this assessment and refused to even meet with the Mufti to hear his case. From the Mufti's point of view, it seemed he was being shut out of Arab plans for Palestine. He felt that the Arab leaders, Salih Jabr and Shukri al-Quwatli in particular, were reneging on previous agreements to let the Palestinians lead the fight for their own country and to limit Arab involvement simply to the supply of arms and money.

Qawuqji was not officially appointed commander in chief of Jaysh al-Inqadh (Arab Liberation Army) until December 6, 1947. His account of the weeks that lay between the October meeting at Aley and his new position are dominated by his descriptions of the Mufti's machinations. Other sources, most notably the diaries of 'Izzat Darwaza and Taha al-Hashimi, confirm that the Mufti continued to work against Qawuqji. Darwaza had worked with Qawuqji during the Palestine Revolt in the late summer and fall of 1936. He and Qawuqji had also met in Basra in late 1936, during the Arab Higher Committee's tour of Iraq. Darwaza had always been concerned about the Mufti's autocratic style of leadership, but he also cooperated with him for the sake of Palestinian unity. Darwaza had left Palestine for Damascus in 1937 because of his involvement in the Palestine Revolt, and he came to be actively involved in the debates in Damascus in 1947 about the defense of Palestine.

Taha al-Hashimi also moved in those circles that debated how best to defend Palestine. He knew Qawuqji from Iraq and, like Qawuqji, had been trained in the Ottoman military system and had fought in World War I. He had done well in the army in Iraq after that war and had served briefly as minister of defense in the late 1930s and even very briefly as prime minister of Iraq in 1941. He served on the Military Committee of the Arab League, and was appointed inspector-general of Jaysh al-Inqadh toward the end of 1947. Both Darwaza and Hashimi wrote detailed memoirs of their careers, which include many pages on the months leading up to the 1948 War. These memoirs, in addition to Qawuqji's own memoirs and documents from his personal archive, offer a glimpse into the world of those desperately trying to grapple with the looming crisis in Palestine in late 1947. Historians have written at length about the divisions between the Arab leaders over Palestine in this period, detailing the mutual suspicions about the intentions of the Iraqis, the Syrians, and the Jordanians in particular. Qawuqji's conflict with the Mufti has hitherto been treated in the context of these suspicions. Was Qawuqji working with King 'Abdullah of Jordan in order to realize 'Abdullah's dream of a Greater Syria in Jordan, Syria, and Palestine? Was he working with Shukri al-Quwatli in order to ensure Syria's dominance in Palestine? These are the kinds of historical questions that have been posed by historians writing about the Arab side in the 1948 War. Because of the Arab defeat in 1948, the scholarly histories and in many cases the memoirs written by the Arab participants all seek to explain the defeat by pointing to the divisions among the Arab states. But this preoccupation with simple divisions does not do justice to the complexity of what was unfolding on the Arab side in the months leading up to the war.

On September 26, 1947, the British declared that they would complete their withdrawal from Palestine by May 14, 1948. The United Nations passed the Partition Resolution just two months later, on November 29, 1947. The resolution gave half of British Mandate Palestine to the European Jewish community in Palestine to establish a permanent Jewish state there. In the map (figure 33), the darker area is the proposed

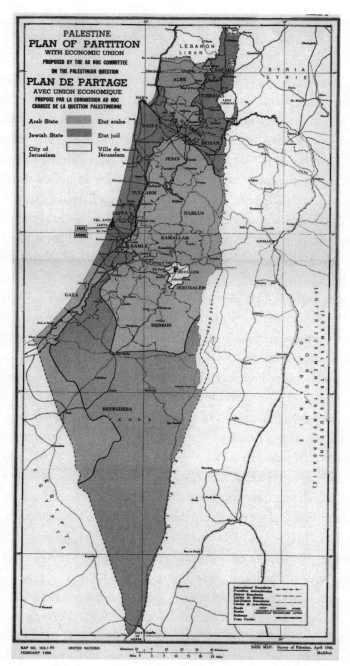

FIGURE 33

territory of the Jewish state. The lighter area is the proposed territory of the Arab state. Jerusalem, in white in the middle, was designated as an international zone.

In spite of the fact that the British would not withdraw their last troops from Palestine until May 14, 1948, fighting broke out between Jews and Palestinians in the days following the issuing of the Partition Resolution. The fighting between December and May 14 marked the first stage of the 1948 War, during which Jews and Palestinians tried to gain as much territory for themselves as they could before the British withdrawal. This phase of the 1948 War is often described as the Civil War. For the Jewish side this was a particularly crucial stage of the war because it knew that once the British withdrew on May 14, it would face an invasion of the armies of the surrounding Arab states. Many Palestinian cities and villages fell to the Haganah (the Jewish army) between December and May 14; they included Haifa, Safad, Baysan, Jaffa, and Acre. The British army maintained a posture of neutrality.

With the passing of the Partition Resolution on November 29, 1947, the leaders of the newly independent Arab states faced a shocking reality. Whereas the end of French and British colonial rule in Syria, Lebanon, Jordan, Iraq, and Egypt had brought full independence, the end of British rule in Palestine would result in the permanent establishment of a European Jewish state in half of the territory. The Arab leaders had not expected the Partition Resolution to pass. In addition, they had just a few weeks to forge a coherent and effective response. Apart from the Arab League, which was only two years old, the Arab states had no joint institutions or history of working together that could provide the foundation to face this crisis. In most cases, their own states were so new that there was also very little state infrastructure to draw upon. With the exception of the British-trained and -commanded Arab Legion in Jordan, their armies were weak and poorly supplied. The accounts of the many meetings that took place in this period show Arab leaders trying to decide how to cope with the impending British withdrawal. Some thought the Arabs could fight and defeat the Jewish forces. Others felt that the Zionists were much better organized and better equipped than the

Arabs and that a fight without the time to prepare properly would bring disaster. Some Palestinians (in particular the Mufti and his circle) did not want the Arab armies to enter Palestine for fear that they would grab territory for themselves and would not support a Palestinian government in Palestine. The overall picture that emerges from the Arabic sources is not one of divisions between groups or policies that were so clearly defined that they alone are sufficient to explain the absence of a coordinated, tightly packaged response. Instead, the picture is diffuse, full of contradictions and shifting patterns. The overarching theme is that of time pressing down. The Arabs found themselves having to respond to a calendar not set by them but made in London and New York. In addition, the Jewish Agency and other Zionist institutions had been preparing for this moment for over thirty years. The fact that 1947 came only two years after the liberation of the Nazi death camps in Europe made the need for a Jewish state appear all the more urgent.

The dispute over who should lead Jaysh al-Inqadh is an important part of the story of the 1948 War, but the Israeli victory in the war so traumatized the Arab side that later accounts of the problems between Qawuqji and the Mufti are colored by the tendency to offer up a simple story of the rivalry between the two men as the main explanation for Arab failure to defeat the Israelis. What follows is an attempt to try to convey the complexity and detail of what happened between them, while at the same time not downplaying the negative political and military effects of their relationship. By this is meant, in particular, the negative effects for the Palestinians, who suffered most because of the Arab defeat.

STRUGGLE FOR JAYSH AL-INQADH

In Qawuqji's boxes there are three pieces of paper stapled together. There is no date, and the title is simply "The Mufti." They are Qawuqji's thoughts—probably written down years after his retirement—about the kind of man the Mufti was:

He is a coward. He never fought on the battlefield of any country. He lays claim to leadership whenever he feels that his life is threatened; then he steals the money and retreats in defeat. He is an ignorant man. He is not a graduate of either a religious school or a secular one. He claims absolute knowledge and authority. He restricts all work in all fields to his person only, and he exerts every effort to destroy any name that starts to shine among the Arabs. He is a conceited man. He believes that each individual must be at his disposal, and if it happens that he disagrees with him, he accuses him of betrayal. His motto is: Either you agree with me or you will play the role of hypocrite and traitor. He is a devious man. Whenever he hears that an influential name has surfaced, he is gripped by a fit of rage and desperation, so he gives his orders to destroy him or assassinate him . . .

Qawuqji's anger toward the Mufti comes from the absolute breakdown in relations that occurred between them in the months preceding the fighting in Palestine. Darwaza gives a detailed account of the intense lobbying that the Mufti undertook in late 1947 to prevent Qawuqji's becoming field commander of Jaysh al-Inqadh. Qawuqji and Darwaza were not close friends, but they had met at key moments over the years. Darwaza describes Qawuqji as sharp and witty, ambitious, energetic, and full of revolutionary spirit. According to Darwaza, Qawuqji was "a charmer" who could get people to work with him. Darwaza tells how the Mufti began a campaign to slander Qawuqji in the fall of 1947. The Mufti spread rumors about Qawuqji's character, saying that his morals were questionable and that he was a drinker and a womanizer. He also said that Qawuqji had sold his services to the British and the French and that he would not hesitate to sell Palestine out to the Zionists. In addition, the Mufti circulated the Badri Qadah text that he had given to the German Foreign Ministry in 1943. This was the first time that this text, which accused Qawuqji of being a British spy, had been circulated in Syria. Darwaza met with the Mufti and asked him about his role in spreading the rumors about Qawuqji and disseminating the Badri

Qadah text. The Mufti denied being involved and claimed that the British or the Jewish Agency must have circulated the text to stir up trouble among the Arab leadership. Darwaza asked the Mufti to publish a statement in the newspapers denying any connection with the report. The denial was never published. Darwaza says in his memoirs that they "all knew that the report had been circulated by the Mufti." In addition to the report, there were rumors in Damascus that the Mufti was offering money to have Qawuqji assassinated. Darwaza asked the Mufti why he was so opposed to Qawuqji. The Mufti replied that he was fearful of what Qawuqji would do once he had beaten the Jewish forces with his volunteer force. The Mufti believed that in the wake of an Arab victory Qawuqji would become a dictator in Palestine and try to extend his rule to Jordan and even to Syria. Darwaza was generally skeptical about the Mufti's abilities to evaluate the situation in Palestine in the lead-up to the war and the threat that the Palestinians faced from Jewish forces.

Taha al-Hashimi's memoirs confirm Darwaza's account of the Mufti's actions during this period. Hashimi supported Qawuqji's candidacy for field commander of Jaysh al-Inqadh because Qawuqji was one of the only candidates upon whom the Syrians, the Jordanians, and the Iraqis could agree. In addition, Hashimi recognized the importance of Qawuqji's ability to command popular support and felt that he was the only person with experience of what Hashimi called guerrilla warfare (*harb al-'isaba*). Other candidates' names, including Isma'il Safwat, were floated. But Safwat was considered too accustomed to conventional warfare (*al-harb al-munazzama*). He had also made it clear that he did not want the job. Preparing a volunteer army and leading it into battle in just a few weeks were daunting tasks. Qawuqji was one of very few willing to take them on. The Mufti kept pushing various Palestinians on Hashimi as alternatives to Qawuqji, but Hashimi dismissed them as having insufficient military training. For Hashimi, who came from the great Arab capital of Baghdad and who been trained in the Ottoman Army, Palestine was a backwater. His memoirs portray the Mufti not as an equal player among the key decision makers but as a pest with an irritatingly persistent agenda. Hashimi's diary also includes details about meetings that took place between the Syrian president Shukri al-Quwatli and the Mufti, during which the Mufti tried to persuade Quwuqji that Qawuqji was not the right person to lead Jaysh al-Inqadh. One account in Hashimi's diary reveals a great deal about both the Mufti and Quwatli and their attitude toward Qawuqji's leadership:

November 8 1947: [Quwatli] told me that the Mufti had visited him in al-Zabadani and had brought up the topic of Fawzi al-Qawuqji. He had tried to persuade him that he was not fit to lead in Palestine. [Quwatli] tried to persuade the Mufti to change his opinion and look to other things and forget about this personal rancor, but to no avail, and the Mufti left. Then the Mufti asked to meet him again in Damascus. Quwatli was expecting the Mufti to open with an important topic concerning Palestine, but he returned to the question of Fawzi al-Qawuqji and how he hadn't graduated from a military school [as Qawuqji claimed] and that he wasn't really an officer. When Shukri [Quwatli] asked him who he thought should be leader, the Mufti replied 'Abd al-Qadir al-Husayni. Shukri replied that he also did not graduate from a military school, and he was also not an officer, in addition to the fact that he didn't have any experience. As for Fawzi, he had taken part in rebellions and was an expert in guerrilla warfare, and he had a reputation. People relied on him. He added that these were serious times, and this was no moment for these kinds of discussions . . . Shukri said to him that if Fawzi acted against our will and went to the Syrian border near Qunaytra, sent out a call to the Arabs, and a hundred Syrians came to his support, then undoubtedly a hundred Palestinians will also join him. Their number will then increase even more; they will enter Palestine and begin to work in spite of you and in spite of me. And if Fawzi announced that he was giving himself up to Palestine and that he wanted to sacrifice his life to save Palestine but Shukri al-Quwatli is forbidding him to go there, what do you think would be the effect of such an announcement on the people of Syria?

This account shows the anxiety that some Arab leaders felt about Qawuqji's ability to command popular support and about how he might channel that popular support for his own political objectives. Qawuqji's reputation for recklessness and his record of not being a team player exacerbated these anxieties. In addition, he had been in exile in Germany for seven years. He had not been involved in the transition from colonial rule to independence in Syria and Lebanon. The fact that his wife was a foreigner further alienated him. This made him a good choice as field commander of Jaysh al-Inqadh because he was not seen to be 'Abdullah's proxy or Quwatli's proxy. Qawuqji was a solution to the problem caused by the competing ambitions of Syria and Jordan. And he was a popular choice among ordinary people. The Mufti didn't like it, but he did not have enough political power to change the minds of men like Quwatli and Hashimi, who had great influence. The dispute over the leadership of Jaysh al-Inqadh also reflected the serious underestimation of the fight that lay ahead. With the exception of Safwat's report that was presented to the Arab League meeting at Aley, most of the contemporaneous sources from the fall and winter of 1947–1948 exude an air of confidence in an Arab victory. This confidence meant that many men—the Mufti is one of the starkest examples—were focused on what would happen *after* the Jewish forces were beaten.

The Mufti's circulation of the Badri Qadah text in Syria had a grave effect on Qawuqji. To be accused in writing of being a British spy and to know that many of his friends and family were reading this text were deeply offensive. Qawuqji had nearly been killed by the British at Palmyra in the summer of 1941. He had also spent most of his adult life fighting against both British and French colonialism. He sent a message to the Mufti through Shawki al-'Abbushi, a member of the Mufti's inner circle. In the message Qawuqji asked the Mufti to stop slandering him or he would start spreading rumors about all the money that the Mufti had managed to gather during the early 1940s in Germany and Italy. He also threatened to tell people that the Mufti had sought German and Italian support to install him as the new caliph of the Islamic world in the wake of an Axis victory in the Middle East. Darwaza describes Qawuqji's response to the Mufti's accusations:

> Of course Fawzi was very affected by it, and he started talking and telling stories [about the Mufti]. In addition, some of the [Palestinian] members of groups that opposed the Mufti, and especially from the Nablus group, began to visit Qawuqji. This added fuel to the Mufti's concerns and complaints, even though it was he who pushed Fawzi hard into this situation. I tried to keep the peace between them and keep things quiet, so that the situation didn't get worse and affect morale, lest our crisis [in Palestine] be the main loser.

WAR PREPARATIONS

By the beginning of December Quwatli, along with some members of the Military Committee, such as Taha al-Hashimi, Mahmud al-Hindi, and Subhi al-'Umari, were becoming anxious about the lack of movement on Palestine. They knew that the issue of who would command Jaysh al-Inqadh needed to be resolved. The controversy over the appointment was paralyzing efforts to move forward. On December 6 the committee met (Safwat, Hashimi, Hindi, and 'Umari were present), and it decided once and for all to appoint Qawuqji field commander. Safwat and Hashimi went straight from the meeting to Qawuqji's house to tell him the news. At the same time that Qawuqji was appointed field commander of Jaysh al-Inqadh, young men in Palestine were organizing a volunteer army under the leadership of 'Abd al-Qadir al-Husayni, the Mufti's nephew.

The Military Committee met several times in Damascus in late December 1947 and early January 1948. Sometimes Qawuqji was present; other times he was not. In at least one meeting Quwatli asked Hashimi if they could meet without Qawuqji and without Qawuqji's friend and patron the minister of defense, Ahmad Sharabati. They were not invited because Quwatli wanted to be able to discuss his concerns about the pace of Qawuqji's attempts to recruit volunteers. There were still many challenges. The Mufti continued to agitate against Qawuqji in spite of the fact that his appointment was now official. In addition, the member states of the Arab League were not making good on their promises to send money, supplies, and men for the new army. In one high-level meeting on December 29, convened by Quwatli and attended by leading members of the Syrian government (the deputy prime minister Muhammad al-'Ayyash and the minister of finance Wahbi al-Hariri) in addition to Hashimi, Darwaza, Sharabati, Mu'in al-Madi, and Qawuqji himself, Hashimi angrily said that there had been four months of talk about Palestine by Arab politicians but still no real action. Syria did not have enough uniforms or supplies for the volunteers who were beginning to join up. Hashimi also emphasized the need for well-trained officers to lead untrained volunteers. He pointed out that this was not like 1936, when armed bands entered Palestine to fight in a popular uprising against the British. This was different. This was modern war. The Arab League's army needed training and sophisticated communications to face the post–World War II British army and the Haganah. This training and organization needed time.

Many Arab politicians had secretly believed that the British would not abandon Palestine and that it would not come to their having to fight against the Zionists for control of Arab and Muslim land. But the date of the British withdrawal (May 14, 1948) had been firmly set, and some British units had started to pull out of the Galilee as early as January 1948. As of December 6, Qawuqji had become responsible for recruiting and organizing a volunteer force that had to be ready to enter Palestine within a few weeks. This meant setting up recruitment stations and training centers. It meant procuring uniforms, arms, food, and money to pay the soldiers. It meant finding and appointing good experienced officers to train inexperienced volunteers. And all this had to be done in the face of a reluctant Arab League, a particularly rainy and cold winter, an outbreak of cholera in Damascus, and the active opposition of the de facto leader of the Palestinians.

In January and February 1948 Qawuqji ran the field command of

Jaysh al-Inqadh from two locations, his home in Damascus and the new training camp based just outside the small town of Qatana, a few miles north of Damascus. Qatana was chosen for the main training camp because it was out of the way but close to Damascus and the Lebanese border. It was also near barren desert hills, which were good for artillery training. During this time, Qawuqji received journalists in his home. On February 2, 1948, *Al-Ahram* published an interview with Qawuqji written up by the United Press correspondent in Damascus, Samir Souqi. Souqi describes the comings and goings at Qawuqji's home in some detail:

> This Arab leader, motivated by utmost resolve, has made of his home a military headquarters guarded by irregulars in American military uniform. Not an hour of the day passes without Bedouins, peasants, and young men in modern clothes turning up on his doorstep demanding to enlist as volunteers in the Arab Liberation Army. He also has headquarters in Qatana, where volunteers are undergoing military training, waiting to be sent to Palestine. He refused to let me visit the place, though, which no journalist has ever seen. In his house there is a special room entered only by trusted people: the room of his aide-de-camp, Mahmoud al-Rifaʻi, a graduate of the Potsdam Military Academy. While we were talking, I noticed that Taha al-Hashimi, who military experts say is one of the greatest military leaders in the Arab world, entered. Al-Qawuqji asked to be excused and took him to another room. I noticed that Hashimi was carrying several large maps of Palestine to review.

There was much enthusiasm about Jaysh al-Inqadh in the Arab press in January, February, and March 1948. This helped the recruitment efforts. Recruiting stations began operating in the major cities of the region, including Baghdad and Cairo. Some recruits also came from tribes in Jordan, Syria, and Iraq. A few even traveled from as far as Tunisia, Morocco, and the Nejd. A few local political figures arrived at Qatana with their supporters. Notable among these was Akram Hourani from Hama, who a few years later became a leading figure in establishing the

Ba'ath Party in Syria. Some officers from the Syrian Army left their positions and joined Jaysh al-Inqadh. In some areas recruitment was less successful. Qawuqji traveled to the Druze Mountain in December 1947 as part of a special effort to involve young Druze men in Jaysh al-Inqadh. Despite the efforts of the governor of the Druze Mountain, very few people came out to greet Qawuqji upon his arrival, and schoolchildren and government officials had to be dragged out to form a suitable reception committee. With typical disdain a British intelligence officer stated: "Qawuqji is reported unsatisfied with the support so far received and appears discouraged. His recruiting trip to Jabal Druze is reported a failure . . . The military attaché comments: Jihad needs a shot in the arm to develop beyond the status of unorganized gang warfare."

Qawuqji also made serious attempts to recruit in Palestine despite the Mufti's opposition to his leadership. In Qawuqji's private papers there is a general recruitment letter dated February 17, 1948, signed by the general leadership of recruitment in Palestine and copied to the military committee in Damascus and to Qawuqji himself. The letter was intended to help local recruiters convince Palestinians that Jaysh al-Inqadh was legitimate:

> The general staff for recruiting will be honored by any person who peruses this letter, in the hope that it will support the recruiting officer in his task of registering the armed forces for the general staff in the region and to follow the necessary procedures to form an independent Palestinian detachment under the command of the field commander of Jaysh al-Inqadh, Fawzi al-Qawuqji. The Military Committee of the Arab League, which has been entrusted to organize the military action that will take place in Palestine, legalized these procedures.

Twenty-five years later, when Qawuqji was sorting through his papers, he picked this letter out and scribbled a comment on a note card that he attached to the document: "Trying to form a leadership and Palestinian force that would be connected with us." The loss of Palestine in 1948 haunted Qawuqji's engagement with his own archive.

The number of recruits was never huge. It is difficult to be precise about numbers because the sources contradict one another; but there were no more than four thousand recruits, and most of these were Syrians and Iraqis. Many left Qatana soon after they arrived because they were not paid or because supplies were meager. Those who stayed often complained about poor training, mainly because of the lack of qualified officers. This was a problem that plagued Jaysh al-Inqadh throughout the war. There were never more than four or five officers in each battalion, and many of the ordinary troops had never fought before. Some battalions, although officially part of Jaysh al-Inqadh, conducted many of their operations independently from Qawuqji's field command. This was certainly the case with the famous Syrian officer Adib Shishakli's battalion. Shishakli, who later became president of Syria, entered the Galilee in January 1948 and set up base there, only in very loose coordination with Qawuqji.

Some historians have described Jaysh al-Inqadh along rigid lines of command and with a clear distribution of battalions. Then they have narrated its fate from the viewpoint of this structure. But this does not do justice to the historical reality and complexity of what actually unfolded. The creation of a new army in a few weeks was an achievement. By March 1948 it had battalions, officers, and ordinary ranks in uniform, some supplies, and rudimentary communications units, including wireless operators. It also had some field hospitals and administration units to take care of pay, publicity, and so on. Jaysh al-Inqadh had a structure, but this structure was always under pressure from older and more established lines of loyalty. Shishakli's battalion is an example of this. Another example was a small Druze battalion under Shakib Wahab, which eventually agreed to participate but only if it remained independent of central command.

Expectations of Qawuqji's success were high, partly because much had been made of the modernness of Jaysh al-Inqadh. People like Hashimi insisted all along that this was not 1936, when armed bands of men entered Palestine independently. The new army had to be modern and organized in order to defeat the British and the Haganah. But because the current of old loyalties ran strong under the surface of the army's modern structure, Qawuqji actually exercised only limited authority. The tension between his responsibility and his lack of real power was the axis around which the war spun out of his control.

CROSSING THE JORDAN

A Jaysh al-Inqadh battalion, under the command of the Iraqi officer Muhammad Safa, moved from Qatana to Palestine in mid-January 1948. This was the first major mobilization of a Jaysh al-Inqadh battalion that Qawuqji had direct responsibility for. Safa's best route to reach the northwest bank of the Jordan River, while avoiding well-guarded Jewish settlements and British patrols, was to travel southwest from Qatana to Dar'a, on the Jordanian border. From there the route would take the battalion due south into Jordan through the desert. It would be hidden from the west by steep desert hills that sloped down toward the Jordan Valley. After a full day's travel, Safa's men would cross the Jordan River at the Damiya Bridge. This was a portable wooden bridge set up by the British amid the ruins of the old Mamluk Bridge, which had been used by travelers and traders up until the fall of the Ottoman Empire at the beginning of the twentieth century. The Damiya Bridge was just a few miles north of the permanent and much busier Allenby Bridge, which in January 1948 was still guarded by soldiers from the British army. At the Damiya Bridge only a few soldiers from the Jordanian Arab Legion stood guard.

Setting Safa's battalion in motion alone required Qawuqji to navigate the fraught politics and competition between Syria and Jordan. In mid-January 1948 Safa's battalion arrived in Dar'a. Qawuqji had traveled with the battalion and arranged for the governor of Irbid (in northern Jordan) to attend a meeting in Dar'a. There Qawuqji explained that he needed permission for the battalion to cross into Palestine through Jordan. The governor checked with the palace of King 'Abdullah and reported back to Qawuqji that it was impossible for the king to grant permission to use Jordanian territory to cross into Palestine because Jordan had a treaty with Britain that prohibited this. Qawuqji telephoned Quwatli and explained the situation. Quwatli sent Isma'il Safwat to see King 'Abdullah. Safwat managed to persuade 'Abdullah to agree to the crossing as long as it was done quietly, carefully, and in stages. Qawuqji ignored this directive to cross in stages because he believed that it would expose his troops to unnecessary danger. The crossing itself took place without incident. A few days later hundreds more Jaysh al-Inqadh troops traveled through Jordan and used the Damiya Bridge to cross into Palestine. When the British discovered that the Damiya Bridge had been used by Jaysh al-Inqadh in this way, they destroyed it, thereby cutting the battalion off from its supply line. From that point on, Qawuqji was forced to send supplies, disguised as regular commodities, through the much bigger Allenby Bridge, which was heavily guarded by British soldiers.

At the beginning of February, Alan Cunningham, the last British high commissioner in Palestine, sent a furious telegram to the secretary of state for the colonies in London. He asked for London's help in controlling the borders of Palestine. Cunningham stressed "once more the necessity of preventive action outside Palestine. This open flouting of our frontier is making both the British Government and our administration here appear ridiculous." Cunningham was targeting British officials such as Glubb Pasha and Alec Kirkbride, both of whom worked with the Jordanian government. Cunningham regarded them as being too close to King 'Abdullah. In Cunningham's view, they were unwilling to take action to stop the incursion of outside Arab troops into Palestine before the British had formally pulled out. In another telegram on the topic of the crossing, sent a few days after the first, Cunningham asked that King 'Abdullah be formally reprimanded. He wrote that 'Abdullah's allowing Jaysh al-Inqadh troops to pass through Jordan "justifies the strongest possible protest, even to a friendly government." This message was passed on to Kirkbride, who sent a cool reply to the Foreign Office:

> Although I am without actual evidence, I believe that a party of volunteers from Syria did pass through Transjordan on the night of the

29th of January . . . I tackled the King and the Transjordan authorities about this informally and received a denial in both cases. As I am without means of substantiation of any allegation I make, it seems difficult to carry the matter any further. I did, however, read the King another lecture on the wickedness of creating difficulties for the Allies.

TELEGRAMS

Safa's battalion was responsible for the area of Palestine bounded by the towns of Nablus to the south and Jenin and Baysan to the north. Soldiers and officers from the battalion spread out in this area, but the small town of Tubas often acted as headquarters because it was located between the three larger towns. Tubas was also quite remote, nestled in quiet grazing land and olive groves. Roughly two weeks after the battalion arrived in Tubas, it was joined by the Hittin Battalion under the command of Madlul 'Abbas as well as by a company of Circassian troops. From late January to mid-March telegrams served as Qawuqji's primary means of contacting his battalions. Each battalion had a wireless operator and a codebook. Qawuqji received and sent these telegrams from his headquarters in Damascus.

The archive of telegrams sent back and forth between Qawuqji and the commanders of the various battalions of Jaysh al-Inqadh over the course of the war is a record of increasing desperation. By April and May of 1948 the telegrams reveal anxiety about lack of supplies and lack of morale as the first major Palestinian cities—Tiberias, Safad, Acre, Haifa, and Jaffa—began to fall to the Haganah. This was in spite of some fierce resistance by Palestinian volunteer fighters. But in January and February 1948, when Qawuqji was still in Damascus, the tone of the telegrams was quite different. Safa was the first to start sending in reports. Logistics were the main concern of those first few weeks: acquiring cars; sorting out the codes for the wireless operators; arranging for food supplies to be sent to the right locations; making sure there was enough cash to pay all the salaries. The telegrams also refer to the behavior of some of the troops. Soldiers were drinking and firing their weapons into the air, bringing various complaints from Palestinian villagers. A few of Safa's telegrams also expose the tension between local Palestinian leaders and several of the Jaysh al-Inqadh officers. The telegrams that Qawuqji sent in response show his commitment to maintaining professional military standards. He urged Safa to be tough on the complaining wireless operators, who felt that they did not have the appropriate equipment and manuals to send messages that were securely coded. Qawuqji also told Safa to take the opportunity to buy British jeeps, being sold illegally to Jaysh al-Inqadh by British soldiers, and to send back any rogue soldiers who were causing trouble in the villages. According to a few telegrams, some local Palestinian leaders joined Jaysh al-Inqadh out of protest against the Mufti and his followers. Other telegrams reported that some local Palestinian villagers were complaining to Jaysh al-Inqadh that they did not want to be led by Palestinian officers because of problems between local families. But Qawuqji did not want the (by then) well-known competition between him and the Mufti to undermine the operating procedures of his army. Qawuqji's view was that there could be formal cooperation between two independent forces but that mixing the two would lead to chaos. In a telegram sent by Qawuqji on February 6, 1948, he is clear about the importance of avoiding quarrels with local Palestinian military leaders:

DO NOT ENTER INTO INTERNAL MATTERS IN THE COUNTRY EXCEPT WHEN YOU NEED TO SECURE YOUR NEEDS THROUGH THE CHANNELS OF THE [PALESTINIAN] NATIONAL COMMITTEES. WE ABSOLUTELY DESIRE THAT THERE SHOULD BE NO STIRRING UP OF EMOTIONS OR EXACERBATING OF DIFFERENCES. IT IS OUR DUTY TO WORK TOWARD A MUTUAL UNDERSTANDING WITH THE CITIZENS [OF PALESTINE] WHATEVER THEIR POLITICAL OUTLOOK. THEY SHOULD HAVE NO RELATIONSHIP WITH US EXCEPT WHEN IT COMES TO MATTERS OF SECURITY AND FIGHTING THE JEWISH FORCES. WE ABSOLUTELY DO NOT CONDONE ANY PROVOCATION ON THE PART OF ANY NATIONALITIES. PLEASE PROCEED ON THIS BASIS.

What is not contained in the telegrams is the news that Safa sent to Qawuqji sometime in February 1948: a group of thugs had been offered money by the Mufti to assassinate Qawuqji. It was widely known that the Mufti was capable of assassinating his political opponents. Only a few months before, in September 1947, he had arranged for the assassination of Sami Taha, a famous Palestinian labor activist and his opponent. Killing political rivals was part of the Mufti's repertoire, just as it was part of the repertoires of some Jewish nationalists in this period. These assassinations were often preceded by accusations of treachery. The Mufti of course had been publicly accusing Qawuqji of treachery since the early 1940s. Although Qawuqji mentions the threat of assassination in his memoirs, he does not talk about how this made him feel. But it is easy to imagine him lying awake in the darkness of those winter nights in his home in Damascus in February and early March 1948, listening for footsteps on the street.

On February 16, 1948, Muhammad Safa's battalion launched a full-scale assault against the Jewish settlement of Tirat-Zvi, which was located in the Baysan Valley just a few miles from the Jordan River. The battalion barraged the settlement using small arms, machine guns, and mortar fire. Then about three hundred soldiers attempted to occupy the settlement. They were met with heavy resistance. The attack failed, and there were many Arab casualties. From the afternoon of February 17 until the early morning of February 18, Qawuqji's and Safa's headquarters exchanged a number of telegrams. It is worth reproducing the full text of these telegrams here because they convey the sense of urgency and exasperation of those hours. Outgoing telegrams were sent from Qawuqji's headquarters in Damascus; incoming telegrams were sent from Safa's headquarters in Palestine:

OUTGOING

17/2

SAFA WHY THIS SILENCE. YOU HAVE BECOME CUT OFF FROM US. HAVE YOUR FORCES ATTACKED THE SETTLEMENTS NEAR BAYSAN. CAN YOU SECURE THE EIGHT-TON CARS.

WE NEED THEM AND ARE READY TO BUY THEM FROM DAMASCUS IF YOU CAN'T GET HOLD OF THEM. WE AWAIT YOUR RESPONSE. FAWZI

INCOMING
17/2 1600
ON MONDAY NIGHT I ATTACKED THE SETTLEMENTS OF THE JORDAN VALLEY WITH THE INTENTION OF TAKING AL-ZIRAʿA. IT WOULD HAVE FALLEN IF IT HADN'T BEEN FOR THE WITHDRAWAL OF A COMPANY WITHOUT ORDERS AND THE LATE ARRIVAL OF REIN-FORCEMENTS, WHICH MEANT THAT THE REMAINING TROOPS WHO HAD BEEN INSIDE THE SETTLEMENT WERE FORCED TO WITHDRAW IN TURN. DETAILS TONIGHT. THE OFFI-CERS ARE SAFE.

INCOMING
17/2 1600
THE ROAD IS CUT OFF, SO NO CITY CARS ARE RISKING IT. AL-HARAWANI AND AL-BIRQAWI WILL TRAVEL SOON. I BOUGHT TWO CARS FOR 224 POUNDS, AND I TOOK OUT A LOAN OF 1,000 POUNDS TO BUY OTHERS. PLEASE SEND THE MONEY TO BUY THE CARS AND THE FUEL.

OUTGOING
17/2 2200
SERGEANT ASIL IS LEAVING FOR YOU AT 1700 HOURS FROM DAMASCUS. YOU MUST LET US KNOW MORNING AND EVENING WHAT THE SITUATION IS YOUR END. WE WAIT IMPATIENTLY FOR DETAILS OF THE BATTLE YESTERDAY. FAWZI

OUTGOING
17/2 2305
WHAT IS THE TYPE OF THE CARS THAT YOU HAVE BOUGHT AND WHAT IS THEIR CAPAC-ITY. FAWZI

OUTGOING
17/2 2305
SAFA—HAVE YOU GOT THE NECESSARY REINFORCEMENTS TO SECURE THE NORTH AND NORTHWEST OF YOUR AREA OF OPERATION IN JENIN AND ITS ENVIRONS. FAWZI

OUTGOING

17/2 2305

WE MUST MAKE CONTACT WITH SAFA AS QUICKLY AS POSSIBLE AND HE MUST INFORM US OF THE DEVELOPMENTS IN THE SITUATION AND THE MOST RECENT POSITION. HAVE OUR FORCES WITHDRAWN. AND WHERE DID THEY REACH. AND WHAT IS THE SITUATION OF THE BRITISH FORCES. FAWZI

OUTGOING

18/2 0110

WHERE IS SAFA. WHO IS READING AND WRITING THE TELEGRAMS. WE ARE WAITING FOR A COMMENT ON THE SITUATION NOW. IT IS ABSOLUTELY NECESSARY THAT YOU INFORM US NOW. FAWZI

OUTGOING

18/2 0320

SAFA AND HIS OFFICERS SHOULD TAKE RESPONSIBILITY FOR THIS SHAMEFUL BREAK IN COMMUNICATIONS. IT IS NOT TENABLE THAT WE ARE HEARING YOUR NEWS FROM PEOPLE AND THEY ARE ASKING US ABOUT THE SITUATION AND WE ARE NOT ABLE TO GIVE ACCURATE INFORMATION. FAWZI

INCOMING

18/2 0810

I HAVE A SUSPICION THAT THE JEWS HAVE WORKED OUT A WAY TO UNRAVEL OUR TELE-GRAMS FROM BEGINNING TO END OF EACH TELEGRAM. PLEASE CHANGE THE CODE QUICKLY. SAFA

INCOMING

18/2

SYNOPSIS OF THE SITUATION: 37 KILLED AND THE SAME NUMBER OF WOUNDED. THE LOSSES OF THE JEWS ACCORDING TO THE CONFIRMED REPORTS OF THE BRITISH COMMANDER IN BAYSAN IS 110 KILLED AND MORE THAN 100 WOUNDED AND 3/4 OF THE HOUSES DESTROYED. THE POSITION OF THE BRITISH WAS EXCELLENT TO THE END. THE CONCENTRATIONS ARE AS FOLLOWS: HITTIN AND THE CIRCASSIANS DID NOT PARTICIPATE WITH THEM IN THE BATTLE. THE REST OF THE HUSAYN BATTALION IS IN

TUBAS, AL-DAYYARBUN IS IN NURIS AND ZARAYN, AND THE YARMUK BATTALION IS IN QABATIYYA.

INCOMING

18/2 0915

THE HEAVY RAIN THAT BEGAN WITH THE BATTLE, AND THAT ONE HAS NEVER SEEN BEFORE IN THIS REGION, PREVENTED US FROM ACHIEVING THE OBJECTIVE THAT WE WERE HOPING FOR. ONE OF THE WORST PROBLEMS THAT WE FACED IN THE BATTLE WAS THE ABSENCE OF COMMUNICATION BETWEEN THE BATTALION AND ITS UNITS AND THE LOSS OF TRANSPORTATION UPON THE RETURN TO THE POINTS OF MILITARY CONCENTRATION. SUPPLY US WITH THE MEANS OF COMMUNICATION AND PROVISIONS, PARTICULARLY DRY GOODS AND MORTAR BOMBS. SAFA

INCOMING

18/2 (72) 0930

I BOUGHT A PICKUP AND A TRUCK OF 3 AND 5 TONS, RESPECTIVELY. YOU ARE DEMANDING THE BUYING OF CARS AND THE STORING OF FUEL, AND YOU ARE INFORMED OF THE AMOUNT THAT SHOULD BE TRANSFERRED TO US AND UP TILL NOW NO MONEY HAS ARRIVED. SAFA

INCOMING

18/2 1420

I DID NOT GIVE DETAILS OF THE BATTLE OWING TO THE FACT THAT I WAS FAR FROM MY STATION AND OWING TO THE ABSENCE OF CONFIRMED INFORMATION AT THAT TIME, AND I DIDN'T INFORM ANYONE BEFORE THE BATTLE OWING TO MY CONCERN THAT THE JEWS KNEW THE CODE. SAFA

The telegrams show Qawuqji's frustration that he was not consulted or informed about the attack on Tirat-Zvi. His frantic appeals for information show his lack of control over what was happening on the ground. But Safa's exasperation is also apparent in this exchange. It is clear that Qawuqji made demands about buying cars without supporting these demands with the cash to pay for them. In the final telegram Safa is angry that he is being reprimanded for not giving details of the battle.

From his perspective, the previous twenty-four hours had been taken up with the business of fighting ("I was far from my station"), not with sending reports. Anxiety about the possibility that the Jewish forces had broken the code of the Arab wireless stations may account for Safa's exaggerated count of the number of Jewish dead. In general, throughout the war Arab reports (both internal and public) exaggerated the number of enemy casualties. This was part of a widely accepted strategy among officers intended to raise morale among the public and the soldiers. The Arab press in particular reported exaggerated accounts of Arab victories and Jewish casualties. Later in the war, as the scale of the Jewish victory became clear, this strategy backfired. The Arab state armies and Jaysh al-Inqadh were exposed to ridicule because of the contrast between their claims and the unfolding evidence of their actual defeat.

INTO PALESTINE

At dusk on March 4 Qawuqji and some fellow officers met in Dar'a on the Syrian-Jordanian border, accompanied by a company of foot soldiers and a small convoy of cars and trucks carrying six heavy guns and ammunition. After resting a little and eating something light, Qawuqji contacted Col. 'Abd al-Qadir al-Jundi, second-in-command of the Jordanian Arab Legion and also a member of the Arab League Military Committee. Qawuqji told him that he wanted to meet with King 'Abdullah. Jundi took a car and driver and made the two-hour journey across the desert to Dar'a in order to drive Qawuqji to the palace in Amman. When Qawuqji and 'Abdullah met, the king made it clear that he had no confidence in the UN or the Partition Resolution, or in President Quwatli, who, in 'Abdullah's view, was against Syrian unity. 'Abdullah told Qawuqji that he was ready to fight for Palestine and that he wanted to make it part of east Jordan. He said that Jordan needed a port, and Haifa could serve as that port.

Historians have written at length about King 'Abdullah's ambitions to rule Greater Syria and his plan to include Palestine within it. They have also suggested that during the 1948 War, Qawuqji was fighting secretly for 'Abdullah and against President Quwatli's interests. This narrative reflects a tendency by many historians of the Arab-Israeli conflict to fix the protagonists in the war firmly on one side or the other. Qawuqji's meeting with 'Abdullah can certainly be read as evidence that he was on the king's side, but it can also be read as a sign of his independence from state interests. In his memoirs Qawuqji is clear about his response toward 'Abdullah: "He expressed his personal admiration of me in addition to his willingness to assist me with the fighting as much as he was able. So I asked him to facilitate our crossing into Palestine, and he said he would get in touch with his officers and order them to give us the necessary assistance."

Qawuqji was a pragmatist. If 'Abdullah could help get him into Palestine, then 'Abdullah was someone with whom he could cooperate. We also know that at least in the late 1940s Qawuqji himself was a Greater Syrianist. He did not believe in the artificial divisions drawn up by Europeans that separated Greater Syria (Bilad al-Sham) into the modern states of Lebanon, Syria, Jordan, and Palestine. Qawuqji was fighting in Palestine to keep Palestine Arab. The line "He expressed his personal admiration of me" is also a part of the story of his relations with King 'Abdullah. Those discussions around who should be the field commander of Jaysh al-Inqadh that took place in the last six months of 1947 must have had an effect on Qawuqji. It took a long time for Shukri al-Quwatli to come out and fully endorse Qawuqji as leader. From Qawuqji's point of view, this was in spite of evidence that the Mufti was untrustworthy and had used unscrupulous methods in his attempts to gain control over Jaysh al-Inqadh. At least at this point in the war King 'Abdullah showed that he was ready to support Qawuqji, and he seemed respectful of Qawuqji's capabilities and the legitimacy of his intentions.

To help Qawuqji get his men across the river, Jundi suggested that Qawuqji arrange a meeting with Glubb Pasha, the British army officer in overall command of the Arab Legion and one of King 'Abdullah's closest advisers. Glubb Pasha had fought against Qawuqji in the Palestine Revolt in 1936 and later at the Rutba Fort in the Iraqi desert in 1941. During their meeting the two men joked about having faced each other before as enemies. But in this instance Glubb Pasha was willing to co-operate with Qawuqji. The Arab Legion had seven infantry companies stationed in Palestine. They were mainly there to protect British installa-tions. The last thing Glubb Pasha wanted was a conflict with Jaysh al-Inqadh. Qawuqji and his men crossed the Allenby Bridge at night and arrived in Tubas on the morning of March 6 just as dawn was breaking. Glubb Pasha had to walk a difficult line during the 1948 War. Officially the Arab Legion was the army of the kingdom of Jordan, yet it was com-manded by a British officer and included other British men in its officer corps. King 'Abdullah certainly followed British advice, and he worked closely with British officials; but Jordanian and British interests did not always coincide. When this happened, Glubb Pasha was caught between two masters, King 'Abdullah and the British government.

Again, Alan Cunningham sent a telegram from Jerusalem to the secretary of state for the colonies upon hearing the rumors that King 'Abdullah had facilitated Qawuqji's crossing into Palestine. He wrote that if it was "correct that Fawzi received Royal Countenance and sup-port in Amman en route here as Commander of the Liberation Army in Palestine, this would hardly seem to accord with King Abdullah's pledge in Amman telegram to Foreign Office no. 39 of 27th of January, not to permit further volunteers to cross Transjordan." Again Kirkbride wrote a cool response. He replied that the presence of Jaysh al-Inqadh in Pales-tine had become a fact on the ground and that King 'Abdullah and the Transjordanian government had "decided that in view of their own plans they must establish some contact with that force and so preclude any possibility of its clashing with the Arab Legion." Kirkbride went on to say that "this no doubt will entail a modification of the original promise about volunteers by King Abdullah to which Jerusalem refers, but it seems to be the only sensible thing to do in the circumstances." Kirk-bride's report mentioned nothing about Qawuqji's meeting with Glubb Pasha. It also seems plausible that men like Kirkbride and Glubb Pasha secretly supported the entrance of an Arab force into Palestine because they wanted to see an Arab victory against the Jewish forces. Some British officials supported the Arab side in the war. In addition to Kirkbride and Glubb Pasha, Brig. Sir Iltyd Clayton, special adviser to the head of the British Middle East office in Cairo, worked closely with a number of Arab leaders to secure an Arab state in Palestine. Clayton was present at most meetings of the Arab League as the crisis unfolded. The support of British individuals did not mean, however, that British government policy was directed toward establishing a Palestinian state in Palestine. Most British officials believed that the best solution was to establish King 'Abdullah as the ruler of the areas allotted to the Arabs in the Partition Resolution. Cunningham was not particularly pro-Jewish or pro-Arab, but as the last high commissioner he had the job of overseeing the orderly dismantling of British rule in Palestine. He wanted to put a stop to anything that made his task more difficult, such as the presence of foreign Arab troops in Palestine before the mandate officially ended.

It rained heavily the night Qawuqji crossed into Palestine. Many of the cars and trucks carrying supplies broke down or got stuck in the mud. For Qawuqji this was an omen of what was to come:

We arrived in Tubas on March 6, 1948. This village was the last I left when the disturbances of 1936 came to an end. Memories came to my mind of heroism and honor, memories of the brave deeds of the group that had come from various Arab countries that had opened up an opportunity before the Arabs, had the "great leaders" only known how to make use of it to solve the Palestine problem once and for all thirteen years before, and then there would have been no need for us to come back to Palestine to fight. Rain fell heavily and incessantly on Tubas. Owing to the ignorance of the drivers or their fatigue, the cars of our convoy lay scattered on the Jericho–Tubas road, either because of problems with the engines or because they were stuck in the mud. Other cars shared the same fate on the Amman–Dar'a road. This problem with the cars and the problem of supply hindered our operations throughout the whole campaign.

Several days after arriving in Tubas, Qawuqji moved his headquarters a few miles due west to the smaller village of Jabʿa. It sat on higher ground than Tubas and commanded a wide view. Qawuqji also felt comfortable in Jabʿa. From there he had fought against the British with some success in the summer of 1936. The photograph (figure 34) was probably taken in Jabʿa a few hours after he arrived there in March 1948.

Qawuqji's area of operation stretched north of Jabʿa to the village of Nuris and west to the city of Tulkaram. He faced many problems in the area under his jurisdiction. Acting almost as a police force, Jaysh al-Inqadh set about trying to control the roads and worked as a guard against banditry. Dysentery and chest infections were spreading among the troops. According to Qawuqji, he also tried to control the distribution by the Mufti's men of pamphlets that called on local Palestinians not to cooperate with Jaysh al-Inqadh. Through the local councils, Qawuqji invited armed Palestinians to join his forces, promising them salaries and uniforms. He also worked out an arrangement with British troops in the

FIGURE 34

area, whereby if they agreed to leave his forces alone, he would not cause them trouble. The British were just a few weeks away from their deadline to withdraw from Palestine. British troops were generally happy to sit tight unless it was absolutely necessary to take action.

In the spring and summer of 1948 the American photo magazine *Life* sent three photographers to Palestine to cover the conflict. The photographs that they took, many of which were not published at the time, now make up a small part of *Life*'s vast archive. The three photographers— John Phillips, Frank Scherschel, and Dmitri Kessel—documented the British army at work, Palestinians leaving their villages for what they thought would be temporary safety in neighboring states, Orthodox Jews under siege in Jerusalem, Haganah soldiers, and some of the Arab volunteers who came to fight in Palestine. The photographs are a fascinating visual account of Palestine in the first months of 1948. But the difference in the way that the Arab and Jewish soldiers were photographed is striking.

Two particular photographs were taken in the late spring and early summer of 1948 by *Life*. John Phillips took the photograph of a small company of Arab fighters (figure 35) and Frank Scherschel took the photograph of a unit of the Haganah (figure 36). Note the boisterous informality of the Haganah soldiers, their cigarettes dangling from their lips; some are crouching, some are standing, and nearly all are smiling. The photograph of the Arab soldiers is oddly staged and formal: men are lying and sitting on divans on top of Oriental carpets, and one seated man is staring straight at the camera in a menacing way. The photograph of the Haganah soldiers is much more intimate. Portrayed in this way, these Haganah fighters would have seemed very familiar to an American audience. They look just like American GIs. On the other hand, the Arab soldiers would have seemed strange, almost feminine. This difference in representation is also present in many of the histories of the 1948 War in written English and Hebrew. The Jewish soldiers are treated as more familiar: men whose motivations can be easily understood. The Arab soldiers, on the other hand, are much more remote characters. Motivations for their actions are often read through the distant and distorting lens of Arab cultural traits.

FIGURE 35

FIGURE 36

FIGURE 37

Phillips also took a photograph of Qawuqji for *Life* (figure 37) at around the same time the other photographs were taken. Again, the photograph is staged in a peculiar way. It is as if the photographer were treating Qawuqji as a typical Arab strongman, and Qawuqji were somehow playing the part.

THE BATTLE FOR MISHMAR HAEMEK

Mishmar Haemek is a kibbutz that in 1948 lay just off the main road between Jenin and Haifa, about thirty miles southeast of Haifa. During World War II it was used as a training camp by the British army. It boasted strong fortifications and underground storage areas that had been built by the British in 1942 in preparation for a German invasion of the Middle East. The photograph (figure 38) was taken just a few years before World War II. In 1948 the kibbutz had a population of about five hundred, mainly members of the Marxist Hashomer Hatzair movement.

Because of its location on the Haifa–Jenin road, the kibbutz served as a command center for Jewish attacks on Arab convoys. The capture of such a Jewish settlement would have been a major strategic victory for the Arab side. In fact the end of March 1948 was a low point for the Jewish community in Palestine. In the north and in the Galilee panhandle, there were many Jewish settlements surrounded by Palestinian villages. These settlements felt cut off and vulnerable to attack. In the hills near Hebron, the Etzion Bloc kibbutzes were under siege. The hundred thousand Jews living in the Old City of Jerusalem were also under siege and rapidly running out of food. The three Jewish convoys of Nabi Daniel, Yehiam, and Khulda, which were attempting to reach besieged communities, had been ambushed and destroyed. It was in this context that the Haganah command drew up the famous Plan Dalet, which historians have analyzed extensively. Plan Dalet was a blueprint for going on the offensive to secure the Jewish state. It included measures for clearing hostile forces out of the interior and establishing territorial contiguity

FIGURE 38

between Jewish populations. The first operation under the new plan was Operation Nahshon, the intent of which was to open the road between Tel Aviv and Jerusalem and thereby lift the siege on the Jewish community in the Old City of Jerusalem. As a result of Operation Nahshon, the beginning of April saw fierce fighting between 'Abd al-Qadir's Palestinian forces and the Haganah on the Tel Aviv–Jerusalem road just a few miles west of Jerusalem.

Qawuqji, based ninety miles to the north, chose this moment to attack Mishmar Haemek. Some Israeli and British historians have assumed that this attack was out of pique that 'Abd al-Qadir al-Husayni was getting so much attention in the Arab press for his fighting on the Jerusalem road. This kind of analysis reduces Qawuqji's motives to vanity and self-promotion. As such they are not serious explanations for why he chose to attack Mishmar Haemek. Hindi, in his account of Jaysh al-Inqadh based on interviews with many of the officers who served with Qawuqji, claims that by attacking Mishmar Haemek, Qawuqji was attempting to relieve the pressure on Husayni's forces. The telegrams that Qawuqji was sending in the first half of April confirm that what unfolded at Mishmar Haemek was linked to what was happening farther south.

The battle for Mishmar Haemek was the first time that artillery was used in the 1948 War. Between 5:00 p.m. and 7:00 p.m. on April 4, Qawuqji bombarded Mishmar Haemek with 75 mm and 105 mm field guns. 'Afif al-Bizri was the commander of the artillery battery. Qawuqji described him as an outstanding artillery commander, comparable only to Captain Rida, with whom he had served in the Ottoman Army during World War I. Three Jewish settlers were killed that first day, and a few wounded. The artillery barrage also destroyed a number of buildings. Qawuqji sent in ground troops in the wake of the bombardment but withdrew them after a few hours. In a telegram to headquarters in Damascus sent on the morning of April 5, he explained his reasons for withdrawing his men:

THE GROUND TROOPS ENTERED THE SETTLEMENT IN THE EVENING. THERE WERE STILL MANY DEFENSIVE POSITIONS HIDDEN UNDERGROUND THAT OUR GUNS HAD NOT BEEN

ABLE TO REACH. THE RAIN WAS COMING DOWN HEAVILY, AND THE MUD WAS GETTING
WORSE. OUT OF FEAR OF INJURIES OCCURRING IN OUR RANKS THAT NIGHT FROM OUR
OWN SOLDIERS BECAUSE OF LACK OF PRECISION AND THE LACK OF NIGHT TRAINING,
I WITHDREW THE SOLDIERS FROM INSIDE THE SETTLEMENT. BECAUSE OF THIS, WE
DID NOT SUFFER ANY CASUALTIES EXCEPT ONE WOUNDED.

Qawuqji continued the bombardment the next day, hoping that artillery alone would be enough to bring about the settlement's surrender.
This could have been a signal of his lack of confidence in the training of
his ground troops or of his underestimation of the strength of Jewish
resistance. By April 7 it appeared that the artillery bombardment had
worked. In a telegram sent that day Qawuqji reported that he had been
visited in his headquarters by a representative of the settlement who came
under the protection of a British army officer. They asked for a truce so that
women and children and wounded could be evacuated from the settlement. He agreed to the truce and guaranteed the safety of their lives and
their property, provided that Mishmar Haemek come under his control.
The same telegram reports the truce as being an indication of the "submission of the settlement and its surrender." In his memoirs the entries
on Mishmar Haemek are contained in two chapters, divided one from
the other by a chapter on Jerusalem and 'Abd al-Qadir's forces. The first
chapter on Mishmar Haemek ends with this truce, which was brokered
by British forces. It seems that on April 7 Qawuqji thought the battle for
Mishmar Haemek was over, and he turned his attention to the crisis
unfolding to his south, in Qastal, on the Tel Aviv–Jerusalem road.

Once the site of an important crusader castle, Qastal was a small
Palestinian village located eight miles to the west of Jerusalem on a hill
above the Tel Aviv–Jerusalem road. By late March 1948 'Abd al-Qadir's
forces were using it as a base from which to maintain the blockade on
the Jerusalem road. On April 2 the Palmach's Harel Brigade attacked
Qastal and occupied the village. A few days later, on April 8, 'Abd
al-Qadir's forces launched a counterattack. The counterattack was successful, and the village returned to Palestinian hands, but 'Abd al-Qadir
was killed in the fighting, along with eighteen Palmach soldiers. During

the Palestinian counterattack, Palestinian messengers from the Jerusalem area arrived at Qawuqji's headquarters in Jab'a asking for Jaysh al-Inqadh to send troops to the Jerusalem front to help maintain the blockade and relieve the pressure on 'Abd al-Qadir's forces. Qawuqji hesitated. He was under strict instructions from Damascus not to interfere with 'Abd al-Qadir's operations. In addition, he was concerned that his motives would be misunderstood, given the atmosphere of mistrust between the Palestinians fighting under 'Abd al-Qadir's leadership and Jaysh al-Inqadh. But he also knew that the help of his forces could make a crucial difference in the battle for control of the road to Jerusalem. As he puts it in his memoirs, he was "on the horns of a dilemma." He decided to go to the aid of the fighters at Qastal. He sent artillery, three armored cars, and a company-size section of his infantry to the Jerusalem area. He telegrammed headquarters in Damascus on the morning of April 8, informing it that he had decided to send reinforcements. Previous telegrams asking permission to send reinforcements had remained unanswered. He placed the force under the command of one of his best officers, Ma'mun al-Bitar.

The Jerusalem front was in a state of chaos as a result of 'Abd al-Qadir's death. Bitar attempted to secure Qastal from Jewish counterattack but was not able to organize the Palestinian forces on the ground in an effective way. Palestinians were devastated by the death of 'Abd al-Qadir, who was a national hero. On April 8 Amin al-Ruwayha, the main medical officer for Jaysh al-Inqadh, arrived in the Qastal area. He confirmed Ma'mun al-Bitar's reports in a telegram sent to headquarters in Damascus that same day, stating that Palestinian forces in the Jerusalem area were disintegrating and that morale was low owing to the death of 'Abd al-Qadir. He wrote that some of the soldiers were calling on Qawuqji to become the commander of the Jerusalem area in order to protect Jerusalem from falling to the Jewish forces. Qawuqji directed Bitar to shell the Jewish quarter of Jerusalem to keep up the pressure on the siege of Jerusalem. This quickly brought the condemnation of the British government. Three British officers came to see Qawuqji at his headquar-

ters in Jab'a to warn him that the British army would have to take action
if he did not stop shelling Jerusalem.

While all this was going on, the worst massacre of civilians during
the 1948 War took place. On April 9, Etzel and Lehi, two Jewish dissi-
dent militias not officially part of the Haganah, attacked the Palestinian
village of Dayr Yasin, which lay on the outskirts of Jerusalem. The attack
on Dayr Yasin was loosely coordinated with Haganah Command as part
of Operation Nahshon. Etzel and Lehi commanders had not expected
serious local resistance, but villagers fought hard to protect Dayr Yasin
from occupation. After overcoming this resistance, Jewish troops mur-
dered hundreds of villagers. The horror of what happened at Dayr Yasin
on April 9 spread throughout the Palestinian community. Awareness of
what happened at Dayr Yasin was one of the reasons that many Palestinians fled their villages and towns in the face of Jewish attacks in the
following months. In just two days, April 8 and April 9, Palestinians
had experienced the death of their most prominent military commander and national hero and the massacre of almost an entire village
by Jewish forces. Maintaining the siege of Jerusalem was impossible. On
April 13 the first Jewish convoy of 160 vehicles from Tel Aviv reached
Jerusalem.

While Qawuqji's attention was focused on events at Qastal, things
started to unravel for Jaysh al-Inqadh at Mishmar Haemek. According
to the account of one of the British officers responsible for negotiating
the truce between Qawuqji's forces and the kibbutz on April 6, the kib-
butzniks had never had any intention of honoring the truce but were
using the time they had bought to allow Haganah and Palmach reinforcements to reach the area. On the morning of April 10 the Haganah
launched a counterattack on Qawuqji's forces outside Mishmar Haemek.
Fierce fighting followed over the next few days, until Qawuqji's forces
had finally been driven back by the Haganah by April 15. Ma'mun al-Bitar,
who had returned with his company from the Jerusalem front to help in
the fighting around Mishmar Haemek, was killed trying to prevent the
Haganah from capturing Jaysh al-Inqadh field guns. Qawuqji sent several

telegrams during the second stage of the fighting around Mishmar Hae-mek asking for Damascus to supply him with ammunition. In one tele-gram, sent on April 13, Qawuqji asked for 81 mortar shells, 105 75 mm artillery shells, and armor-piercing ammunition. He received the follow-ing telegram from Taha al-Hashimi on April 14:

> THE BATTLE FOR MISHMAR HAEMEK HAS BECOME A BATTLE OF ATTRITION. SITUATION
> REGARDING AMMUNITION, PARTICULARLY FRENCH, IS BAD. IT APPEARS THAT YOUR
> ARMAMENTS ARE NOT SUFFICIENT TO REPEL THE ENEMY AND HOLD OUT. DO YOU NOT
> THINK THAT IT WOULD BE BETTER TO END THE FIGHTING AND WITHDRAW YOUR
> FORCES? WE HOPE THE LEAGUE WILL HELP US WITH ARMS.

Years later, in the early 1970s, when going through his papers Qawuqji scribbled a note on this telegram from Taha al-Hashimi: "Order to retreat from Mishmar, threat to stop providing supplies, the hope to get some supplies from the league." Again, Qawuqji's engagement with his own archive shows how he tried to forge a narrative of what hap-pened at Mishmar Haemek. By the 1970s Qawuqji, as well as Arab na-tionalist soldiers of his generation, had been discredited by a barrage of criticism in others' memoirs and histories about 1948. Qawuqji intended to counter this critique by producing a detailed narrative of how those two weeks in April 1948 had unfolded. The exchange of telegrams between Qawuqji and headquarters in Damascus does not resolve the issue of what really happened at Mishmar Haemek. There is something detached about the exchange. When Qawuqji asked for such large amounts of ammunition, did he really believe that it was possible for Damascus to procure and transport this quantity of ammunition to Mishmar Haemek in a few days? Or was Qawuqji's April 13 telegram, sent during a time of desperate retreat, part of a preemptive attempt to exonerate himself from responsibility for the defeat?

In the course of the fighting for Mishmar Haemek, the Haganah destroyed a number of Palestinian villages that lay close to the kibbutz and expelled their inhabitants. Plan Dalet was being implemented in full force. There is a poignant document in Qawuqji's private papers that gives us a glimpse of the devastation that these events brought to the lives of those villagers who were expelled. It is a letter signed by representatives of the villages of Abu Shusha, Abu Zurayq, al-Naghnaghiyya, al-Ghubayya, and al-Mansi:

At five o'clock in the evening on Friday, April 9, 1948, around one thousand Jews attacked the village of Abu Shusha al-'Arabiyya, which was located about fifty meters from the Jewish settlement of Mishmar Haemek. After a fierce battle they took over a section of the village. On Saturday, April 10, they were joined by reinforcements, and we couldn't hold them back when no Arab reinforcements came to our aid, given that we did not have enough ammunition. They took the rest of the village. After that they burned and destroyed everything in the village while our dead and wounded were still in the field of battle. They did the same in the neighboring village of Abu Zurayq, and they blew up a number of houses in the village of al-Naghnaghiyya and al-Ghubayya and al-Mansi. All these villages are now occupied. We are now displaced and scattered in the area of Jenin with nothing except what the sky can give us and only our blankets as protectors. So we have come to you in desperation to ask you to look into this situation with compassion and help us get our fields back, which are in that area.

In his memoirs Qawuqji tries to rehabilitate his reputation by claiming that Mishmar Haemek was a victory. But the documents in his archive—documents that were written at the time—provide evidence that Mishmar Haemek was a disaster for the Arab side. The defeat at Mishmar Haemek occurred in the context of other disasters: the death of the Palestinian leader 'Abd al-Qadir al-Husayni and the massacre of hundreds of civilians at Dayr Yasin. From the Jewish perspective, the Yishuv had gone from being under Arab siege in several areas, including Jerusalem, to being on the offensive. This change of fortune is evoked in the triumphalist diary entry that Yosef Weitz, the director of the Jewish National Fund's Land Department, wrote on April 21, 1948: "Our army is steadily conquering Arab villages, and their inhabitants are afraid and flee like mice . . . Villages are steadily emptying, and if we continue on this course—and we shall certainly do so as our strength increases— then villages will empty of their inhabitants."

Historians have often pointed the finger of blame at Qawuqji for this. Qawuqji certainly made serious mistakes. He naively trusted the Jewish forces to honor the truce and the British to enforce it, underestimating the lengths that the Haganah would go to prevent Mishmar Haemek's being occupied by Jaysh al-Inqadh. But this was Qawuqji's first real en- counter with the strength of the Jewish forces. The fact that the kibbutz appealed for a truce under the protection of the British army within a day of being shelled appeared to Qawuqji like an easy victory. It was also a relief not to have to send Jaysh al-Inqadh ground troops into the kib- butz, given that he had little confidence in their training and that the heavy rain had made the terrain difficult. The fact that the appeal for a truce coincided with an unfolding crisis for 'Abd al-Qadir's forces on the outskirts of Jerusalem and that Qawuqji was asked for help by a delega- tion from the Jerusalem area led him to make the decision to send Ma'mun al-Bitar to Jerusalem. At that moment it seemed to be the right one. How could he refuse to help when it seemed that Mishmar Haemek was quiet? After the Haganah broke the truce at Mishmar Haemek and launched a counteroffensive against Jaysh al-Inqadh, the fighting was fierce. Qawuqji fought hard to maintain his control, and one of his best officers, Ma'mun al-Bitar, now returned from Jerusalem, was killed in the fighting. Because of Qawuqji's underestimation of the Haganah's ca- pacity, he did not have enough ammunition for sustained battles, and his untrained troops were beginning to desert. But this misjudgment reflected the general attitude of the Arab League's Military Committee, which underestimated the potential of the Jewish forces. This collective misperception could account for the strangely detached exchange of telegrams between Qawuqji and Damascus about sending more ammuni- tion. The human tragedy that unfolded in the Palestinian villages around

Mishmar Haemek as a result of the battle and that is brought back to us from the past through the villager's appeal later haunted Qawuqji. His anxious jotting on his own carefully kept archive testifies to this.

One reason for the later criticism of Qawuqji was a report that he met with Jewish Agency officials shortly before the battle for Mishmar Haemek. In interviews given long after the war, Yehoshua Palmon, who worked for SHAI, the intelligence unit of the Haganah, said he met with Qawuqji and a number of his officers on April 1, 1948. In these interviews Palmon claimed that during this meeting he secured Qawuqji's agreement that he would not come to the aid of the Mufti's fighters in the Jerusalem area and that Jaysh al-Inqadh and the Haganah would refrain from attacking each other. Palmon knew that the Mufti had accused Qawuqji of being a British spy in Berlin, and he tried to use this knowledge to secure guarantees from Qawuqji concerning his intentions toward the Jewish forces. But Palmon's later recollections are contradicted by a written report made at the time. In the written report Palmon says that Qawuqji was loyal to the Arab League and would follow its orders whether those were to fight the Jews or to make an agreement with them. Palmon was in contact with several Arab army officers during 1948. His activities were part of a Jewish Agency policy to make as many connections as possible with Arab officers and politicians in order to undermine the possibility of unity among the Arab forces in 1948. From the Jewish perspective this was a crucial tactic. A united Arab assault posed the greatest threat to the establishment of a Jewish state. Palmon also contacted Shakib Wahab, the commander of the Syrian Druze Battalion of Jaysh al-Inqadh in mid-April 1948, to try to recruit him to the Jewish side. The case of Shakib Wahab is well-known. Wahab made a binding agreement with Palmon that was one factor in the defection of many Druze officers and soldiers from the Druze Battalion to the Haganah. (The descendants of those Syrian Druze soldiers still serve in the Israel Defense Forces today.) Qawuqji, by contrast, continued to fight against the Jewish forces for the duration of the war. He may well have met with Palmon on April 1, as Palmon claimed, but we only have Palmon's (somewhat confused) account of what was said at that meeting.

We cannot know what Qawuqji's intentions were in meeting with Palmon. The fact that Qawuqji attacked the major Jewish settlement of Mishmar Haemek just a few days after the meeting implies that Palmon's attempts to secure Qawuqji's cooperation had little effect. In addition, the fact that Qawuqji brought other Jaysh al-Inqadh officers to meet with Palmon on April 1 indicates that Qawuqji did not see the meeting—at the time—as something that needed to be kept secret.

JAFFA FALLS

The last half of April and the first two weeks of May saw the capture, by Jewish forces, of the Palestinian cities of Tiberias, Safad, Acre, Haifa, and Jaffa. The fall of these cities had a devastating effect on the morale of Palestinians as well as Jaysh al-Inqadh soldiers. Many of the Palestinian inhabitants of these cities were expelled or fled to Lebanon, frightened by stories of Jewish massacres, although expecting to return a few weeks later once the British mandate had formally expired and the combined armies of the Arab states had recaptured their towns from Jewish forces. But this reconquest failed. These few weeks of exile turned into decades, and the grandchildren of those refugees are still living in camps in Lebanon. Palestinian villagers were also displaced internally, fleeing to areas that they believed to be under the control of Qawuqji's forces. Several telegrams sent by Qawuqji to Damascus in this period show that he found himself dealing with the human crisis that was created by this internal displacement. Hungry, homeless Palestinians were taking refuge in Palestinian towns, such as Jenin, which were already facing dwindling supplies of food because of the war. On April 30 Qawuqji sent the following telegram to Damascus:

TO HIGH COMMAND: THE NUMBER OF REFUGEES FROM IMPORTANT VILLAGES IS NOW VERY LARGE. THE PALESTINIAN TOWNS IN OUR AREA HAVE BARELY ENOUGH FOOD SUPPLIES FOR THEMSELVES, SO THEY CANNOT SUPPLY THE REFUGEES. I THEREFORE

REQUEST YOU TAKE URGENT MEASURES TO HELP THEM BY ENSURING THEM SUPPLIES OF FOOD. FAWZI

Qawuqji was also receiving petitions from the heads of villages asking for Jaysh al-Inqadh's help in rounding up young men who were leaving the villages for the safety of Jordan. The heads of the villages were calling on the troops to help bring these young men back to fight. Out of fear of starvation, some villagers began negotiating with Jewish forces. They promised not to resist Jewish occupation if in turn they were allowed access to their fields. Qawuqji later scribbled notes on many of these petitions: "they think of migrating and negotiating a truce with the Jews at the smallest event," "taking refuge in Jordan to escape the shooting and the occupation." Qawuqji's notes contain a trace of bitterness toward the very people that he was in Palestine to fight for. It is as if the desperation of frightened civilians were partly responsible for his military failure.

Qawuqji also had to cope with desertions from Jaysh al-Inqadh because of low morale, dwindling food supplies, and late paychecks. In the first two weeks of May he sent several telegrams that addressed the problem of desertions. Men were handing in their arms and asking to be discharged because their pay was weeks late. In addition, their uniforms were too shabby for them to appear in public. Whole units within battalions were leaving Jaysh al-Inqadh and going back home to Syria or Lebanon to join their state armies. Soldiers were borrowing money from local moneylenders and not paying it back. Qawuqji's archive contains letters of complaint about a group of men from Jaysh al-Inqadh who had not paid their debts to lenders in the villages of Tubas and Tayasir. The letters request that Qawuqji launch an investigation and force the soldiers to pay their debts. Some deserting soldiers went to Palestinian towns like Jenin and created havoc by firing their rifles. One of the letters in Qawuqji's papers is from a doctor in Nablus who claimed that one of the Jaysh al-Inqadh battalion commanders had stolen eight carloads of wheat that had been sent from Jaffa to Nablus to relieve its inhabitants, who were

FIGURE 39

beginning to starve. For some Palestinians, Qawuqji's army was more of a menace than a solution. The fact that this army had been assembled at such short notice and with very little training was beginning to show as some units started unraveling in late April and early May 1948. This was the setting for Jaffa's fall in mid-May 1948.

After Jerusalem, Jaffa was the second most important city in Palestine. It lay on the coast just south of the new Jewish city of Tel Aviv. In 1947 it had a population of about one hundred thousand. The port of Jaffa was the hub of Palestine's citrus industry. The city had a thriving professional middle class. It also contained poor shantytowns that housed migrant workers from Syria, who came to work in the citrus industry. The photograph of Jaffa (figure 39), taken by an American in the late 1800s, shows the city from the sea.

By the time fighting broke out in Palestine in December 1947, Jewish neighborhoods had surrounded Jaffa: Holon and Bat Yam to the south, Hatikva and Mikve Yisrael to the east, and Tel Aviv to the north. Jaffa was thus particularly vulnerable to Jewish attack. The divide between the prosperous middle class and the poor migrant workers also made it difficult for local leaders to coordinate a unified response to Jewish assaults on the city. The Iraqi officer 'Adil Najm al-Din led the Jaysh al-Inqadh garrison in Jaffa. By March and April 1948 Jaysh al-Inqadh troops had become very unpopular among the residents of Jaffa. Mainly Iraqis and Syrians, some of the troops treated the Palestinians with disdain, and there had been incidents when Jaysh al-Inqadh soldiers indulged in looting. By April 28, when the Haganah and Etzel launched their attack against Jaffa, many from the upper and middle classes of the city—with the exception of the mayor and other members of the Jaffa National Committee—had left to take temporary refuge in the interior of Palestine. Others had left by boat for Lebanon or Egypt.

On April 29 Qawuqji, who was still based somewhere north of Jeru-salem, away from the action in Jaffa, received a panicked telegram from Isma'il Safwat requesting that he do everything he could to save Jaffa while at the same time protecting Jerusalem. In his memoirs Qawuqji comments on the way in which the telegram revealed the acute psycho-logical crisis that Safwat was undergoing in the face of the collapse of Jaffa. The Jaysh al-Inqadh garrison in Jaffa was disintegrating in the face of the Haganah assault. Qawuqji ordered the Ajnadayn Battalion, under the command of Michel 'Isa, a capable officer, to reinforce the Jaffa garrison. 'Isa was also directed to take over Najm al-Din's command of Jaysh al-Inqadh troops in Jaffa. The Ajnadayn Battalion fought hard on arrival and in coordination with some garrison troops managed to re-capture Tel al-Rish, a rural suburb, from the Haganah. But by May 2 'Isa was facing desertions and Najm al-Din had left the city by sea along with most of his men. On May 3, Qawuqji sent the following telegram to the command in Damascus:

SITUATION IN JAFFA DISTRESSING. 'ADIL AND HIS MEN HAVE WITHDRAWN AND THE SITUATION IS CONFUSED. AJNADAYN INFECTED BY PANIC FLIGHT. ONLY A FEW MEN LEFT WITH MICHEL 'ISA. JAFFA ALMOST EMPTY. ARMS IN STORES AND STREETS. AMMUNITION BEING THROWN INTO THE SEA. GROUP MUST BE SENT BY SEA TO COL-LECT ARMS AND TAKE THEM TO SEA TO BEIRUT AND DAMASCUS. THERE WERE ARMED CLASHES BETWEEN THE AJNADAYN BATTALION AND THE IRAQIS SERVING UNDER 'ADIL IN AN UNSUCCESSFUL ATTEMPT TO PREVENT THEM FROM FLEEING. NEW ARMS BEING SOLD WHOLESALE AND RETAIL IN ALL AREAS.

By May 10 only a handful of soldiers remained with 'Isa, and Jaffa was left effectively unprotected. William Fuller, the British district commissioner, persuaded the mayor of Jaffa and the remaining members of the Jaffa National Council to declare it an undefended city. The British were leaving in four days, and Fuller believed that the status of undefended city might protect Jaffa from wholesale destruction when Jewish forces entered in full force on the morning of May 14. The fall of Jaffa to the Haganah occurred in the same few weeks as the fall of Tiberias, Haifa, Acre, and Safad. In addition, the Haganah was gaining strength around Jerusalem. Safwat resigned from the Military Committee of the Arab League a few days after the fall of Jaffa. He had drafted the Aley report for the Arab League about the extent of Jewish military capabilities, and he was devastated by the unfolding disaster in Palestine. But he did not have the power to overcome the political inertia that prevented the Arab League from fulfilling its promise to supply Jaysh al-Inqadh properly. As the field commander of Jaysh al-Inqadh Qawuqji had directed movements in Jaffa from afar. But the telegrams he sent back to headquarters in Damascus show that he had little control over what was actually happening inside the city. His decision to replace 'Adil Najm al-Din with Michel 'Isa came much too late for Jaffa.

As Jaffa fell and the scale of the defeats in Palestine became clear, the Syrian Foreign Ministry attempted to forge a reconciliation between the Mufti and Qawuqji. The Mufti was not in Palestine. During the war he lived in exile in Cairo. But he nevertheless attempted to direct the operations of the Palestinian forces from a distance, first through 'Abd al-Qadir al-Husayni (until he was killed) and then through the Palestinian commander Hasan Salama. On May 9, 1948, five days before the British withdrawal, the Syrian foreign minister Muhsin al-Barazi (later prime minister under Husni Za'im) sent Qawuqji a letter on behalf of President Quwatli. It mentioned a letter that the Mufti had sent to Qawuqji through Quwatli, which attested to the Mufti's willingness to cooperate with Qawuqji. Through Barazi, Quwatli was sending the message to Qawuqji that he was satisfied by the genuineness of the Mufti's gesture and that Qawuqji should be too:

His Excellency the President perused the letter sent to you by His Eminence the Mufti, Amin al-Husayni, and was satisfied by its truthfulness and by the fact that it shows cooperation and collaboration, something that we badly need in these critical times.

Publicly, and as far as the Syrian government was concerned, Qawuqji seems to have accepted this letter from the Mufti, but privately he believed that nothing had really changed or, as he expressed it through an Arabic proverb, "that Halima returns to her old habits." Much later he scribbled some comments onto the letter:

> All the accusations that the Mufti disavowed in the newspapers and then declared again, that I am a spy (English or French) and that I am conniving with the Jews, were futile and did not benefit him, nor the revolt that he set up against us, nor the corruption of some of our troops to the point of desertion . . . After all this and all his failures, he could find no better behavior to show than his approaching me through Shukri al-Quwatli, and to write a letter, which is praising me and complimenting my nationalism. So I welcomed his repentance, but yet Halima returns to her old habits.

Barazi thus managed to negotiate an official reconciliation between the Mufti and Qawuqji in May 1948. The Mufti's letter, also in Qawuqji's papers, did indeed praise him and compliment him on his nationalism and on his commitment to the struggle against colonialism; but Qawuqji's later thoughts were also scribbled on this letter:

> His Eminence accuses me of spying for the benefit of the English and the French in collusion with the Jews. Then he comes to me in this letter saying all this stuff about what I have accomplished by way of great deeds and struggle and defense of the land and that my name will be mentioned with appreciation, blah, blah, blah . . . Where is the truth in all of this? Is it in the spying or in the great national deeds? He is not truthful. There is hypocrisy in his letter.

Qawuqji did succeed in uniting with Palestinian forces in the last few days before the final British withdrawal on May 14, in order to try to protect Jerusalem from the Haganah's advance. Palestinian irregulars and units of Jaysh al-Inqadh garrisoned in central Palestine under Qawuqji's direct control countered Haganah attempts to control the road to Jerusalem. Intense battles were fought around Latrun, Bab al-Wad, and Bayt Mahsir. David Ben-Gurion later claimed that this was some of the fiercest fighting faced by the Haganah throughout the war.

FIGHTING FOR THE NORTH

At midnight on May 14, 1948, the British mandate over Palestine expired, the State of Israel was declared, and the Haganah became the Israel Defense Forces (IDF). The next morning the Arab armies invaded, marking the beginning of the interstate phase of the 1948 War. The Syrian Army was the main threat to the Israel Defense Forces in the north. To the south, they faced the Iraqi Army; in Jerusalem and the surrounding area they faced the Jordanian Arab Legion, the most formidable of the Arab armies and the one that was to inflict the heaviest losses on Israeli forces. In the far south the IDF faced the Egyptian Army. Qawuqji was appointed field commander of the northern front of Jaysh al-Inqadh, which continued to operate but in a much-reduced capacity. Now the pressure was on the Arab state armies to regain the cities and towns that had fallen to the Haganah in March, April, and early May. Palestinian refugees were glued to their radios, hopeful that the IDF would be defeated and they would be able to return to their homes. Qawuqji's role was far less pivotal than it had been before May 14. He spent less time in Palestine itself and more time shuttling between meetings with leaders of the Arab states and meetings with 'Azzam Pasha at the headquarters of the Arab League in Cairo in an attempt to procure arms and supplies for Jaysh al-Inqadh. Out of frustration with the Arab League he twice submitted a letter of resignation to 'Azzam Pasha. He used the threat of resignation to try to force the league to produce more arms. On both occasions he was persuaded to remain in his position as commander of the northern front. Jaysh al-Inqadh was overshadowed by the Arab state armies during the final months of the war. Qawuqji constantly struggled for supplies, yet somewhere between one and two thousand Jaysh al-Inqadh soldiers stayed in the field until the end. Sometimes they retreated in the face of the growing strength of the IDF. Other times they fought hard: at Malkiyya on the Lebanese border in late May and early June, at Sejera (near Nazareth) in July, and in the villages of the northern Galilee in October during the final Haganah push to secure complete control of the north in the last few weeks before the end of the fighting.

Malkiyya was a small town on the border between Lebanon and Palestine in the Galilee panhandle. It stood in the hills overlooking the roads that ran from 'Aytarun to Sa'sa' and from 'Aytarun to Blida. The same hills also commanded the Huleh Plain along the border between Syria and Lebanon. As such they were an important site from which to protect Bint al-Jubayl in Lebanon and the south of Jabal 'Amil. By the end of May 1948 the IDF had captured Malkiyya as part of its attempt to secure the border between Lebanon and Palestine. On June 5–6 a coordinated Arab attack was launched on the Galilee as part of a plan to retake the northern Galilee's military sites lost by Adib Shishakli's forces in March, April, and May. The attack was launched from the east and the west with the cooperation of Syrian and Lebanese forces and Jaysh al-Inqadh. As part of this attack Malkiyya was successfully recaptured from the Haganah. Qawuqji, along with Lt. Col. Shawkat Shuqayr, a regular Lebanese Army officer, planned and coordinated the attack.

In his memoirs Qawuqji lays out in careful detail the way in which the battle was executed in coordination with the Syrian Air Force and the Lebanese Army. He watched the fighting through his binoculars from a neighboring hill, along with the Lebanese minister of defense, Majid Arslan, and Gen. Fu'ad Shahab, the commander of the Lebanese forces. It was a hard battle, with casualties on both sides, but the combined Arab forces broke through into the village at dawn on June 7. Most of the Haganah fighters were dead. Qawuqji remarks that many of the dead were wearing bandages, and he comments on their courage for fighting while they were wounded. Many of the Haganah soldiers were Russians. Qawuqji knew something of their reputation as tenacious fighters from his experience of being in Berlin in the summer of 1945, when the Russians overran the city.

The battle of Malkiyya has since been claimed by the Lebanese Army as a victory. Malkiyya even played an important role as a symbol for antisectarian unity in the Lebanese Army during the period of the civil war in the late 1970s and 1980s. Most historians do not recognize the role that Jaysh al-Inqadh played in the battle. However, Qawuqji's close cooperation with the Lebanese Army was a sign of a shift of allegiance. During the interstate war Qawuqji worked closely with Arslan, Shahab, and Riyad al-Sulh, the Lebanese prime minister. He praises Arslan and Sulh in his memoirs for supplying the arms, supplies, and support that Jaysh al-Inqadh needed. In his view this was genuine assistance, in contrast with the empty promises of Taha al-Hashimi and the Arab League. Malkiyya had shown Qawuqji that he could rely on the support of the Lebanese government, more than on King 'Abdullah and on the Syrians. Qawuqji was awarded the Medal of the Cedar by the Lebanese government for Jaysh al-Inqadh's role in Malkiyya.

SOLDIERS AND POLITICIANS

Two days after the victory at Malkiyya, on June 8, 1948, Qawuqji traveled briefly to Beirut, where he met with Riyad al-Sulh as well as with 'Azzam Pasha. The British, the Americans, and the UN were putting pressure on the Arab League to get the Arab state armies to accept a cease-fire; everybody in Beirut spoke about it. 'Azzam Pasha met with Qawuqji and asked him what he thought about the impending truce. Qawuqji was unequivocal in his response:

> An armistice is usually made after the defeat of the enemy who then asks for it. Nothing of this kind has happened. We are not defeated

or crushed, nor are the Jewish forces, yet our position is comparatively better than theirs . . . It is an opportunity for them to increase their armaments and strengthen their fortifications and reorganize their fronts after having tested the strength of our armies and our preparations.

Three days later, on June 11, the so-called first truce of the war went into effect. It lasted exactly a month and was followed by the Ten Days War, during which the IDF captured the Palestinian towns of Lydda, Ramle, and Nazareth, in addition to dozens of smaller towns and villages in Palestine, including eventually Sejera, which was the site of fighting between Jaysh al-Inqadh and the Israel Defense Forces. Qawuqji tried to use the period of the first truce to assess the state of play in the Galilee and to shore up arms and fortifications for when hostilities resumed. He traveled the Galilee, examining the main roads between towns, in order to plan how best to secure them against IDF attack. In a report dated June 20 he provided details on the main roads and his estimation of how the IDF would try to use them to take key towns like Sejera, Tarshiha, Shefa 'Amr, and Majd al-Kurum. He evaluated how many men and arms would be required to defend these towns and others. He stated that the "enemy intends to bring in fighter planes and field guns during the truce and that once this occurs the enemy will be equal with the combined Arab forces as far as the quality of arms is concerned." The report ends with the assertion that the IDF would not dare attack Nazareth because of the particular strength of its fortifications.

Riyad al-Sulh supported Qawuqji's efforts to secure arms. While in Cairo, Sulh wrote a letter supporting Qawuqji's repeated requests for a reliable supply of arms from the Military Committee of the Arab League. Sulh's letter is in Qawuqji's private papers, and the letter is filed under the heading "Riyad works in Cairo to guarantee our needs from Damascus." Like so many of the key documents in his archive, he scribbled a note: "Deep inside me, the thermometer of hope rose to a high degree, after it had dropped to zero following the conduct of the Syrian authorities and Taha al-Hashimi. It was as if I were that thermometer tossed by the hand of a child in a bathroom, at one time rising up by the water's heat and then dropping down by the water's coldness."

During the period of the first truce, Jaysh al-Inqadh was restructured. A single operational and logistical staff was established with one field headquarters at 'Aytarun, in Lebanon. Shawkat Shuqayr, the Lebanese army officer who had been so successful at Malkiyya, was made chief of staff, and Amir Hasak was made chief of operations and intelligence. This allowed Qawuqji to focus on securing arms and other material support for the army. He spent large amounts of time in the last few months of the war traveling to Damascus, Beirut, and Cairo and meeting with leaders of the various Arab states, in addition to 'Azzam Pasha and other high-ranking bureaucrats in the Arab League. Jaysh al-Inqadh stayed in the field until the bitter end. During the fighting that broke out after the first truce, its soldiers fought hard at Sejera as part of the effort to protect Nazareth. But both Nazareth and Sejera were in Jewish hands by the time the second truce began on July 18.

When describing these last few months of the war in his memoirs, Qawuqji travels between the soldier's space (fighting and anxiety about supplies) and the politician's space (summits and meetings in Damascus and Beirut). He paints a picture of these two spaces existing independently from each other and always portrays himself as a stranger among the politicians, shocked at their disconnectedness from the reality of the fighting. Whenever he meets with them—and "them" is usually Taha al-Hashimi, Jamil Mardam, Shukri al-Quwatli, 'Azzam Pasha, and even Riyad al-Sulh—he pleads for them to respond positively to his requests for supplies.

In September 1948 Jaysh al-Inqadh held some of the high ground that rises above the Huleh Plain, northeast of Safad. This included the town of Marus, which was being held by the 'Alawite Battalion of Jaysh al-Inqadh under the command of Ghassan Jadid. IDF attacks on the Marus area were intended to dislodge Jaysh al-Inqadh forces from their commanding position over the Huleh Plain. Qawuqji received daily telegrams from Jadid asking for reinforcements and ammunition, so Qawuqji approached the commander of the Syrian Army, Husni Za'im, who was occupying Mishmar Ha-Yarden, a few miles to the east, to ask for his cooperation in defending the Marus region. Za'im persuaded Qawuqji to go with him to Damascus so that they could try together to persuade the politicians to supply ammunition. Qawuqji, Husni Za'im, Jamil Mardam, Riyad al-Sulh, and Quwatli met in the Presidential Palace in Damascus on September 13. Qawuqji asked for mortar bombs and guns to help him defend Marus, but according to his account, Quwatli turned to him and said, "Why do you provoke the Jews? Don't you see that they have us by the neck? You had better withdraw from Marus." Qawuqji left the meeting filled with despair: "These words were a severe blow to me. I never expected anything like this. What disturbed me more now was not the question of ammunition but the mentality, this strange and surprising mentality, in the heads of 'the heads.'"

By the fall of 1948 Jaysh al-Inqadh soldiers were in a desperate state. Stationed mainly in the hills in northern Palestine and southern Lebanon, many were without shoes and warm winter coats. Dysentery and other diseases were rife in the Arab Liberation Army camps. In spite of this, some soldiers continued to fight under Qawuqji's direction. On October 22, 1948, Jaysh al-Inqadh troops managed to occupy an IDF position near Kibbutz Manara, in the upper Galilee. The IDF tried to retake the military post but failed. Thirty-three IDF soldiers were killed and forty wounded in the attempt.

The incident at Manara convinced Ben-Gurion that the IDF had to clear Jaysh al-Inqadh from the Galilee once and for all. At the end of October the IDF launched Operation Hiram, which was intended to oust Jaysh al-Inqadh and to complete the Israeli occupation of the Galilee. Jaysh al-Inqadh troops fought hard against the IDF in some Galilee villages, even though the IDF had put four brigades (about six thousand men) into the field. These troops were supported by massive artillery and aerial bombardments. Jaysh al-Inqadh had about fifteen hundred men spread out across two partial-strength brigades. They fought with the little artillery they had left and with rifles. Palestinian farmers, armed mainly with old Ottoman rifles, also tried to defend their villages. Operation Hiram saw some of the worst massacres of Palestinians by Israeli forces during the war, including at al-Dawayima, Safsaf, Saliha, 'Eilabun, and Hula. By this point in the war it was clear to Palestinians in the Galilee that the promised Arab victory was not coming. They were hearing reports of the deplorable conditions in refugee camps just a few miles north across the Lebanese border. Some fled to Lebanon, but many decided to stay and take their chances under Israeli rule.

The IDF position near Manara was recaptured by the IDF during Operation Hiram. Qawuqji understood that the IDF had superior forces and that without being resupplied he could not expect his troops to continue fighting. His main focus during Operation Hiram was managing the organized withdrawal of his forces. Most of the remaining Jaysh al-Inqadh troops and weapons were safely withdrawn to Nabatiya in Lebanon, in late October and early November 1948. However, approximately two hundred Jaysh al-Inqadh soldiers died during the retreat, while some were taken prisoner by Israeli forces.

It was a particularly cold and rainy November in the hills of southern Lebanon. Mahmoud Fahmi Darwish, the general secretary of the League for the Liberation of Palestine in Baghdad, visited the Iraqi troops serving with Jaysh al-Inqadh in order to hand out cigarettes and candy as a show of support from the Iraqi people. Qawuqji told him that the men needed clothing much more than cigarettes and candy. Darwish was moved by the deprivation that he saw among the troops, and he immediately telegraphed his committee back in Baghdad to send three thousand blankets. A few days later Taha al-Hashimi ordered that Jaysh al-Inqadh be disbanded because the Arab League no longer had the resources to pay its salaries. Some Jaysh al-Inqadh troops were reassigned to the Syrian Army under the command of Husni Za'im. Qawuqji was relieved of his command.

By the end of the war, the new State of Israel had captured much more of Palestine than it had originally been allotted in the Partition Resolution. Those parts of Palestine not contained in the new State of Israel were under either Jordanian or Egyptian control: Jordan had occupied the West Bank of the Jordan River and East Jerusalem, Egypt had occupied the Gaza Strip. In addition, 750,000 Palestinians, over half the Arab population of

FIGURE 40

Palestine, had left in fear or had been directly expelled by Jewish forces. Refugee camps for the Palestinians were hastily assembled in Syria, Jordan, and Lebanon. A photograph taken in 1951 (figure 40) shows Nahr al-Barid Refugee Camp, near Qawuqji's hometown of Tripoli, Lebanon.

After the end of the war the Mufti, who in September 1948 established himself as the president of something called the All-Palestine Government, was officially based in the city of Gaza in southwestern Palestine. Gaza fell under Egyptian control after the conclusion of armistice agreements between Egypt and Israel in the spring of 1949. In defiance of the Israeli victory, the All-Palestine Government pronounced its jurisdiction over all of Palestine with Jerusalem as its capital, but it had no army and no civil service. It was also dependent upon Egyptian support. The Mufti continued to serve as its president long after the war, living in Cairo until the Egyptian government dissolved the All-Palestine Government in 1959. He lived out the rest of his life in relative obscurity in Beirut.

EPILOGUE

In his account of the war, Qawuqji admits no mistakes of his own. His silence about his misjudgments during 1948 was probably a defensive reaction to the way he had been scapegoated in the decades after the war. He was accused of a long list of crimes: plotting to use Jaysh al-Inqadh troops to overthrow the Syrian government; spying for the British; spying for the Israelis; spying for the French; secretly working with King ʿAbdullah; working only for Syrian interests; refusing to cooperate with the Palestinians; refusing to cooperate with the Arab League; being a coward; and presiding over his troops' looting of Palestinian towns. These accusations rattled about amid the cacophony of recriminations in the post-1948 Arab world.

Qawuqji certainly made mistakes. Like other Arab army officers and politicians, he underestimated the potential of the Jewish forces. This led to his decision to attack settlements like Mishmar Haemek without adequate preparation and planning. He was unable to prevent troops who were officially under his general command from looting and from engaging in other thuggish behavior. This was particularly acute in the case of Jaffa, where his inability to control the garrison there was one of the factors that led to the fall of the city. There is also no question that the animosity between him and the Mufti clouded Qawuqji's judgment during the war and affected his ability to work with the Palestinians. But Qawuqji faced an extremely difficult situation in 1948. The Arab League was weak and disorganized. The Military Committee of the league could hardly provide even the basic supplies necessary for Jaysh al-Inqadh to fight. Many of its soldiers fought bravely, but some were former criminals who enlisted simply to loot Palestinian towns and villages. There had also been no time to build trust between the officers of Jaysh al-Inqadh. After all, it was an army created from nothing in just a few weeks. There was no coherent command structure that held firm under pressure. Qawuqji had responsibility for the army but little power over its operation. In hindsight, Qawuqji's greatest misjudgment may have been agreeing to lead this army into the field in the first place. There is little doubt that his reputation—particularly among Palestinians, most of whom had thought highly of him before 1948—would have been less tarnished if he had turned down the command. But Qawuqji was genuinely committed to fighting for Palestine. He did not give up on that commitment until the Arab states signed armistice agreements with Israel at the end of 1948 and the beginning of 1949. Unlike some officers and politicians who had been involved in the war, Qawuqji did not go on to have a political career in the years following 1948. He was easy to scapegoat because there was little price to be paid for pointing the finger of blame at him. What is more, Qawuqji never fought for any particular Arab state in 1948. Ever since he joined the Syrian Revolt in October 1925, Qawuqji's military career was as a transnational fighter. This left him without a veteran's place in a particular nation-state and defenseless in the face of post-1948 recriminations.

At the end of Qawuqji's memoirs there is a short essay written by him in 1950, just two years after the war ended. The essay contained a list of recommendations for the Arabs to follow if they wanted to avoid a new catastrophe. His recommendations all focused on the importance of Arab unity. He suggested the establishment of an Arab army that should be operationally separate from politics and politicians. He called on all the Arab states to contribute to this army with money and manpower in the spirit of genuine trust and sincerity. The memoirs end with his declaration that the future of the Arab people would not be secure without this kind of bold undertaking:

> The Arab people cannot be sure of their future without taking a new leap, which should spring from a new mentality and which should operate in new ways in order to secure a strong unity that can confront the many threats to their existence.

But Qawuqji's commitment to an Arab unity that existed separately from the interests of nation-states was already out of date in 1950. The time of ex-Ottoman soldiers like Qawuqji, who fought in and traveled across Arab lands as if there were no borders, was over. He played no role in the dramatic events that gripped the Arab world between 1948 and his death in 1976. Because of this, there is very little information about his life after 1948. We know that in the 1950s he made a few formal visits to various Arab states, where he was politely received as an ex-Arab commander. One photograph taken in Cairo in the 1950s (figure 41) shows him sitting somewhat forlornly at a banquet held in his honor and attended by assorted dignitaries, including the Palestinian newspaper editor Mohamed Ali Eltaher, the Saudi ambassador to Egypt, and an ex–Egyptian minister of war, Salih Harb Pasha.

Also in the 1950s Qawuqji, as a representative of the Lebanese Army, traveled to Argentina, where he met Juan and Eva Perón. They gave Qawuqji the latest model of a submachine gun as a gift from the Argentinian people. He later toyed with the possibility of standing for the Lebanese parliament as a representative from Tripoli. Letters in his archive show that he had some strong support, but the plans never came to fruition. Qawuqji's disdain for politicians was a barrier to any serious political engagement.

For most of his post-1948 life, Qawuqji, Anneliese, and their three

FIGURE 41

sons lived on a small income in an apartment in Bir al-'Abid, a lower-middle-class neighborhood in the southern suburbs of Beirut. The apartment was on the ground floor, and at the back was a garden with fruit trees, where Qawuqji spent much of his time. He received a tiny pension from the Saudi government for his role in training the Saudi Army in the early 1930s. He also received a modest salary as a consultant for the Lebanese Army. Whatever perks the family enjoyed came from the generosity of friends. This kind of generosity paid for a small villa in the Beirut beach resort of Saint Michel, where he received old comrades, as well as journalists wanting to hear stories about his past. But those who knew him well talked of his struggles with money and his efforts to support his wife and children in Beirut.

In 1957 Qawuqji wrote to Shukri al-Quwatli, who was president of Syria, asking for funds: "I have already complained to you about this matter and I have made clear that my children can only expect a terrible future in light of the pathetic pension that I receive, an amount that wouldn't even be enough for a floor sweeper in your palace. And this after the long battle that I fought against the colonialist in every Arab land and after the fact that I have filled the pages of history." There is no reply to this letter in Qawuqji's archive. Like so many of Qawuqji's dispatches from the field during the 1948 War, it appears that this appeal fell on deaf ears.

As Qawuqji struggled to find a role for himself in the post-1948 Arab world, a younger generation of army officers rose to prominence in Arab politics. In Iraq in 1958 the radical anti-British Army officer 'Abd al-Karim Qasim launched a successful coup against the pro-British civilian government. Syria had been rocked by power struggles since the end of the 1948 War; in 1963 Ba'athists launched a coup that eventually brought Hafez al-Asad to power in 1970. In Egypt Gamal 'Abd al-Nasser rose to power in the mid-1950s, replacing the Egyptian monarchy. All these men had come of age long after the collapse of the Ottoman Empire. They were part of a new state-driven militarism that dominated politics in the Arab world. Even a figure like Nasser, who was a champion of Pan-Arabism, saw Egypt as the leader and center of Arab unity. The Arab League, the official organ of Arab unity, continued to meet in airy conference centers, but it was widely regarded as a toothless organization without the will to effect real change.

Qawuqji's lifetime saw three more Arab-Israeli wars. In 1956 Britain, France, and Israel secretly agreed to attack Egypt and attempted to topple the Nasser regime. Nasser, who was extremely popular in Egypt and the rest of the Arab world, came out of the 1956 War politically unscathed and went on to fight Israel again in the 1967 War. Like 1948, 1967 was another disaster for the Arab armies, which lost the Sinai Peninsula, the Gaza Strip, the Golan Heights, and the West Bank of the Jordan River to Israeli occupation. In the wake of the 1967 defeat, Palestinians decided to take matters into their own hands, and the Palestine Liberation Organization rose to prominence. Under the leadership of Yasser Arafat, the PLO became a key player in Arab politics in the late 1960s and 1970s. The PLO was particularly influential in Lebanon, the country that had become its main base.

The last Arab-Israeli war that Qawuqji watched from the sidelines was the October 1973 War, when Egypt launched a surprise attack on Israel in an attempt to retrieve the Sinai Peninsula. This was the time when the Lebanese journalist Jan Daya, aiming to find out what an aging Arab commander thought about the progress of the war, interviewed Qawuqji. Although Daya's article began in 1973 in the middle of the war between Egypt and Israel, he quickly turned to Qawuqji's past and especially to Qawuqji's return to Tripoli from Paris in the spring of 1947. Daya tells us little about the Qawuqji of 1973, apart from noting his surprise that Qawuqji was living in a simple apartment without attendants and pomp.

Relations between Lebanese and Palestinians soured in the 1970s as a result of the PLO's ascendancy in Lebanon. Some historians go so far as to blame the Palestinian presence in Lebanon for the outbreak of the civil war there in April 1975. The Lebanese civil war had many causes, but the beginning of the violence was sparked by clashes between Palestinians and Lebanese Christian militias. The first phase of the civil war came to a close in October 1976, just a few weeks before Qawuqji died on December 15, 1976. Between April 1975 and October 1976 Lebanese militias massacred thousands of Palestinians, including at the Tel al-Za'atar Refugee Camp in northeastern Beirut in August 1976. Tel al-Za'atar was home to Palestinians who had been expelled from northern Palestine in the 1948 War. In the last year of his life, Qawuqji saw the violent effects of 1948 reverberating just a few miles from his apartment building in Beirut.

The apartment in Bir al-'Abid lay right at an intersection of warring militias during the Lebanese civil war. There were explosions and fighting in the streets every day. Qawuqji's sons, who had left home by the mid-1970s, begged Qawuqji and Anneliese to move to a safer neighborhood. Qawuqji joked that he had been through much harder times than this and that he had his Argentinian submachine gun and an old Luger pistol to protect him and Anneliese. But eventually the couple were persuaded and moved into an empty apartment in the same building as their son Ossama and his family, in the quieter area of Verdun in West Beirut. It was in the Verdun apartment that Qawuqji spent the last few months of his life. He died at home after a short illness. Anneliese later told family members that right before he died, she heard Qawuqji speaking Turkish, as if he were back in the Ottoman Army talking to his fellow officers.

Qawuqji's funeral was held in his hometown of Tripoli on December 16, 1976. Tripolitan merchants closed up their stores that day, and mourning posters were pasted on the walls announcing the death of "one of the great commanders of the two Arab revolutions in Syria and Palestine." People watched from the streets and from their balconies as Qawuqji's funeral convoy moved slowly through the streets of Tripoli, past al-Taal Square. This was the same square where Qawuqji had watched from a friend's balcony British soldiers laughing and talking, fifty-eight years before, following the defeat of the Ottoman Army in World War I. After prayers in the Mansouri Mosque, Qawuqji was buried in the family plot in the main graveyard in Tripoli. In addition to his family, numerous Lebanese, Syrian, and Palestinian dignitaries, as well as old comrades from the various revolts that he had fought in, paid their respects. Palestinians were represented at the funeral by Abu Ta'an, a high-ranking PLO official based in Tripoli. His speech was quoted at length in the newspaper coverage of the funeral:

> The PLO bids farewell to an exceptional Lebanese and Arab leader who devoted his life and struggle for the Arabness of Palestine. The PLO feels deep sadness and huge grief for the loss of this great Arab leader, whose life and struggle for the sake of Palestine was an achievement, an epic and a glowing flash of light in this historic struggle that has united the Lebanese and Palestinian people. All the legends of heroism and sacrifice, which the two peoples have inscribed in the face of conspiracies and challenges, are only a continuity of the deep-rooted traditions of struggle in which the late Fawzi al-Qawuqji had the honor of initiative and the honor of revolutionary leadership.

Abu Ta'an delivered his eulogy just a few weeks after Lebanese militias and Palestinians stopped fighting each other. The Lebanese Army was out in force at Qawuqji's funeral because Lebanon was still extremely unstable in December 1976. By mentioning the "deep-rooted traditions of struggle," Abu Taʿan reminded Lebanese and Palestinians of an earlier, simpler time. Qawuqji was a painful symbol of the failure of Arab nationalism to achieve its goal of unity. But remembering him also evoked a past when the future was open to possibility, when ordinary Arab soldiers fought together under his leadership against a clear colonial enemy.

Visitors to Qawuqji's grave today have to search long and hard to find it, resting amid the tightly clustered headstones. He lies next to his father. Surrounding the two of them are the graves of ordinary Tripolitans, as if in death Qawuqji were lost amid the crowd that had embraced him upon his return to his hometown in March 1947.

NOTES ON SOURCES

I have used a wide range of original sources to construct the narrative in this book. The most important archive I consulted is the private archive of Fawzi al-Qawuqji in Beirut. I am very grateful to his family, in particular Ossama El-Kaoukji and Dwan El-Kaoukji, for allowing me access to this archive. Informal conversations with Ossama El-Kaoukji and Dwan El-Kaoukji have also informed my narrative. I consulted the following two Arab archives in the Middle East that contain materials relating directly to Qawuqji: the Center for Historical Documents [Markaz al-Watha'iq al-Tarikhiyya] in Damascus and the Institute for Palestine Studies [Mu'assasat al-Dirasat al-Filastiniyya] in Beirut. Some of the documents available in the above three archives have also been published in the second (1995) edition of Qawuqji's memoirs: Khayriyya Qasimiyya, ed., *Mudhakkirat Fawzi al-Qawuqji* [The Memoirs of Fawzi al-Qawuqji], (Damascus: Dar al-Namir, 1995). Qawuqji's memoirs were prepared for publication by the late Palestinian historian Khayriyya Qasimiyya. My book would not have been possible without Professor Qasimiyya's efforts in making Qawuqji's story available to us. I also draw on archival material from the National Archives (London); Service Historique de la Défense (Vincennes, Paris); Centre des Archives Diplomatiques de Nantes (Nantes); Ha-Arkhiyon Ha-Tziyoni Ha-Merkazi [the Central Zionist Archive] (Jerusalem); Ginzakh Ha-Medina [the Israel State Archive] (Jerusalem); the papers of Nabih and 'Adil al-'Azma at the Exeter University Library (Exeter); and the Middle East Centre Archive at St. Antony's College (Oxford). For archival material relating to Qawuqji's connection with German officials, I have relied on the published work of Gerhard Höpp, in addition to Höpp's private archive housed at the Zentrum Moderner Orient (Berlin).

Other important primary sources are the Arabic memoirs of soldiers and politicians who knew Qawuqji or were directly involved in events in which he played an important part; these include Ja'far Pasha al-'Askari, Sa'id Taqi al-Din, 'Izzat Darwaza, Taha al-Hashimi, Hajj Amin al-Husayni, Nabih and 'Adil al-'Azma, Kamal Haddad, Salah al-Din al-Sabbagh, Khidr al-'Ali Mahfuz, Sa'id al-Tarmanini, 'Abd al-Rahman Shahbandar, Sa'id al-'As, Subhi al-'Umari, Bahjat Abu Gharbiyya, Nasser Eddin Nashashibi, Salah Ibrahim al-Nazer, and Mohammad Said Ishkuntana. The memoirs of the Syrian journalist Munir al-Rayyis, who was with Qawuqji during many of the events narrated in this book, were a particularly rich resource. I also consulted contemporaneous newspaper articles in English, French, and Arabic. Although the large amount of scholarship that has been published in European languages on the history of the modern Middle East contains very little information on Qawuqji himself, it has helped me contextualize the historical events that he participated in.

The notes below provide a detailed account of the sources used for each chapter. They also include page numbers for the quotations that appear in the main text.

Abbreviations Used in the Notes

CADN   Centre des Archives Diplomatiques de Nantes (Nantes)
CHD   Center for Historical Documents (Damascus)
CO   Colonial Office
CZA   Central Zionist Archives (Jerusalem)
FO   Foreign Office
IPS   Institute of Palestine Studies (Beirut)
ISA   Israel State Archive (Jerusalem)
MAE   Ministère des Affaires Étrangères
NA   National Archives (Britain)
QPP   Qawuqji's Private Papers (Beirut)
SAC/MEC   St. Antony's College, Middle East Centre (Oxford)
SHD   Service Historique de la Défense (Vincennes)
T   Telegrams

1. Ottoman Officer

For the opening line of Qawuqji's memoirs: Qasimiyya, ed. *Mudhakkirat*, 15. For the methodological challenges that arise in using memoirs (including Qawuqji's) as a source: Laila Parsons, "Micro-narrative and the Historiography of the Middle East," *History Compass* 9/1 (2011), 84–96; and Laila Parsons, "Some Thoughts on Biography and the Historiography of the Early 20th-Century Arab World," *Journal of the Canadian Historical Association* 21/2 (2010), 5–20. Details about his parents and his early childhood come from conversations with his son, Ossama El-Kaoukji. For more on Qawuqiji's great-grandfather, see the entry "Muhammad ibn Khalil al-Mashishi al-Qawuqji al-Tarabulusi al-Sha'mi al-Hanafi," in Carl Brockelmann, *Geschichte der arabischen Litteratur: Supplement*, vol. 2 (Leiden: Brill, 1943), 776. Brockelmann lists eleven works by him and states that he was born in 1810 and died in 1888. For background on the establishment of the Ottoman military schools: Mesut Uyar, "Ottoman Arab Officers Between Nationalism and Loyalty During the First World War," *War in History* 20/4 (2013), 526–44; Michael Provence, "Ottoman Modernity, Colonialism, and Insurgency in the Interwar Arab East," *International Journal of Middle East Studies* 43 (2011), 205–25. Sultan Abdul Hamid also established special tribal schools for the sons of tribal shaykhs: Eugene Rogan, "Aserit Mektebi: Abdulhamid II's School for Tribes (1892–1907)," *International Journal of Middle East Studies* 28/1 (1996), 83–107. For the physical description of life in the Ottoman school system: Ben Fortna, *Imperial Classroom: Islam, Education, and the State in the Late Ottoman Empire* (Oxford: Oxford University Press, 2002), ch. 4, 5, and 6; Andrew Mango, *Ataturk* (London: John Murray, 2004), ch. 2; William Facey and Najdat Fathi Safwat, eds., *A Soldier's Story: From Ottoman Rule to Independent Iraq. The Memoirs of Ja'afar Pasha al-Askari*, 1885–1936 (London: Arabian Publishing, 2003), 15–19; Merwin Albert Griffiths, "The Reorganization of the Ottoman Army Under Abdulhamid II, 1880–1897" (unpublished Ph.D. dissertation, University of California—Los Angeles, 1966); James Madison McGarity, "Foreign Influence on the Ottoman Turkish Army, 1880–1918" (unpublished Ph.D. dissertation, American University, 1968). For the Mauser rifle and the Ottoman Army: J. Grant, "The Sword of the Sultan: Ottoman Arms Imports, 1854–1914," *Journal of Military History* 66/1 (2002), 9–36 (24).

For the quotations about "the army of freedom" and the fight between the Turkish and Arab students: Qasimiyya, ed., *Mudhakkirat*, 15 and 16, respectively. The story about being given bad food because he was an Arab comes from Rita Awad, who served as his assistant when he was working on his memoirs in the early 1970s. The Hamidian map of the Ottoman Empire: Fortna, *Imperial Classroom*, 189. For Qawuqji's journey to Mosul: Qasimiyya, ed., *Mudhakkirat*, 17–18. Ja'far al-'Askari, who had attended the War College a few years earlier (he was graduated in 1904) and who ended up joining the Arab Revolt of 1916, describes a similar *kalak* journey down the Tigris in 1897: Facey and Safwat, eds., *Soldier's Story*, 15–17. 'Askari also confirms that the normal route for officers in the Ottoman Army traveling between Baghdad and Istanbul was by the Euphrates, not the Tigris. The stopping points on the way were Dayr al-Zur and Aleppo and then finally Alexandretta, where they could board a ship to Istanbul. For the quote about the tribes: Qasimiyya, ed., *Mudhakkirat*, 17–18. Romanticizing the tribes was not restricted to Qawuqji but was part of a broader revolutionary nationalist discourse. Both the memoirs of Munir al-Rayyis, a Syrian revolutionary and friend of Qawuqji's, and those of Salah al-Din al-Sabbagh, the Iraqi nationalist officer who participated in the coup of 1941 and was executed in 1945, contain romantic images of the tribes as warriors against colonialism. The archetypal Arab fighter represented on the covers of their books is a tribesman with a rifle and either a flag or the outline of a map signifying the nation: Salah al-Din al-Sabbagh, *Fursan al-'Uruba: Mudhakkirat al-Shahid al-'Aqid al-Rukn Salah al-din al-Sabbagh* [Horsemen of Arabism: Memoirs of the Martyr, Staff Colonel Salah al-Din al-Sabbagh], (Rabat: 1994; first published 1956), 16; Munir al-Rayyis, *Al-Kitab al-Dhahabi li-l-Thawrat al-Wataniyya fi al-Mashriq al-'Arabi: Thawrat Filastin 'Am 1936* [The Golden Book of National Revolts in the Arab East: The Palestinian Revolt, 1936], (Damascus: Alif Ba', 1977), cover.

For the idea that anticolonial memoirs tell a public story of nation rather than offer up a more personal account: Dipesh Chakrabarty, "Postcoloniality and the Artifice of History: Who Speaks for 'Indian' Pasts?," *Provincializing Europe: Postcolonial Thought and Historical Difference* (Princeton: Princeton University Press, 2000), 27–46. My account of Arab nationalism is as Qawuqji presents it; the emergence of Arabism from Ottomanism in Greater Syria was in fact a very complicated story. Hasan Kayali explains this complexity well in *Arabs and Young Turks: Ottomanism, Arabism, and Islamism in the Second Constitutional Period of the Ottoman Empire, 1909–1918* (Berkeley: University of California Press, 1997). For the Rashid Rida quote: Qasimiyya, ed., *Mudhakkirat*, 18. For more on Islamic modernism as represented by Afghani, 'Abduh, and Rida: David Commins, "Religious Reformers and Arabists in Damascus, 1885–1914," *International Journal of Middle Eastern Studies* 18 (1987), 405–25. For an analysis of Rida as journalist: Dyala Hamza, "From '*ilm* to *sihafa* or the Politics of the Public Interest (*maslaha*): Muhammad Rashid Rida and his Journal al-Manar," in Hamza, ed., *The Making of the Arab Intellectual: Empire, Public Sphere and the Colonial Coordinates of Selfhood* (London: Routledge, 2012), 90–103. For the Turanid and Qahtanid quote: Qasimiyya, ed., *Mudhakkirat*, 16. For more on Turkification in this period: Kayali, *Arabs and Young Turks*, 88–96. For 'Aziz 'Ali al-Masri and the Qahtaniyya: Facey and Safwat, eds., *Soldier's Story*, 102.

For Qawuqji's joining al-'Ahd: Sa'id al-'As, *Safha min al-Ayyam al-Hamra: Mudhakkirat al-Qa'id Sa'id al-'As* [A Page from the Red Days: The Memoirs of the Commander Sa'id al-'As], (Beirut: al-Mu'assasa al-'Arabiyya li-l-Dirasat wa-al-Nashr, 1988; first published in 1935), 20. For more on al-Qahtaniyya and al-'Ahd: Eliezer Tauber, *The Emergence of the Arab Movement* (London: Frank Cass, 1993), 98–100 and 213–36. For a social history of Mosul and the struggle to collect taxes from the Shammar: Sarah Shields, *Mosul Before Iraq: Like Bees Making Five-Sided Cells* (Buffalo: SUNY Press, 2000). For Qawuqji's account of his time in Mosul: Qasimiyya, ed., *Mudhakkirat*, 18–24. For the quote about Turks being more effective than Arabs: ibid., 20. Information on the Mesopotamian campaign is taken from Eric Erikson, *Ordered to Die: A History of the Ottoman Army in the First World War* (New York: Praeger, 2000), 66–68. For a comprehensive history of the Ottomans in World War I: Eugene Rogan, *The Fall of the Ottomans: The Great War in the Middle East* (New York: Basic Books, 2015). For Qawuqji's account of the fighting in Iraq, his meeting with Jamal Pasha in Jounieh, and his journey to Bir Sab'a: Qasimiyya, ed., *Mudhakkirat*, 27–32. For the quote that describes Bir Sab'a: ibid., 32. For the reconnaissance missions, the battle of Nabi Samuel, and winning the Iron Cross: ibid., 32–51; documents relating to Qawuqji's Iron Cross can also be found in Private Papers (Fawzi al-Qawuqji), Center for Historical Documents, Damascus [CHD].

For the quote about the battle for Nabi Samuel: Qasimiyya, ed., *Mudhakkirat*, 50. For the meeting with Liman von Sanders: ibid., 52. For Qawuqji's early encounters with von Leyser: ibid., 33. For Jamal Pasha's inspection: ibid., 34–35. For the train crash and the Ottoman government's accusations against Qawuqji: ibid., 39–45. For von Leyser's letter: ibid., 517, and Qawuqji's Private Papers [QPP]. For Qawuqji's thoughts on the Arab Revolt: ibid., 37–38. For the fact that most Arab officers in the Ottoman Army did not join the Arab Revolt: Uyar, "Ottoman Arab Officers Between Nationalism and Loyalty." For the passage where Qawuqji describes pretending to be an Arab defecting from the Ottoman Army: Qasimiyya, ed., *Mudhakkirat*, 45. For the account of Qawuqji's journey through the last days of the war until his arrival home in Tripoli: ibid., 51–71. Other sources consulted to provide context for this section include Munir al-Rayyis, *Al-Kitab al-Dhahabi li-l-Thawrat al-Wataniyya fi al-Mashriq al-'Arabi: al-Thawra al-Suriyya al-Kubra* [The Golden Book of National Revolts in the Arab East: The Great Syrian Revolt], (Beirut: Dar al-Tali'a li-l-Taba'a wa-l-Nashr, 1969), 91–93; Liman von Sanders, *Five Years in Turkey* (Annapolis: United States Naval Institute, 1927), 198–254; Subhi al-'Umari, *al-Ma'arik al-'Ula: al-Tariq ila Dimashq* [The First Battles: The Road to Damascus], (London: Riad al-Rayyes Books, 1991), 288–99; Mango, *Ataturk*, 179–82; David R. Woodward, *Hell in the Holy Land: World War I in the Middle East* (Lexington: University Press of Kentucky, 2006), 138–206. For the quote about the famine: Qasimiyya, ed., *Mudhakkirat*, 51. For Qawuqji's account of what Mustafa Kemal said after being rescued: ibid., 64. For Qawuqji's description of Damascus and his depiction of the railway station's being "like a slice of watermelon in the desert covered with flies": ibid., 68. For the quote about his final conversation with Mustafa Kemal in Homs: ibid., 71.

2. Syria in Revolt

For the location of his apartment in Berlin: Gerhard Höpp, "Ruhmloses Zwischenspiel. Fawzi al-Qawuqji in Deutschland, 1941–1947" [Inglorious Interlude. Fawzi al-Qawuqji in Germany, 1941–1947], in Peter Heine, ed., *Al-Rafidayn: Jahrbuch zur Geschichte und Kultur des modernen Iraq* (Würzburg: Ergon Verlag, 1995), 19–46, 30. For the report on the tribes of Syria: University of Exeter Documentation Centre, Private Papers of Nabih and 'Adil al-'Azma, MS215. For the report "Reasons for the Revolution": Private Papers (Fawzi al-Qawuqji), CHD. Information about the pronunciation of Suriya's name comes from conversations with Qawuqji's family. For the Safarjalani reference: Muhyi al-Din al-Safarjalani, *Tarikh al-Thawra al-Suriyya* [History of the Syrian Revolt], (Damascus: Dar al-Yaqdha al-'Arabiyya, 1961). For Qawuqji's studio portrait and short testimony: ibid., 16–17. For Qawuqji's account of watching the British army enter Midan al-Taal and the quotation: Qasimiyya, ed., *Mudhakkirat*, 74. For Faysal's tour of the Syrian cities: Subhi al-Umari, *Maysalun: Niyahat 'Ahd* [Maysalun: End of a Regime], (London: Riyad al-Rayyes Books, 1991), 19–20. For the account of the Arab Army, the hiring of Hashimi, and information about salaries: ibid., 33–38. For Qawuqji's account of his meeting with Faysal and the quotation: Qasimiyya, ed., *Mudhakkirat*,

75. For the copy of his ID card: Private Papers (Fawzi al-Qawuqji), CHD. For the fact that Ottoman institutions did not generally divide religion from nationality: Uyar, "Ottoman Officers," footnote 16.

For details on the structure of the Arab Army: (No author), *Tarikh al-Jaysh al-'Arabi al-Suri* [History of the Syrian Arab Army], vol. 1 (Damascus: Markaz al-Dirasat al-'Askariyya, 2002), 60–90. For background on the Arab Army and the disputes between Yasin al-Hashimi and Yusuf al-'Azma: Malcolm Russell, *The First Modern Arab State: Syria Under Faysal, 1918–1920* (Minneapolis: Bibliotheca Islamica, 1918), 180–81. For Qawuqji's account of al-Mu'allaqa: Qasimiyya, ed., *Mudhakkirat*, 79–80. For the meeting with Faysal in his house in Damascus: ibid., 83. For background information about Nuri Sha'lan: Dawn Chatty, "The Bedouin in Contemporary Syria: The Persistence of Tribal Authority and Control," *Middle East Journal* (Winter 2010), 29–49. For Qawuqji's account of the fall of Damascus to the French: Qasimiyya, ed., *Mudhakkirat*, 85–89. For the quotation: ibid., 87.

For the French *Copie du Livret Matricule* from the Syrian Legion: QPP; also Service Historique de la Défense [SHD], 4H151. Details about his first wife come from conversations with his son, Ossama El-Kaoukji. For accounts that he believed he was joining a national army: 'Abd al-Rahman Shahbandar, *Mudhakkirat al-Duktur 'Abd al-Rahman Shahbandar* [The Memoirs of Dr. 'Abd al-Rahman Shahbandar], (Beirut: Dar al-Irshad, 1968), 150–51. For the story of Qawuqji's recruitment into the Syrian Legion: Qasimiyya, ed., *Mudhakkirat*, 91–92. For the quote from Captain Hak: ibid., 91. For the letters from Catroux and Hillier: QPP; also 4H151, SHD. For his account of Captain Mike's behavior: Qasimiyya, ed., *Mudhakkirat*, 92; and Shahbandar, *Mudhakkirat*, 150–51. For the French officer in southern Lebanon and his dog: Malek Abisaab, "Shi'ite Peasants and a New Nation in Colonial Lebanon: The Intifada (Uprising) of Bint Jubayl, 1936," *Comparative Studies of South Asia, Africa and the Middle East* 29/3 (November 2009), 483–501. For the Tarmanini quote, see the reference to the Tarmanini manuscript below. In his book *Being Modern in the Middle East: Revolution, Nationalism, Colonialism and the Arab Middle Class* (Princeton: Princeton University Press, 2012), Keith Watenpaugh makes a forceful argument for Ottoman continuity in the early 1920s in Syria. He is critical in particular of James Gelvin, whose book *Divided Loyalties: Nationalism and Mass Politics in Syria at the Close of Empire* (Berkeley: University of California Press, 1999) argues for the existence of an organic Syrian nationalism in the late 1910s and early 1920s. For the quote about Mustafa Kemal's revolt in Anatolia and Qawuqji's admiration of 'Abd al-Karim al-Khattabi: Qasimiyya, ed., *Mudhakkirat*, 101.

For Qawuqji's list of the names of those who cooperated with him and his account of trying to get closer to the religious scholars: ibid., 102–104. For the importance of ex-Ottoman officer networks in the Syrian Revolt: Michael Provence, *The Great Syrian Revolt and the Rise of Arab Nationalism* (Austin: Texas University Press, 2005), 38–42. Provence's book is the only detailed narrative in English of the revolt. For an expanded analysis of the role of ex-Ottoman officer networks in anticolonial rebellions across the Middle East: Provence, "Ottoman Modernity, Colonialism, and Insurgency." Sa'id al-Tarmanini's account is drawn from the typed manuscript of his memoir: Private Papers (Fawzi al-Qawuqji), CHD (no pagination). Here is the list of names of people recruited in the planning stage of the revolt that Tarmanini mentions: 'Abd al-Salam al-Farji, Faraj al-Farji, 'Uthman al-Hawrani, Mahmud al-'Uthman, Najib Agha al-Barazi, Muhammad Agha al-Barazi, Tawfiq al-Shishakli, Khalid al-Khatib, Muhammad 'Ali al-Shawwaf, al-Hajj Mustafa al-Dib, 'Abd al-Qadir Malishu, 'Ali al-Daghistani, Salih al-Daghistani, Sulayman Sami al-Daghistani, Mustafa 'Ashur, 'Abd al-Rahman al-'Atr, Mustafa al-Bashri, Muhammad Sa'id al-Kurdi, Qasim Qunbar, Akram bin 'Ala al-Din Kaylani, Mahmud bin al-Shaykh, Muhammad al-Hinawi, Mahmud Tafuja, 'Uday al-Quwaydar, Kayru al-Hazza'a, Hassan al-'Abdu, Husayn al-Kamash, Yusuf al-Ma'aluk, Munir al-Rayyis, and Mudhir al-Siba'i. For information on Hizb al-Sha'ab [People's Party] and Sultan al-Atrash's approaches: Provence, *Great Syrian Revolt*, 69–72. For the quote from Shabandar: ibid., 72. For Qawuqji's statement about the loyalty of Nahas, Firkali, and Maghribi: Qasimiyya, ed., *Mudhakkirat*, 108. For the quote about the tribes' being "the flame of the fire of the revolt": ibid., 111. For more on constitutionalism (including Syrian constitutionalism) and its history in the modern Middle East: Elizabeth Thompson, *Justice Interrupted: The Struggle for Constitutional Government in the Middle East* (Cambridge: Harvard University Press, 2013). For Qawuqji's earlier account of his meeting with the tribes: 'As, *Safha min al-Ayyam al-Hamra*, 10. Provence dates this account to 1935, *Great Syrian Revolt*, 96. For Qawuqji's account of meeting with Barazi: Qasimiyya, ed., *Mudhakkirat*, 106. For Tarmanini's visit to Hananu: Tarmanini Memoir, Private Papers (Fawzi al-Qawuqji), CHD (no pagination). For the account of the meeting with Sultan al-Atrash in Jabal Druze: Rayyis, *Al-Kitab al-Dhahabi li-l-Thawrat al-Wataniyya fi al-Mashriq al-'Arabi: al-Thawra al-Suriyya al-Kubra*, 209–10.

For the account of the revolt itself, including the account of the false start: Qasimiyya, ed., *Mudhakkirat*, 111–16; Tarmanini Memoir, Private Papers (Fawzi al-Qawuqji), CHD; Qawuqji's account of Hama and a report to the Palestinian/Syrian Conference of 1926: in Safarjalani, *Tarikh al-Thawra al-Suriyya*, 182–202; French military reports from 4H151, SHD, and reports from the Ministère des Affaires Étrangères [MAE] in Centre des Archives Diplomatiques de Nantes (Nantes) [CADN]. For the report of the telephone call from Marthot: "Telegram Received on the Night of October 4, 1925," October 5, 1925, 4H151, SHD. For Gerbail's (undated) account of his kidnapping on October 3, 1925: 4H151, SHD. The long Gerbail quote is also taken from this document. For the Farid al-Kaylani quote at the meeting as the revolt is failing: Tarmanini Memoir, Private Papers (Fawzi al-Qawuqji), CHD (no pagination). Martin's report on October 7 and the quote about Qawuqji's having "actually organized the Bedouin": 4H151, SHD. For the French intelligence reports that contain the (translated) texts of letters that Qawuqji sent to Hama notables in December 1925: MAE, Box 1704, CADN.

For the account of Qawuqji's journey to the northeast and his return and time in Qalamun: Qasimiyya, ed., *Mudhakkirat*, 117–26. Najras al-Ka'ud's name is misspelled in the memoirs as al-'Aqud. For a detailed account of the rebellion in Damascus in October 1925 and the French bombing of the city: Provence, *Great Syrian Revolt*, 103–107;

Philip Khoury, *Syria and the French Mandate: The Politics of Arab Nationalism, 1920–1945* (Princeton: Princeton University Press), 174–80. For the letter dated February 17, 1926, from Qawuqji to the Isma'ilis: MAE, Box 1706, CADN. For a detailed account of the various rebel groups operating in the Ghouta, including the letters that they sent to notable families: Provence, *Great Syrian Revolt*, 108–25. Provence also discusses differences among Syrian Christians regarding the revolt, 123. For Provence's account of the trial of Ramadan Shallash: ibid., 134–38. For the letter written on June 24, 1926, confirming Qawuqji as leader of the revolt in the Ghouta: QPP. Qawuqji also has an account of his being appointed leader in his memoirs: Qasimiyya, ed., *Mudhakkirat*, 126–28. For a French intelligence report dated June 23, 1926, confirming Qawuqji's appointment as leader: MAE, Box 1706, CADN. The French report says that he replaced Mustafa Wasfi as leader of the revolt in the Ghouta.

For the French intelligence report dated August 17, 1926, concerning Qawuqji's trying to force Salim Hamada to pay tax to the rebels: MAE, Box 1706, CADN. For Qawuqji's list of men who stayed loyal to the revolt: Qasimiyya, ed., *Mudhakkirat*, 127. For the report of Qawuqji's having been wounded during the fighting in the Ghouta: intelligence report entitled "About the Gangs," July 29, 1926, MAE, Box 1706, CADN. For Shahbandar's letter dated October 5, 1926: QPP. For Qawuqji's December 1926 report from the Ghouta and the line about punishing villages that cooperated with French orders to set up guards: QPP. For Qawuqji's travels in Jordan and his return and infiltration into Damascus: Qasimiyya, ed., *Mudhakkirat*, 135–37. For Qawuqji's note: ibid., 136. Qawuqji's long reports on rekindling the revolt are in Private Papers (Fawzi al-Qawuqji), CHD. Some of these are also reproduced in Qasimiyya, ed., *Mudhakkirat*, 548–64. For Qawuqji's account of his travels to Turkey to rekindle the revolt and his various meetings with old contacts in Turkey: Qasimiyya, ed., *Mudhakkirat*, 144–47. For letters sent between Qawuqji and Haydar between November 1927 and July 1928: QPP. For the quote about watching Ataturk arrive in Istanbul: ibid., 144. For the French pardoning of rebels and the exiling of other rebels to Wadi al-Sirhan: Provence, *Great Syrian Revolt*, 138–53.

Qawuqji's time in Saudi Arabia is covered in Qasimiyya, ed., *Mudhakkirat*, 149–72. Information on Nabih al-'Azma's time there is in Khayriyya Qasimiyya, *Al-Ra'il al-'Arabi al-Awwal: Hayat wa-Awraq Nabih wa-'Adil al-'Azma* [The First Arab Vanguard: The Life and Papers of Nabih and 'Adil al-'Azma], (London: Riyad al-Rayyes Books, 1991), 47–49, 200–204, 206, 234, 235, 240; also Khayriyya Qasimiyya, ed., *Jawanib Min Siyasat al-Malik 'Abd al-'Aziz: Tijah al-Qadaya al-'Arabiyya, Dirasat Tahliliyya Min Khilal Awraq Nabih al-'Azma* [Aspects of the Policy of King 'Abd al-'Aziz Toward the Arab Question: An Analytical Study from the Papers of Nabih al-'Azma"], (Riyadh: Darat al-Malik 'Abd al-'Aziz, 1999), whole book. Munir al-Rayyis also traveled to the Hijaz in 1934. He has an account of this in his memoirs: Rayyis, *Al-Kitab al-Dhahabi li-l-Thawrat al-Wataniyya fi al-Mashriq al-'Arabi: Thawrat Filastin 'Am 1936*, 120–38. For information on "the Syrians" at Ibn Sa'ud's court, including Fu'ad Hamza and Yusuf al-Yasin: "Leading Personalities in Saudi Arabia," National Archive [NA], Foreign Office [FO], 464/5; also Mohammed Almana, *Arabia Unified: A Por-*

trait of Ibn Saud (London: Hutchinson Benham, 1980), 187–99. For St. John Philby in Jidda: H. Stj. B. Philby, *Arabian Days: An Autobiography* (London: Robert Hale Ltd., 1948), 237–320. For a list of the rebels in Wadi Sirhan: NA, FO 371/13805, 1929. For the Qawuqji quote about his feelings as he approached Jidda: Qasimiyya, ed., *Mudhakkirat*, 149. For Qawuqji's account of the Syrians he met in his first few days in Jidda: ibid., 150–51. For meeting with Ibn Saʿud and Qawuqji's observing that Arslan could not understand Ibn Saʿud's Arabic: ibid., 150. For Ibn Saʿud's complaints about Qawuqji's fair skin: ibid., 152. For examples of Qawuqji's views on Philby: ibid., 153, 158. For an account of Philby's conversion to Islam and Fuʾad Hamza's role: Philby, *Arabian Days*, 275–320.

For Nabih al-ʿAzma's letter to his brother ʿAdil: Qasimiyya, ed., *Jawanib Min Siya-sat*, 35. The two brothers also exchanged letters during this time about the economic plight of the Syrian rebels in Wadi Sirhan and the possibility of obtaining Ibn Saʿud's help. For Qawuqji's account of the obstacles they faced trying to inspect the king's army: Qasimiyya, ed., *Mudhakkirat*, 157. For the official letter of complaint: Qasimiyya, ed., *Al-Raʿil al-ʿArabi al-Awwal*, 199. For the long report on the state of the king's army and the required improvements: ibid., 200–203. For other letters that Nabih al-ʿAzma sent to Ibn Saʿud that contain a superior tone: ibid., 206. For the editor's account of why ʿAzma left the Hijaz: ibid., 47–49. For Qawuqji's account of his centralizing the army and setting up a training program for officers: Qasimiyya, ed., *Mudhakkirat*, 159–60. For Philby's description of Ryan: Philby, *Arabian Days*, 276. For Ryan's account of the parade: Sir A. Ryan to Mr. A. Henderson, Jedda, January 12, 1931, NA, FO 406/67. For Qawuqji's account of the parade and his discovery that the Wahhabi religious scholars regarded the military parade as polytheism and had persuaded Ibn Saʿud to cancel further parades: Qasimiyya, ed., *Mudhakkirat*, 160. For Qawuqji's complaints to Ibn Saʿud about Sulayman, and the account of Ibn Saʿud's reprimanding Sulayman in front of Qawuqji: ibid., 161. For the letter from Ibn Saʿud to Qawuqji asking him to stay in the kingdom: QPP; also, Qasimiyya, ed., *Mudhakkirat*, 573. Details about his marriage to a woman from the Banu Thaqif and his daughter Suriya come from conversations with Ossama El-Kaoukji.

For Ryan's account of the arrests of people suspected of being connected to a Hashemite plot: Ryan to Sir John Simon, Jedda, July 17, 1932, NA, FO 406/70. Ryan mentions Qawuqji by name as someone arrested in this context. For Qawuqji's account of his arrest and interrogation: Qasimiyya, ed., *Mudhakkirat*, 168–70. For Qawuqji's thoughts as the steamer left Jidda for Egypt: ibid., 172. Where I have translated the Arabic as "over the previous years," the Arabic text in fact says "over the previous two and a half years." I am assuming that this is a mistake, given the fact that Qawuqji is clear elsewhere that he spent four years in the kingdom.

3. Palestine 1936

For more on Qawuqji's place in the historiography on Palestine: Laila Parsons, "Soldiering for Arab Nationalism: Fawzi al-Qawuqji in Palestine," *Journal of Palestine*

Studies, 36/4 (2007), 33–48; and Laila Parsons, "Rebels Without Borders: Southern Syria and Palestine, 1919–1936," in Cyrus Shayegh and Andrew Arsan, eds., *The Routledge Handbook of the History of the Middle East Mandates* (London: Routledge, 2015), 395–408. For Qawuqji's contacts in Baghdad: Höpp, "Ruhmloses Zwischenspiel," 20–22. For information on the Iraqi ex-Ottoman officers: Hanna Batatu, *The Old Social Classes and the Revolutionary Movements of Iraq* (Princeton: Princeton University Press, 1978), 319–61. For Qawuqji's conversations with Faysal: Qasimiyya, ed., *Mudhakkirat*, 175–76. For his journeys to Palestine and his plans for revolt there: *The Times*, April 1, 1937; Qasimiyya, ed., *Mudhakkirat*, 177–79. For information on Hajj Amin al-Husayni: Philip Matar, *The Mufti of Jerusalem: Muhammad Amin al-Husayni and the Palestinian Question* (New York: Columbia University Press, 1988), 1–18. For information on the 'Azma brothers: Qasimiyya, *Al-Ra'il al-'Arabi al-Awwal*, 10. For the 'Adil al-'Azma quote: ibid., 66–67. For a recent article on 'Izz al-Din al-Qassam: Mark Sanagan, "Teacher, Preacher, Soldier, Martyr: Rethinking 'Izz al-Din al-Qassam," *Die Welt des Islams* 53/3–4 (2013), 315–52. For Qawuqji's meeting with the Mufti in Baghdad: Qasimiyya, ed., *Mudhakkirat*, 185. For the Mufti's renovations of the Dome of the Rock and al-Aqsa Mosque: Gudrun Kramer, *A History of Palestine: From the Ottoman Conquest to the Founding of the State of Israel* (Princeton: Princeton University Press, 2008), 222–23. For the description of the different units and the journeys that the men made: Qasimiyya, ed., *Mudhakkirat*, 190–98; Khidr al-'Ali Mahfuz, *Tahta Rayat al-Qawuqji* [Under Qawuqji's Banner], (Damascus: no pub., 1973), 44–47; Rayyis, *Al-Kitab al-Dhahabi li-l-Thawrat al-Wataniyya fi al-Mashriq al-'Arabi: Thawrat Filastin 'Am 1936*, 199–225; also Yehoshua Porath, *The Palestinian Arab National Movement: From Riots to Rebellion, 1929–1939*, vol. 2 (London: Frank Cass, 1977), 188–90; and Sonia Nimr, "The Arab Revolt in Palestine, 1936–1939: A Study Based on Oral Sources" (unpublished Ph.D. thesis, University of Exeter, 1990), 95–96.

For Qawuqji's meeting with the rebels in Jabal Jarish and the organization of the units: Qasimiyya, ed., *Mudhakkirat*, 199; Nimr, "Arab Revolt," 96; Porath, *Palestinian Arab National Movement*, 189. For the Newsletter of the Second Battalion of the Lincolnshire Regiment: St. Antony's College, Middle East Centre [SAC/MEC], Tibawi Papers, Box 3/File 5 (my thanks to Mark Sanagan for alerting me to this file). For the text of Bayan #1: SAC/MEC, Tibawi Papers, Box 3/File 5; also Mahfuz, *Tahta Rayat al-Qawuqji*, 47–51; and Bayan al-Hout, ed., *Watha'iq al-Haraka al-Wataniyya al-Filastiniyya, 1918–1939: Min Awraq Akram Zu'aytar* [Documents of the Palestinian Nationalist Movement, 1918–1939: From the Papers of Akram Zu'aytar], (Beirut: Institute for Palestine Studies, 1979), 448–49. Most subsequent bayanat are signed the same way except that some place the word "Palestine" in brackets after "Southern Syria." Many bayanat also talk explicitly about the indivisibility of Syria and Palestine. For some reason, Mahfuz's reproduction of Bayan #1 has "Palestine" in brackets after "Southern Syria," but the other reproductions do not. For an example of a bayan that talks at length about the indivisibility of Palestine from Syria: Bayan #8, also in SAC/MEC, Tibawi Papers, Box 3/File 5. Most of the bayanat were also published in the weekly journal of the Muslim Brotherhood in Egypt, *Jaridat al-Ikhwan al-Muslimin*.

For more on the bayanat in this journal: Israel Gershoni, "The Muslim Brothers and the Arab Revolt in Palestine," *Middle East Studies* 22/3 (1986), 377. About Qawuqji's appealing to the Syrianism of Palestinian peasants, it is worth noting that the popular Palestinian rebel leader 'Arif 'Abd al-Raziq also called himself commander in chief of the rebels in Southern Syria toward the end of the revolt. Porath attributes this to the fact that 'Abd al-Raziq was being funded by a special committee based in Damascus: Porath, *Palestinian Arab National Movement*, 246. But it is also likely that this name gave 'Abd al-Raziq popular support in the villages in the north of Palestine (I am grateful to Saleh 'Abd al-Jawad for pointing this out to me).

For the Fadwa Tuqan quote: Fadwa Tuqan, *A Mountainous Journey: An Autobiography* (St. Paul: Graywolf Press, 1990), 84. For the argument about Qawuqji's appealing to the urban middle class: Ted Swedenburg, *Memories of the Revolt* (Minneapolis: University of Minnesota Press, 1995), 82. For the Mufti's response to Qawuqji's referring to Palestine as Southern Syria: Mustafa Kabha, *Al-Thawra al-Kubra, 1936–1939* [The Great Revolt, 1936–1939], (Nazareth: Maktaba al-Qabas al-Nasira, 1988), 77–80; see also Porath, *Palestinian Arab National Movement*, 191–93. Porath claims that Qawuqji was allied with Jerusalem's Nashashibis. Sonia Nimr questions this claim, saying that Qawuqji's allegiances to particular Palestinians were based on factors local to the Jenin area. For Bahjat Abu Gharbiyya's account: Bahjat Abu Gharbiyya, *Mudhakkirat al-Munadil Bahjat Abu Gharbiyya* [Memoirs of the Fighter Bahjat Abu Gharbiyya], (Beirut: Institute of Palestine Studies, 1993), 79–80. Matthew Hughes has an article on Bahjat Abu Gharbiyya's involvement in the ambush of a car containing two British police officers. The article is based on an interview with Abu Gharbiyya when he was in his early nineties: Matthew Hughes, "Assassination in Jerusalem: Bahjat Abu Gharbiyah and Sami al-Ansari's Shooting of British Assistant Superintendent Alan Sigrist, 12th of June 1936," *Jerusalem Quarterly* 44 (2010), 5–13.

For the setting up of the courts and the execution of Barmaki: Mahfuz, *Tahta Rayat al-Qawuqji*, 55–60 (the quotation is on pp. 54–55); Abu Gharbiyya, *Mudhakkirat*, 81. Mustafa Kabha's important article on the revolutionary courts deals mainly with the post-Qawuqji period. He does not include an account of Barmaki's trial: Mustafa Kabha, "The Courts of the Palestinian Arab Revolt," in Amy Singer, Christoph K. Neumann, and Aksin Somel, eds., *Untold Histories of the Middle East: Recovering Voices from the 19th and 20th Centuries* (London: Routledge, 2011), 197–213. Information on Bal'a is taken from an interview with Salim Hassan Abdulla (conducted by his granddaughter), contained on the website palestine.remembered.com. For Qawuqji's quote about the Bal'a ambush: Qasimiyya, ed., *Mudhakkirat*, 206. For the account of Bal'a in the (September) Newsletter of the Second Battalion of the Lincolnshire Regiment: SAC/MEC, Tibawi Papers, Box 3/File 5; also "Official Communiqué of the Lincolnshire Regiment," Central Zionist Archives [CZA], S25/11295. For Munir al-Rayyis on Bal'a: Rayyis, *Al-Kitab al-Dhahabi li-l-Thawrat al-Wataniyya fi al-Mashriq al-'Arabi: Thawrat Filastin 'Am 1936*, 228–36. For the bayan about Bal'a: Mahfuz, *Tahta Rayat al-Qawuqji*, 71. For Mahfuz's account of Bal'a as a whole: ibid., 62–72. For Qawuqji's quote about the performance of the Palestinians at Bal'a: Qasimiyya, ed., *Mudhakkirat*,

208; and "Note of Interview Between a Prominent Egyptian Publicist and Fawzi El Kaoukji Early in April, 1937," CZA Z4/32069; also see Nimr, "The Arab Revolt in Palestine," 97.

The testimony of the villager about the destruction wrought by the British army is taken from an interview with Salim Hassan Abdulla (conducted by his granddaughter) on palestine.remembered.com. Matthew Hughes also has an article on British reprisal raids during the Palestine Revolt: Hughes, "The Banality of Brutality: British Armed Forces and the Repression of the Arab Revolt in Palestine, 1936–1939," *English Historical Review* 124 (2009), 313–54. For Rayyis on the truce: *Al-Kitab al-Dhahabi li-l-Thawra al-Wataniya fi al-Mashriq al-'Arabi: Thawrat Filastin 'Am 1936*, 241. For a detailed account of the truce negotiations and the British military pressure on Qawuqji to leave: Porath, *Palestinian Arab National Movement*, 203–15. For the full text of the October 20 bayan: Qasimiyya, ed., *Mudhakkirat*, 578. For the withdrawal bayan published in *Al-Ayyam*: ibid., 580. For more on the Peel Commission: Penny Sinanoglu, "The Peel Commission and Partition, 1936–1938," in Rory Miller, ed., *Britain, Palestine and Empire: The Mandate Years* (Burlington: Ashgate, 2010), 119–40. Palestinian leaders initially boycotted the Commission, but they broke the boycott in January 1937 and gave evidence. For the letter from Hamadi dated October 14, 1936, and the letter from 'Adil al-'Azma also probably written in mid-October: QPP. For the account of Qawuqji's departure from Palestine: Qasimiyya, ed., *Mudhakkirat*, 242–55. For a brief British report on Qawuqji's passage: Jordan: "Report on the Political Situation for the Month of October, 1936," in Robert L. Jarman, ed., *Political Diaries of the Arab World: Palestine and Jordan, 1924–1936*, vol. 2 (London: Archive Editions, 2001), 768–71. On November 8, 1936, *Al-Difa'* newspaper published a letter that Qawuqji wrote to Amir 'Abdullah thanking him for his assistance in granting Qawuqji safe passage through Transjordan. The Qawuqji Papers in the Institute for Palestine Studies in Beirut include correspondence between 'Abdullah and Qawuqji written in mid–late October 1936 concerning the safe passage: Qawuqji Papers, Institute for Palestine Studies [IPS], File 5. For Qawuqji's manifesto in *Alif Ba'*: NA, AIR 2/1764 (only the English translation is available). For Qawuqji's visit to Basra: 'Izzat Darwaza, *Mudhakkirat 'Izzat Darwaza*, vol. 2, 350. Although Qawuqji did not return to Palestine to rejoin the revolt, which broke out again in earnest in late 1937, rumors about his involvement continued to circulate. There is a British Foreign Office file in the National Archives in London devoted to Arabic newspaper reports circulating in the fall of 1937 that claimed Qawuqji had "placed a price" on the head of General Dill, the British general directing the British army's suppression of the revolt in Palestine. Qawuqji vehemently denied these reports in an article published in *Al-Istiqlal* on October 13, 1937: NA, FO 684/10. British intelligence reports in 1937 and 1938 also reported rumors circulating in northern Palestine in 1937 and 1938 that Qawuqji had returned to Palestine to fight. Although never confirmed, these rumors worried the British because Qawuqji, in the words of one British intelligence officer, was "looked upon [by the Palestinians] as a national hero": Daily Intelligence Summary, Palestine Police, February 28, 1938, SAC/MEC, Tegart Papers, Box 5/File 2.

4. Baghdad to Berlin

For information on the Bakr al-Sidqi coup: Adeed Dawisha, *Iraq: A Political History* (Princeton: Princeton University Press, 2013), 136–37; Charles Tripp, *A History of Iraq* (Cambridge: Cambridge University Press, 2007), 86–97. For the correspondence between Clark Kerr and the FCO in December 1936 and January 1937: NA, AIR 2/1764. The quote about Kirkuk is from Clark Kerr to FCO, January 25, 1937. For the Daniel Oliver quote: Daniel Oliver to Ayles, March 10, 1937, NA, CO 733/344 file 75550/A59. For the articles in the Iraqi press in 1937 about Qawuqji: QPP. For the Canadian and American newspaper articles about him in 1937: *The Winnipeg Tribune*, July 16, 1937; *Portsmouth Daily Times*, February 26, 1937; *The Morning Herald*, July 16, 1937. The image is from *The Salt Lake Tribune*, March 7, 1937. For the fact that banners at Nabi Musa had images of Qawuqji: Munir al-Rayyis, *Al-Kitab al-Dhahabi li-l-Thawrat al-Wataniyya fi al-Mashriq al-'Arabi: Harb al-'Iraq, 1941* [The Golden Book of the Arab Revolts in the Arab East: The Iraq War, 1941], (Damascus: Alif Ba', 1977), 102. For the quote about recording his memoirs and his arrival in Kirkuk: Qasimiyya, ed., *Mudhakkirat*, 11–12. For Qawuqji's plans to resurrect revolt in Transjordan: ibid., *Mudhakkirat*, 263–78. For the letter from Rayyis to Qawuqji, July 15, 1937: QPP. For the letter from 'Umar al-'Umari to Subhi al-'Umari, October 27, 1937: QPP. For the letter from 'Umar al-'Umari to Subhi al-'Umari, November 11, 1937: QPP. For the letter to Ibn Sa'ud, and the list of the tribes: QPP. For a different version of the letter to Ibn Sa'ud: Qasimiyya, ed., *Mudhakkirat*, 601. For Ibn Sa'ud's reply: ibid., 602. For the rumors that the British were onto Qawuqji's plans: ibid., 276.

For information on Fritz Grobba: Wolfgang G. Schwanitz, "The Jinnee and the Magic Bottle: Fritz Grobba and German Middle East Policy, 1900–1945," in Schwanitz, ed., *Germany and the Middle East, 1871–1945* (Princeton: Markus Wiener Publishers, 2004), 87–118. For a good article on the Arabs and their relations with the Axis: Basheer M. Nafi, "The Arabs and the Axis: 1933–1940," *Arab Studies Quarterly* 19/2 (1997). For specific information on Qawuqji's early meetings with Grobba: Höpp, "Ruhmloses Zwischenspiel," 20–23. For the meeting with Helmuth Groscurth: ibid., 22. For the meetings with Salah al-Din al-Sabbagh: Sabbagh, *Fursan al-'Uruba*, 138–41. For information about the establishment of the Desert Forces and the Mufti's mistrust of Qawuqji: Rayyis, *Al-Kitab al-Dhahabi li-l-Thawrat al-Wataniyya fi al-Mashriq al-'Arabi: Harb al-'Iraq, 1941*, 101–104. For Rayyis's account of his meeting with Qawuqji as Qawuqji was preparing to leave Baghdad: ibid., 54. For Qawuqji's few pages of diary entries on his involvement in the coup: Qasimiyya, ed., *Mudhakkirat*, 282–87. For Glubb Pasha's account of Rutba: John Bagot Glubb, *The Story of the Arab Legion* (London: Hodder and Stoughton, 1948), 266–68. For Kemal Haddad's accusations against Qawuqji: Kemal Haddad, *Haraka Rashid 'Ali al-Kaylani* [The Rashid 'Ali al-Kaylani Movement], (Sidon: Al-Maktaba al-'Asriyya, 1948), 118. For the Mufti's involvement in setting up the Desert Forces and his desire to be rid of Palestinian troublemakers in his circle: Rayyis, *Al-Kitab al-Dhahabi li-l-Thawrat al-Wataniyya fi al-Mashriq al-'Arabi: Harb al-'Iraq, 1941*, 101–104. For the Glubb Pasha quote on the H4 pumping station: Glubb,

Story of the Arab Legion, 258. For British documents describing the looting of the pumping stations: "Report of the Special Operations Executive, June 14, 1941," NA, HS3/154. For the Rayyis quote: Rayyis, *Al-Kitab al-Dhahabi li-l-Thawrat al-Wataniyya fi al-Mashriq al-'Arabi: Harb al-'Iraq, 1941,* 77.

For the conversation between Jamil al-Midfa'i and Qawuqji on the telephone: Rayyis, *Al-Kitab al-Dhahabi li-l-Thawrat al-Wataniyya fi al-Mashriq al-'Arabi: Harb al-'Iraq, 1941,* 80. For the contact between Qawuqji and Rahn: Höpp, "Ruhmloses Zwischenspiel," 24–25. For the meeting between Qawuqji and the French officers: Rayyis, *Al-Kitab al-Dhahabi li-l-Thawrat al-Wataniyya fi al-Mashriq al-'Arabi: Harb al-'Iraq, 1941,* 88. For the report that describes Qawuqji as a scallywag: "Report of the Special Operations Executive, June 14, 1941": NA, HS3/154. My thanks to Steven Wagner for his thoughts on what "DPX" might mean. For the British report sent on July 2 about the al-Ghaim pumping station: NA, HS3/154. For Qawuqji's meeting with family and friends: Rayyis, *Al-Kitab al-Dhahabi li-l-Thawrat al-Wataniyya fi al-Mashriq al-'Arabi: Harb al-'Iraq, 1941,* 100–101, 114. For Qawuqji's planning to defend the T3 station in cooperation with the French: ibid., 117–18. For the long Rayyis quote about Qawuqji's injuries: ibid., 119. For the account of Qawuqji's operation in Dayr al-Zur: ibid., 123. For evidence that the British knew about his movements: British intelligence reports show that the British were monitoring Vichy communications in Syria and knew all about Qawuqji's presence in Dayr al-Zur by July 1941: NA, HW41/208 (I am grateful to Steven Wagner for pointing this document out to me). For his stay in the hospital in Berlin and the death of Majdi: Qasimiyya, ed., *Mudhakkirat,* 288–89, and Rayyis, *Al-Kitab al-Dhahabi li-l-Thawrat al-Wataniyya fi al Mashriq al-'Arabi: Harb al-'Iraq 1941,* 174–76. For more information on his transfer to Germany and his stay in the hospital: Höpp, "Ruhmloses Zwischenspiel," 25–27. For his lifelong headaches and his wearing a hat indoors on cold days: conversation with his son Ossama El-Kaoukji. For information on his apartment: Höpp, "Ruhmloses Zwischenspiel," 30. For the trip to Paris and the argument with the German official: Rayyis, *Al-Kitab al-Dhahabi li-l-Thawrat al-Wataniyya fi al-Mashriq al-'Arabi: Harb al-'Iraq, 1941,* 243–51. For the report on the tribes of Syria probably written in late 1941: University of Exeter Documentation Centre, Private Papers of Nabih and 'Adil al-'Azma, MS215. For the other reports based on his fighting in Iraq: Höpp, "Ruhmloses Zwischenspiel," 28.

For a scholarly book on Arab responses to the Holocaust: Meir Litvak and Esther Webman, *From Empathy to Denial: Arab Responses to the Holocaust* (New York: Columbia University Press, 2009). For the letters from Qawuqji to 'Adil al-'Azma: Qasimiyya, ed., *Al-Ra'il al-'Arabi al-Awwal,* 427 and 429. For the text of the denunciation: "Tarjamat Hayat al-Batal Fawzi al-Qawuqji Sadira 'an Maktab al-Mufti al-Akbar bi-Birlin" [The Life of the "Hero" Fawzi al-Qawuqji Issued by the Office of the Grand Mufti in Berlin] (no date, no publisher). This document is also in the Israel State Archive in a file on Qawuqji, ISA 946/15. Domvile was indeed a British intelligence officer based in Baghdad from late 1936: Steven Wagner, "British Intelligence and Policy in the Palestine Mandate, 1919–1939" (unpublished D.Phil. thesis, Oxford, 2014). For the Mufti's attempts to silence his opponents by accusing them of treachery: Höpp, "Ruhmloses

Zwischenspiel," 34. For Grobba's concerns about Qawuqji's political ambitions: Götz Nordbruch, *Nazism in Syria and Lebanon: The Ambivalence of the German Option, 1933–1945* (London: Routledge, 2009), 174. Nordbruch's account is based on a report by Grobba in the German archives. For Rayyis on setting up the army in Greece: Rayyis, *Al-Kitab al-Dhahabi li-l-Thawrat al-Wataniyya fi al-Mashriq al-'Arabi: Harb al-'Iraq, 1941,* 176–80. For Qawuqji's memoirs on trying to set up the army: Qasimiyya, ed., *Mudhakkirat,* 293–303; also Höpp, "Ruhmloses Zwischenspiel," 34–35. For Qawuqji's view of the secret exchange of notes: ibid., 31. For Qawuqji's mention of the Mufti's desire to be caliph: Qasimiyya, ed., *Mudhakkirat,* 297. Qawuqji's private archive contains a typescript, with handwritten corrections, of an unattributed English draft translation of the memoirs, starting from his arrival in Berlin. In most places this translation corresponds to the published Arabic memoirs (i.e., the *Mudhakkirat,* edited by Qasimiyya), but sometimes the English version contains material that does not appear there, indicating that there probably was an earlier Arabic draft of the memoirs. The issue of the Mufti and the caliphate is one of these occasions. In the English version Qawuqji devotes several pages to the question, whereas the published Arabic memoirs contain just a brief mention of it. My account here draws mainly on the English version: English typescript of the memoirs, 13–16, QPP.

For examples of works on the collaboration between the Mufti and the Nazis: B. Schechtman, *The Mufti and the Fuehrer: The Rise and Fall of Haj Amin al-Husseini* (New York and London: Thomas Yoseloff, 1965); Maurice Pearlman, *Mufti of Jerusalem: The Story of Haj Amin el Husseini* (London: Gollancz, 1947). For information on the Mufti in Germany and his visit to a concentration camp: Gerhard Höpp, "In the Shadow of the Moon: Arab Inmates in Nazi Concentration Camps," in Schwanitz, ed., *Germany and the Middle East,* 221. For the Ilan Pappe quote: Ilan Pappe, *The Rise and Fall of a Palestinian Dynasty: The Husaynis, 1700–1948* (Berkeley: University of California Press, 2010), 316. For the Qawuqji quote about Berlin in 1945: Qasimiyya, ed., *Mudhakkirat,* 304. For information on Qawuqji's time in Berlin after the Russian occupation until his escape to Paris: ibid., 304–309. For the fact that he used the Mufti's denunciation as proof to the Russians of his split with the Nazis: English typescript of the memoirs, 26–27, QPP. For the letter to 'Adil and Nabih al-'Azma in 1946: Qasimiyya, *Al-Ra'il al-'Arabi al-Awwal,* 469. It is in this letter that Qawuqji also talks about the deaths of Yumni and Nizar, something he does not mention in his memoirs. For British correspondence in October and November 1946 concerning Qawuqji's request for help from the British military government: NA, CO 537/1316. For the quote: Letter from R. Thistlethwaite [Snuffbox, the code name for MI5] to J. Beith at the Foreign Office, November 1, 1946. This correspondence also shows that the British considered other reactions to Qawuqji's request. These included agreeing to meet with him and then arresting him once he was in the British zone and agreeing to meet with him in order to hand him over to British intelligence. For the Qawuqji quote about arriving at the Syrian Legation in Paris: Qasimiyya, ed., *Mudhakkirat,* 308.

5. Palestine 1948

The Jan Daya articles are in *Al-Hayat*, February 9 and February 10, 1998. (The quote from the *Al-Hayat* interview with Qawuqji in Paris is cited in the February 9 article.) For British documents concerning his return to the Middle East: NA, FO 371/62138. For the British report that Qawuqji met with the Mufti in Cairo: R. Campbell, Telegram from Cairo to the Foreign Office, February 25, 1947, NA, FO 371/62138. For reports about British pressure on the Lebanese government not to allow Qawuqji's return to Lebanon: Mr. Young, Beirut to Foreign Office, February 20, 1947, NA, FO 371/62138. In addition to the material I cite for this chapter, there are also documents in NA, FO 371/62138, pertaining to parliamentary questions raised about the British government's failure to arrest Qawuqji at Lod. For the *Al-Ahram* articles from his time in Cairo: *Al-Ahram*, February 24, February 25, and February 27, 1947. For David Horowitz's account of the plane journey: David Horowitz, *A State in the Making* (New York: Knopf, 1953), 146–50 (the quote is on p. 150; I am grateful to Neil Caplan for alerting me to this source). For Qawuqji's account of his journey back to the Middle East and his arrival in Tripoli: Qasimiyya, ed., *Mudhakkirat*, 309–19. For the quotation about his anxiously waiting on the plane at Lod: ibid., 310. For the long quotation about his arrival in Tripoli: ibid., 317. For his return to Lebanon and what happened in Tripoli, also see Oren Barak, "Intra-communal and Inter-communal Dimensions of Conflict and Peace in Lebanon," *International Journal of Middle East Studies* 34 (2002), 619–44. For telegrams of congratulation (early March 1947) upon Qawuqji's arrival in Tripoli: QPP.

    For the Meminger visit to Qawuqji in Damascus and the British report on it: Report from the British Legation in Damascus to the Foreign Office, November 3, 1947, NA, FO 371/62138. For background on the conference at Aley: Khalidi, "The Arab Perspective," in William Roger Louis and Robert W. Stookey, eds., *The End of the Palestine Mandate* (Austin: University of Texas Press, 1986), 104–36. For the fact that the Mufti turned up unexpectedly: ibid., 119. For 'Arif al-'Arif's visit to Safwat: 'Arif al-'Arif, *Nakbat Filastin wa-l-Firdaws al-Mafkud* [The Catastrophe of Palestine and Paradise Lost], (Sidon: 1956–1958), vol. 1, 18–19. Khalidi also has a synopsis of the Safwat report: Khalidi, "Arab Perspective," 119; see also Khalidi, "Selected Documents on the 1948 Palestine War," *Journal of Palestine Studies* 27 (Spring 1998), 62–72. An account of the meeting at Aley can also be found in the Iraqi Parliamentary Commission of Enquiry into the Palestine Question, *Taqrir Lajnat al-Tahqiq al-Niyabiyya fi Qadiyat Filastin* [Report of the Committee of Enquiry into the Palestine Question], (Baghdad: Matba'a al-Hukuma, 1949), 65–69 and 78. (The full text of Safwat's report is contained in the Appendix, 131–36.) For the Mufti's account of Aley: Hajj Amin al-Husayni, *Haqa'iq 'an Qadiyat Filastin* [The Facts About Palestine], (Cairo: Dar al-Kitab al-'Arabi, 1956), 179–80. For Qawuqji's account of Aley: Qasimiyya, ed., *Mudhakkirat*, 324–26. Historians who have written about Arab rivalries in the lead-up to the war include Avi Shlaim, *Collusion Across the Jordan* (Oxford: Clarendon Press, 1988); Haim Levenburg, *Military Preparations of the Arab Community in Palestine* (London: Routledge, 1993); and Joshua Landis, "Syria and the 1948 War," in Eugene Rogan and Avi Shlaim, eds., *The War for*

Palestine (Cambridge: Cambridge University Press, 2007). Landis argues that Qawuqji was firmly in the Syrian camp and accuses him of not being serious about fighting for Palestine. Ronen Yitzhak argues that Qawuqji was firmly in 'Abdullah's camp: Ronen Yitzhak, "Fauzi al-Qawuqji and the Arab Liberation Army in the 1948 War: Toward the Attainment of King 'Abdullah's Political Ambitions in Palestine," *Comparative Studies of South Asia, Africa and the Middle East* 28/3 (2008), 459–66.

For Qawuqji's later undated handwritten comments on the Mufti: QPP. For 'Izzat Darwaza's account of Qawuqji's character: Izzat Darwaza, *Mudhakkirat 'Izzat Dar-waza*, vol. 2, 114. For his account of the Mufti's slandering of Qawuqji: ibid., vol. 5, 612–15. For the quote from Darwaza about how Qawuqji was affected by the Mufti's slander: ibid., 614. For Taha al-Hashimi's account: Khaldun Sati' al-Husari, ed., *Mud-hakkirat Taha al-Hashimi* [The Memoirs of Taha al-Hashimi], (Beirut: Dar al-Tali'a li-l-Tiba'a wa-l-Nashr, no date), vol. 2, 155–69. For the quotation from Hashimi about the Mufti's meeting with Quwatli: ibid., 165. For the account of Qawuqji's appoint-ment as commander of Jaysh al-Inqadh on December 6: ibid., 178. For the account of the meeting on December 29: ibid., 184–85. For Samir Souqi's visit to Qawuqji's house: Mona Anis and Omayma Abdel-Latif, "Fawzi al-Qawuqji: Yesterday's Hero," *Al-Ahram Weekly*, 1998 (issue 367). For enthusiasm in the Arab press about Qawuqji: *Filastin*, February 3, February 5, February 10, and February 14, 1948. For the account of Qawuqji's visit to the Druze Mountain and the report from the British intelligence officer, January 17, 1948: CZA S25/3045; also discussed in Laila Parsons, *The Druze Between Palestine and Israel, 1947–49* (London: Macmillan, 2000), 57. Druze sources indicate, however, that Qawuqji did meet with Sultan al-Atrash during his visit to Jabal Druze and Atrash agreed to help him organize a Druze unit: Kais Firro, *The Druzes in the Jewish State: A Brief History* (Leiden: Brill, 1999), 43–44. (I am grateful to Shay Hazkani for pointing this out.) For the recruiting letter from the General Staff, Febru-ary 17, 1948: QPP. For more information on recruiting methods: Avraham Sela, "'Tzava Ha-Hatzla' Ba-Galil Ba-Milhemet Ha-Atzma'ot 1948" [The "Salvation Army" in the Galilee in the 1948 War], in Alon Kadish, ed., *Milhemet Ha-Atzma'ot, 1948–1949* [The War of Independence, 1948–1949], (Israel: Ministry of Defense Press, 2004), 207–67. Sela's article is based on Jaysh al-Inqadh papers in the Israeli archives. Addi-tional information on recruiting and on the debates over leadership is taken from Hani al-Hindi's excellent book: Hani al-Hindi, *Jaysh al-Inqadh* [The Arab Liberation Army], (Beirut: Shams al-Muthallath, 1992), which contains interviews with former officers from Jaysh al-Inqadh. For an attempt to understand Jaysh al-Inqadh as a conventional army: Levenburg, *Military Preparations of the Arab Community*.

For the account of Jaysh al-Inqadh troops' crossing into Palestine: Qasimiyya, ed., *Mudhakkirat*, 342–43. Sela's article describes the crossing of the Second Yarmuk Battalion, under the command of Adib Shishakli, into the Galilee in mid-January: Sela, "'Tzava Ha-Hatzla,'" 214–15. This was before Muhammad Safa crossed into Pal-estine through Jordan. It appears that Shishakli operated almost completely indepen-dently from Qawuqji's command, in spite of Qawuqji's claims to the contrary in his memoirs. Sela's article focuses on Jaysh al-Inqadh's operations in the Galilee. For

Cunningham's telegram: Alan Cunningham to the secretary of state for the colonies, February 1, 1948, NA, FO 371/68366. The second telegram from Cunningham is dated February 4. For the telegram from Kirkbride: Alec Kirkbride to Foreign Office, February 6, 1948, NA, FO 371/68366. For information on Tubas: 'Arif, *Al-Nakba*, 39. For Qawuqji's fears of assassination: Qasimiyya, ed., *Mudhakkirat*, 345–47. Jaysh al-Inqadh telegrams [T] are from the private collection of Walid Khalidi, also housed in the Institute for Palestine Studies in Beirut. For Qawuqji's account of his journey until he arrived in Tubas: Qasimiyya, ed., *Mudhakkirat*, 352–58. For the quote "I saw that he had personal admiration for me . . .": ibid., 353. For the long Tubas quote: ibid., 357. Qawuqji also mentions the rain in the official report of mobilization that he sent to Safwat on March 7, 1948: QPP. He talks in this document about requiring 'Abdullah's permission (which was granted) to cross from Syria into Transjordan so that he could then cross into Palestine at the Allenby Bridge. For King 'Abdullah's ambitions in Palestine: Shlaim, *Collusion Across the Jordan*, and Mary Wilson, *King Abdullah, Britain, and the Making of Jordan* (Cambridge: Cambridge University Press, 1990).

For Cunningham's telegram about Qawuqji's crossing: Alan Cunningham to the secretary of state for the colonies, March 18, 1948, NA, FO 371/68369. For Kirkbride's response: Kirkbride to the Foreign Office, March 20, 1948, NA, FO 371/68369. For Qawuqji's account of Mishmar Haemek: Qasimiyya, ed., *Mudhakkirat*, 362–70; also for Mishmar Haemek, see the unattributed English translation in "Fawzi al-Qawuqji: Memoirs, 1948. Part I," *Journal of Palestine Studies* 1/4 (Summer 1972), 27–58. Qawuqji's published Arabic memoirs differ somewhat from the memoirs that the *Journal of Palestine Studies* translated into English and published in 1972. For example, the published Arabic memoirs do not contain most of the telegrams that the *JPS* article weaves into the narrative of Mishmar Haemek. Hani al-Hindi's chapter on Mishmar Haemek also provides material for my account of the battle: Hani al-Hindi, *Jaysh al-Inqadh*, 93–102. Three Jewish residents of Mishmar Haemek were killed on the first day. Over the following days of battle, two more were killed. For the telegram that Qawuqji sent on April 5, 1948, about why he withdrew from Mishmar Haemek: T. For his decision about whether to go to the aid of the forces around al-Qastal and his comment that he was "on the horns of a dilemma": Qasimiyya, ed., *Mudhakkirat*, 365. For the shelling of Jerusalem and the British officers' telling him to stop: ibid., 367. For the British officer's account that Mishmar Haemek had never intended to honor the truce: Dan Kurzman, *Genesis, 1948: The First Arab-Israeli War* (London: Valentine, Mitchell, 1972), 129. (For his account Kurzman interviewed the British officer involved.) For the telegram that Taha al-Hashimi sent Qawuqji on April 14: "Fawzi al-Qawuqji: Memoirs, 1948. Part I," 46. For Qawuqji's handwritten note on a different copy of the same message: QPP. For the telegram that Qawuqji sent Taha al-Hashimi on April 13: "Fawzi al-Qawuqji: Memoirs, 1948. Part I," 46. Yoav Gelber's account of Mishmar Haemek, based mainly on Israeli sources, holds that Qawuqji lied in his memoirs about sending reinforcements to help 'Abd al-Qadir at Qastal in the middle of the battle for Mishmar Haemek: Yoav Gelber, *Palestine: 1948* (Portland: Sussex Academic Press, 2001), 88–89. For the letter of appeal from the five villages: QPP. For Yosef Weitz's diary entry: Benny Morris, *Birth of the Palestinian Refugee Crisis, 1947–1949* (Cambridge: Cambridge University Press, 1987), 117. For the meeting with Palmon: Shlaim, *Collusion Across the Jordan*, 157–58. Shlaim's account is based on a later interview with Palmon and on an unsourced account of the same meeting in Dan Kurzman's 1972 book *Genesis 1948*, 67–69. According to Shlaim's account, Qawuqji asked Palmon for one military victory to make up for the earlier defeat at Tirat-Zvi. Palmon's description of his meeting with Qawuqji and his description of his meeting with Shakib Wahab are nearly identical. In *Collusion Across the Jordan* Shlaim accuses Qawuqji of being "theatrical," but much the same could be said of Palmon, the self-styled local expert, whose accounts of his meetings with these two Arab military commanders paint an Oriental backdrop where tricky Arabs make bargains in secret. For the meeting between Palmon and Shakib Wahab and the agreement struck with Wahab: Israel Defense Forces Archive, 922/75/44; David Koren, *Kesher Ne'eman* [Steadfast Alliance], (Tel Aviv: Ministry of Defense, 1991), 61; also discussed in Parsons, *Druze Between Palestine and Israel*, 72–74. Gelber too has an account of Palmon's meeting with Qawuqji, but it differs from Shlaim's. In Gelber's account, which is based on Palmon's report from the time (now in the Haganah Archive), Palmon concluded from the meeting that Qawuqji was loyal to the Arab League: Gelber, *Palestine: 1948*, 71–73. Gelber has an account of Qawuqji's supposedly being in contact with Ezra Danin, another Jewish intelligence officer, a few weeks earlier. But this is based on accounts of a Palestinian serving in Jaysh al-Inqadh who was in fact working as an informant for SHAI (Jewish military intelligence). Informant accounts are notoriously unreliable: Gelber, *Palestine: 1948*, 56–57. For another transcript of an interview with Palmon about the meeting with Qawuqji: Uri Milstein, *Arkhiyyon Milhemot Israel* [The Archive of the Wars of Israel], (Israel: Meitar-Milshtain, 1984), 28/868, 21–23.

For the telegram to Damascus about refugees needing food: "Fawzi al-Qawuqji: Memoirs, 1948. Part II," *Journal of Palestine Studies* 2/1 (Autumn 1972), 3–33 at 4. For petitions from villagers and Qawuqji's scribbled notes on April 19 and 27 and May 5, 1948: QPP. For the letter from the doctor in Nablus on May 6, 1948: QPP. A batch of letters sent in April 1948 about Jaysh al-Ingadh soldiers not paying their debts is also in QPP. For the fall of Jaffa: "Fawzi al-Qawuqji: Memoirs, 1948. Part I," 55–57; also Itamar Radai, "Jaffa, 1948: The Fall of a City," *Journal of Israeli History: Politics, Society, Culture* 30/1 (2011), 23–43; and Nasser Eddin Nashashibi, Salah Ibrahim al-Nazer, and Mohammad Said Ishkuntana, *Jaffa Forever* (Beirut: Arab Institute for Research and Publishing, 2013). I am grateful to Salim Tamari for alerting me to the existence of this book, which was written by a group of Jaffans. It accuses the Arab League's Military Committee of negligence in the fall of Jaffa. This book gives a different account of why Qawuqji fired 'Adil Najm al-Din. According to the account of Mohammad Said Ishkuntana, the radio station of Jaysh al-Inqadh was broadcasting the news that Jaysh al-Inqadh had bombed and destroyed the nearby Jewish settlement of Netter. 'Adil Najm al-Din denied publicly that this had happened, and Qawuqji was so angry at the public humiliation that he fired him as the commander of the battalion. For Qawuqji's account of events at Jaffa: Qasimiyya, ed., *Mudhakkirat*, 372–93. For Qawuqji's telegram to Safwat:

"Fawzi al-Qawuqji: Memoirs, 1948. Part I," 57, where the name Ajnadayn is mistransliterated as Ajnadin.

For the fighting around Bab al-Wad: Qasimiyya, ed., *Mudhakkirat*, 399–405. For Barazi's letter and the Mufti's letter, both dated May 9, 1948: QPP. Qawuqji also has an account of the letters in Qasimiyya, ed., *Mudhakkirat*, 393–94. For Qawuqji's resignation letters to 'Azzam Pasha on August 5, 1948, and September 22, 1948: QPP. For the battle of Malkiyya: Qasimiyya, ed., *Mudhakkirat*, 416–20. Avraham Sela describes the battle of Malkiyya as "one of the most efficient and successful offensives carried out by the Arabs in the entire war": Sela, " 'Tzava Ha-Hatzla,' " 103. For an argument about how the battle of Malkiyya was later used in the construction of Lebanese identity: Barak, "Intra-communal and Inter-communal Dimensions." Patrick Seale also has a good account of the battle of Malkiyya in *The Struggle for Arab Independence: Riad el-Solh and the Makers of the Modern Middle East* (Cambridge: Cambridge University Press, 2010), 646–50. This includes the information that Qawuqji received the Medal of the Cedar. For Lebanon's role in the 1948 War, including an account of Malkiyya: Matthew Hughes, "Collusion Across the Litani? Lebanon and the 1948 War," in Avi Shlaim and Eugene Rogan, eds., *The War for Palestine: Rewriting the History of 1948* (Cambridge: Cambridge University Press, 2007), 204–27. Hughes downplays the significance of the Lebanese victory at Malkiyya.

For the first truce: Hassan al-Badri, *Al-Harb fi Ard al-Salam* [War in the Land of Peace], 231. Badri cites an interview given by David Ben-Gurion to the newspaper *Palestine* on December 27, 1948. There Ben-Gurion claims that the first truce "allowed Israel the opportunity to increase the number of volunteers [to the IDF] and arms and supplies and reorganization of the army." For Qawuqji on the truce: Qasimiyya, ed., *Mudhakkirat*, 420–22. For the quote about Qawuqji's opinion on the truce: ibid., 421. For the report from 'Ayntarun on June 20, 1948, in which Qawuqji surveys the enemy's new capabilities following the first truce: QPP. For Riyad al-Sulh's letter supporting Qawuqji's attempts to get more supplies from the Arab League, July 5, 1948: QPP. For the quote about the meeting in Quwatli's palace: Qasimiyya, ed., *Mudhakkirat*, 467. Further examples of Qawuqji's alienation during such meetings can be found throughout the memoirs, but this is the most graphic. In addition, telegrams sent by Qawuqji and other Jaysh al-Inqadh battalion commanders from July to October 1948 attest to the increasing demands for supplies and wages. On some of these telegrams Qawuqji wrote: "no reply": QPP. For an account of the Jaysh al-Inqadh attack on the IDF position near Manara: Qasimiyya, ed., *Mudhakkirat*, 479–81; and Gelber, *Palestine: 1948*, 223. The numbers of Israeli dead and wounded are taken from Gelber. For Operation Hiram and the withdrawal of Jaysh al-Inqadh: Qasimiyya, ed., *Mudhakkirat*, 487–93, and Gelber, *Palestine: 1948*, 223–28; also Sela, "Tzava Ha-Hatzla,' " 247–48. Sela puts the number of soldiers killed during the retreat at four hundred. Half of these were soldiers from the Syrian Army. For the visit by Darwish to Jaysh al-Inqadh troops and the orders to demobilize Jaysh al-Inqadh: Qasimiyya, ed., *Mudhakkirat*, 497–502. For more on the Mufti's All-Palestine Government and how its establishment was connected with the rivalry between Egypt and the Arab League, on the one hand, and

King 'Abdullah, on the other: Avi Shlaim, "The Rise and Fall of the All-Palestine Government in Gaza," *Journal of Palestine Studies* 20/1 (Autumn 1990), 37–53.

Epilogue

Concerning Qawuqji's reputation after the war: Sa'id Taqi al-Din, in his account of his interview with Qawuqji, lists all the accusations commonly heard about him in the 1950s: Sa'id Taqi al-Din, *Al-Majmu'a al-Kamila: Al-Maqalat al-Siyasiyya* [The Complete Collection: Political Articles], (Beirut: Dar al-Nahar, 1969), 187 (I am grateful to Sameeh Hammoudeh for alerting me to this source). Qawuqji mentions the fact that leaders in Damascus suspected that he would launch a coup against them in the last days of the war: Qasimiyya, ed., *Mudhakkirat*, 504–505. He describes how he was sent to Cairo to meet with 'Azzam Pasha so that he would be far from Damascus. In his memoirs he refutes this claim, saying that he made it clear in both private and public gatherings that he would not consider such a thing when his country was facing dangers from beyond its borders: 505. Palestinian accounts of the war tend to be very critical of Qawuqji. Perhaps the most well-known is Muhammad Nimr al-Hawari, *Sirr al-Nakba* [Secret of the Catastrophe], (Nazareth: no publisher, 1955). Hawari was scathing about the entire Arab leadership in 1948, including the Mufti. For an example of his critique of Qawuqji: 199–200. The Iraqi Parliamentary Commission of Enquiry into the Palestine Question, published in 1949, hardly mentions Qawuqji by name. Rather it singles out the Mufti as one of the causes of the defeat: *Taqrir Lajnat al-Tahqiq al-Niyabiyya fi Qadiyat Filastin*, 128. Accusations against Qawuqji continue to appear—e.g., Ma'ruf al-Duwaylibi's memoirs, serialized in *Sharq al-Awsat* (June 26, 2005). Popular songs in Palestine also ridiculed Qawuqji for working with King 'Abdullah; examples of these can be found in al-Nakba Archive, www.nakba-archive.org. For the essay on Arab unity written by Qawuqji in 1950: Qasimiyya, ed., *Mudhakkirat*, 508–11 (the quote is on p. 511).

Information on Qawuqji's life after 1948, including his visit to Argentina, is from conversations with Ossama El-Kaoukji. For evidence that he had support to run as a candidate for the Lebanese parliament: letter from the Lebanese journalist Joseph Sedky to Khalil al-Khoury, January 18, 1951, QPP. Evidence that he was living on a modest income is from conversations with his family and from Sa'id Taqi al-Din, *Al-Majmu'a al-Kamila*. For the 1957 letter to Quwatli asking for money: QPP. Other members of his family also struggled to make ends meet. In August 2003 the newspaper *Al-Sharq* published a long article about Qawuqji's daughter Haifa. Then in her eighties, she was living in poverty and appealed to the government of Kuwait for financial help on the basis of her father's record as a fighter against French and British colonialism: *Al-Sharq*, August 16, 2003. For the account of Qawuqji's death and funeral in 1976: *Al-Nahar*, December 16 and December 18, 1976. The PLO speech is in the first article. For the detail that he was speaking Turkish right before he died and for the description of his grave: conversation with Ossama El-Kaoukji.

ACKNOWLEDGMENTS

My first debt of gratitude is to Fawzi's son Ossama El-Kaoukji and granddaughter Dwan El-Kaoukji. This book would have been much thinner if Ossama had not given me access to Fawzi's private papers in Beirut and allowed me to photocopy everything I wanted. Ossama also made himself available for discussion on several occasions when I came across a gap in the sources, particularly to do with family history, and needed specific help. Ossama's and Dwan's generosity, humor, and respect for my independence as a historian have been wonderful. I am also grateful to May Farhat, Nadine Hatab, Ula Hatab, and Stephanie Thomas for their help in Beirut.

Thanks are due to the hardworking archivists at the Institute for Palestine Studies in Beirut, the Center for Historical Documents in Damascus, the National Archives in London, the Service Historique de la Défense in Vincennes, the Centre des Archives Diplomatiques in Nantes, and the Central Zionist Archive in Jerusalem. Steven Wagner generously shared documents that he had found in the Israeli archives and gave me access to his personal database of mandate sources, and Mark Sanagan found documents for me in the Middle East Studies Centre Archive, St. Antony's College, Oxford. Others helped by forwarding or pointing me toward various sources; they include Martin Bunton, Adel Allouche, Oren Barak, Neil Caplan, and Sameeh Hammoudeh. Walid Khalidi also provided me with some crucial documents relating to Fawzi's role in 1948. A generous grant from the Canadian Social Studies and Humanities Research Council helped propel my research, as did start-up research funds from Yale and McGill Universities.

Michael Provence read an earlier draft of this book; his help over the years has been invaluable, and his own work has been an inspiration. Eugene Rogan also read the manuscript. Eugene has been a kind and supportive mentor ever since I was a student at Oxford in the early 1990s. Ben Fortna kindly read an earlier version of my account of Qawuqji in the Ottoman school system. Charles Tripp read the section on Qawuqji in Iraq. Steven Wagner read Chapters 1–4. Shay Hazkani read the chapter on 1948. Other colleagues made crucial comments, suggestions, and critiques at the many papers that I have given over the years on Qawuqji. They include Salim Tamari (Institute of Palestine Studies, Ramallah, April 2014); Sameeh Hammoudeh (Birzeit University, April 2014); Orit Bashkin and Cyrus Schayegh (Princeton University, October 2013); Hasan Kayyali and Gershon Shafir (University of California—San Diego, 2010); Rita Awad (School of Oriental and African Studies, London, December 2008); Katarina Lange (Zentrum Moderner Orient, Berlin, June 2008); William Granara and Ilham Makdisi (Harvard University, May 2007); and Abbas Amanat and Mridu Rai (Yale University, December 2002).

I have had important and formative conversations about my project with colleagues and friends in Montreal. They include Rula Jurdi Abisaab, Dyala Hamza, Michelle Hartman, Wilson Jacob, and Setrag Manoukian. Brian Lewis gave me confidence in the project and encouraged me to take an interest in the genre of biography. Malek Abisaab made key observations that forced me to think in new ways about Fawzi's world and also directed me to some important sources. Chris Anzalone, Fadia Bahgat, Katy Kalemkerian, Rachel Haliva, and Mark Sanagan all helped with the research for this book. My Ph.D. student and research assistant Hussam Ahmed has been absolutely invaluable. He has found sources, checked my translations, worked on obtaining copyrights for the photographs, and much more. I am deeply grateful to him for his hard work, intelligence, and professionalism. The late Noel Abdulahad helped me translate some of the more difficult handwritten documents. The incisive and detailed comments of Alex Star, my editor at Hill and Wang, made this a much better piece of narrative history. My thanks also to Thomas LeBien for his enthusiasm at the beginning of this project.

Other colleagues and friends provided more general support, both intellectual and emotional: Hosam Aboul-Ela, Diana Allan, Tassos Anastassiadis, Sahar Bazzaz, Harry Bone, Holly Buss, Anne Christie, Kate Creasey, Kate Desbarats, Nicholas Dew, Ayman El-Desouky, Elizabeth Elbourne, Claudia Fabbricatore, Shokry Gohar, John Hall, Wael Hallaq, Prashant Keshavmurthy, Lynn Kozak, Catherine LeGrand, Catherine Lu, Lorenz Luthi, Ilham Makdisi, Josée Malouin, Khalid Medani, Sue Morton, Michelle Murphy, David Nancekivell, Vrinda Narain, Jason Opal, Colleen Parish, Nancy Partner, Carl Pearson, Matt Price, Jamil Ragep, Sally Ragep, Will Robins, Vincent Romani, Carne Ross, Karmen Ross, Jarrett Rudy, Anaïs Salamon, Pouneh Shabani-Jadidi, Kaleem Siddiqi, Adina Sigartau, Jon Soske, Andrew Staples, Sean Swanick, Judith Szapor, Stephanie Thomas, Eve Troutt-Powell, and, last but not least, Griet Vankeerberghen. My thanks also to Avi Shlaim for his wise guidance as I was just starting out on this project. Lovely dinners with Amelia Jones and Paul Donald made West-mount seem like home for the first time. The friendship and intellectual companion-ship of Carrie Rentschler and Jonathan Sterne made me a happier person. Bill Granara has been there for me through good times and bad. He is my dear friend and teacher.

My American parents-in-law, Joe and Mary Wisnovsky, have loved and supported me since I first showed up twenty-eight years ago. My father-in-law, who worked all his life as an editor, read the book in manuscript form, and his approval has meant the world to me. My brother-in-law Peter Wisnovsky and his husband, Alejandro Mendoza Castillo, have also been a source of warm support. My own parents, Anthony and Sheila Parsons, and my brothers, Simon and Rupert Parsons, all have died. I miss them very much and wish they were here to see this book published. My father was a British diplomat who lived most of his life in the Middle East. The experience and knowledge that he passed on to me are embedded in my work. Happily, much of my English family is still alive, and they sustained me with their love: my smart, outspoken nieces, Rosie Lee and Rebecca Parsons; my thoughtful, humorous nephews, Patrick Lee and Simon Parsons; and my wise, beloved sister-in-law, Anne Parsons. And the recent ar-rival of Leila Azmayesh-Lee into the world has brightened it enormously. It is hard to put into words what my sister Emma Parsons has meant to me. She is my sister, my dear friend and confidante, and my guide. She also read the whole manuscript of this book. It was when she said that she liked it that I started to believe that others might as well. My son, Simon Wisnovsky, was born in 1990, three weeks before I began my D.Phil. on the Druze in the 1948 Arab-Israeli War. He is an intelligent, kind, and thoughtful person, and I am proud to be his mum. I also count myself very lucky that he has a partner as smart and funny as Caroline Cawley. My sixteen-year-old daughter, Jasmine Parsons, took great interest in what I would say about her in these acknowl-edgments. In fact we discussed the matter at length, and she decided that we could encapsulate all her many attributes with one phrase: awe-inspiring.

This book is dedicated to Rob Wisnovsky, my husband of twenty-seven years. Rob and I rigmaroled about every aspect of this book. He read the manuscript multiple times and made crucial interventions. I could not have written it without him. But beyond this intellectual support, his love and his confidence in me are part of who I am.

INDEX

Page numbers in *italics* refer to illustrations.

Qadah, Badri, 157, 158, 162, 172–73, 178, 188, 200–201, 203
Qahtaniyya, al-, 15
Qahtan tribe, 14
Qanawati, Muhammad 'Ali al-, 166
Qarnail, 190
Qasim, 'Abd al-Karim, 253
Qassam, 'Izz al-Din al-, xv, 114
Qastal, 227–29
Qatana, 206–209
Qawuqji, 'Abd al-Majid al- (Fawzi's father), 3, 19, 53, 256
Qawuqji, Bahjat al- (Fawzi's brother), 3, 148
Qawuqji, Fawzi al-: at Aley conference, 193–95; anticolonialism and Arab nationalism of, xiv–xvi, 42–43, 58–59, 62–63, 108, 149–52, 169, 171, 190, 250–53; in Arab-Israeli War of 1948, 195, 209–21, 224, *224*, 226–46, 249–50; in Berlin during World War II, xvi, 38, 166–77; in Cairo, 105–106, 182, 184–89, 191; childhood of, 3; children of, 39, 104, 105, 170, 177–79, 251–52, 254; death of, 254–56; in Faysal's Arab Army, 43–52, *47*, 54, 107; in French Army's Syrian Legion, 53–61; German officers and, 26–31, 152, 169; Grobba and, 152–53; Iraq exile of, 106, 108–110, *110*, 139–45, 147–48; Islamic observances of, 60–62; marriages of, 54–55, 104, 105 (*see also* Müller, Anneliese); medals awarded to, 23, 25, 33; military education of, 3–10, 42, 47; Mosul posting of, 10–19; Mufti's antagonistic relationship with, 113–17, 172–76, 192–96, 199–204; newspaper articles about, 145–46, *147*; in Palestine Revolt of 1936, 110–11, 118–38, *121*, 148, 149, 155, 159, 190, 195; during pro-British Arab Revolt, 31–32; recruitment and training of Jaysh al-Inqadh volunteers by, 204–209; retirement in

Beirut of, 104, 167, 182, 199, 253–54; in retreat after Ottoman defeat, 34–36, 41–42; returns from Europe to Tripoli, 180–91; in Saudi Arabia, 83–105, 108; siblings of, 3, 148, 167, 170, 179; in Soviet occupied Germany, 176–79, 181, 184; Sulayman's role in arrest of, 104–105; in Syrian Revolt, 38–40, 62–63, 66–75, 77–93, 107, 108, 149, 190–91, 250; in Transjordan, 138–39; World War I Ottoman Army unit commanded by, 20–34, 41, 42; in World War II in Iraq and Syria, xiv, 139, 154–67, 190
Qawuqji, Haifa al- (Fawzi's daughter), 55, 165
Qawuqji, Majdi al- (Fawzi's son), 55, 90, 165, 167, 170, 179
Qawugji, Qadri al- (Fawzi's brother), 3, 148
Qawugji, Yumni al- (Fawzi's brother), 3, 167, 170, 179, 148
Qawugji, Zafir al- (Fawzi's brother), 3, 148
Qunaytra, 202
Qunbaz, Salih, 76
Quran, 18, 62, 63
Qurna, al-, 19
Quwatli, Shukri al-, 193, 196, 204, 210, 244, 245, 252; and 'Abdullah's Greater Syria ambitions, 217–18; Mufti and, 195, 202–203, 238, 239

Rabwa, al-, 35
Rahn, Rudolf, 161–63, 167
Ramadan, 5
Ramadi, xiii, xiv, 139, 161
Ramallah, xiv, 20, 23, 26, 33
Ramle, 243
Rasas, 69
Rashayya, 48

A NOTE ABOUT THE AUTHOR

Laila Parsons is an associate professor of history and Islamic studies at McGill University. She is the author of *The Druze Between Palestine and Israel, 1947–49*.